Collins

English GCSE for AQA

English
Targeting Grade A/A*
Student Book

Keith Brindle
and Mike Gould

Matches the new
GCSE Specification

Approve
D0997794

Published by Collins Education
An imprint of HarperCollins Publishers
77-85 Fulham Palace Road
Hammersmith
London
W6 8JB

Browse the complete Collins catalogue at
www.collinseducation.com

© HarperCollins Publishers Limited 2010

10 9 8 7 6 5 4 3 2 1

ISBN 978 0 00 734220 4

Keith Brindle and Mike Gould assert their moral rights to be
identified as the authors of this work.

All rights reserved. No part of this publication may be
reproduced, stored in a retrieval system, or transmitted in any
form or by any means, electronic, mechanical, photocopying,
recording or otherwise, without the prior written permission of
the Publisher or a licence permitting restricted copying in the
United Kingdom issued by the Copyright Licensing Agency Ltd,
90 Tottenham Court Road, London W1T 4LP.

British Library Cataloguing in Publication Data.
A Catalogue record for this publication is available from the
British Library.

Editor: Catherine Martin
Design and typesetting by EMC Design
Cover Design by Angela English
Printed and bound by L.E.G.O. S.p.A., Italy

Mixed Sources

Product group from well-managed
forests and other controlled sources
www.fsc.org Cert no. SW-COC-001806
© 1996 Forest Stewardship Council

FSC

FSC is a non-profit international organisation established to promote the
responsible management of the world's forests. Products carrying the FSC
label are independently certified to assure consumers that they come
from forests that are managed to meet the social, economic and
ecological needs of present and future generations.

Find out more about HarperCollins and the environment at
www.harpercollins.co.uk/green

Contents

What's it all about?

Being able to analyse the different non-fiction texts that we meet every day is an important life skill. It helps you understand how writers try to influence their readers. For the exam, you need to be able to move beyond describing what a text is about into explaining how effects are achieved and analysing why particular features are effective. If you can interpret how language, structure and presentation are used by writers and are able to compare texts, you will be able to cope well with the demands of the exam.

How will I be assessed?

You will get **20% of your English marks** for your ability to deal with close-reading questions in the exam.

You will have to complete **four** questions based on your reading of **three** non-fiction texts. You will not have seen these texts before the exam.

The four questions will carry a total of **40 marks**.

This forms Section A of the exam paper and you will have **one hour** to complete it.

What is being tested?

You are being examined on your ability to

- read and respond to the texts, focusing on the questions asked
- select material from the texts to answer the questions
- interpret the texts
- use evidence from the texts to support your answers
- compare the language used in the texts
- explain and evaluate how writers use language, grammar, structure and presentational features to achieve effects and engage and influence the reader.

This chapter will develop and offer you practice in the necessary skills.

Understanding Non-fiction Texts and Writers' Choices

Introduction

This section of Chapter 1 shows you how to

- explore a range of non-fiction texts and their features
- prepare to analyse texts in the exam
- practise a range of reading skills to boost your performance.

Why is the close reading of different texts important?

- In everyday life, we are surrounded by texts which attempt to influence us, so knowledge of how they work is vital.
- You will be tested on your understanding of non-fiction texts in the exam.

A **Grade C** candidate will

- understand and demonstrate how meaning and information are conveyed in a range of texts
- make personal and critical responses, referring to specific aspects of language, grammar, structure and presentational devices to justify their views.

C

A **Grade A/A★** candidate will

- develop perceptive interpretations of texts
- respond personally and persuasively to texts
- employ apt quotations to support detailed understanding
- comment perceptively on thoughts, feelings and ideas in texts.

A **A★**

Prior learning

Before you begin this unit, think about

- the many kinds of non-fiction texts you read in a day, and how and why they are different
- the different purposes of those texts
- what you learnt about non-fiction texts at Key Stage 3.

> Can you list them all? What are the main features of each one?

> Are they informing you, persuading you, entertaining you?

> How many technical terms for features can you use: headline, caption, pull-quote?

Forms and conventions of non-fiction texts

Learning objectives

- To consider the range of non-fiction texts.
- To begin to identify what makes them different.

What does non-fiction mean?

In the exam, you will have to answer questions on three non-fiction texts, which are likely to be from different **genres** or forms of non-fiction. There will not be any form of fiction such as a novel extract, short story, play or poetry.

Non-fiction forms include journalistic texts (newspaper reports, articles or leaders), leaflets and travel writing.

Checklist for success

Try to read a different kind of non-fiction text every day and ask yourself these questions:

- How do the presentational features and pictures attract the reader's attention?
- What is the audience for this text? How do I know?
- What does the writer want me to think about this topic?
- Is there anything interesting about the language used?

Focus for development: Conventions

Each form of non-fiction text has its own **conventions**. These are the typical features that help you recognise what kind of text you are reading. Conventions can be to do with **language** (style), **structure** (how the text has been organised) or **layout** and **presentation**.

Writers adapt these conventions according to their **audience** (who they are writing for) and their **purpose** (why they are writing).

ACTIVITY

In groups, list as many different forms of non-fiction text as you can think of.

Be specific: don't just write 'newspaper article' but try to think of all the types of newspaper article you might encounter – for example, a leader, a news report, a feature or a column.

ACTIVITY

Look at the two texts opposite. In groups, work out what form each text is, and pick out the textual and presentational features that tell you this.

Think about

- **language and style**
  What kind of words and phrases are used? Is the tone formal or chatty? Are the sentences long and elaborate, or short and snappy?
- **structure**
  Does the text use paragraphs or bullet points to organise the information?

- **presentation and layout**
  What presentational features do you notice – pictures, headlines and so on? Why are they used and how has the text been arranged on the page?

Use the annotations to help you.
Finally, try to explain why you think each text has been written, organised and presented in this way. What is its **purpose**?

Today's television

SUNDAY 26 JULY

Star of show in remote and threatening setting – appealing to audience

Picks of the day

✴ CHOICE

RIVERS WITH GRIFF RHYS JONES

BBC1, 9PM

A new five-part series, in which Griff Rhys Jones explores how "the forgotten highways into the heart of Britain" have influenced our lives throughout history. He begins in Scotland, travelling upstream from Kinlochleven into one of the most remote areas of the country and following the course of the water downstream to Perth. He milks fish for their eggs, goes canyoning and canoes a fast-flowing river that pine trees, ripped from the banks, have turned into an obstacle course. An informative, enthusiastic perspective.

Programme title clearly highlighted

Why is the picture used?

What purposes are shown here?

What form of text does this indicate?

EXAM TASK

- Who do you think the texts have been written for? How do you know?
- Find details from the texts to support your answer.

Remember

- Analyse non-fiction texts by examining their most significant features.
- Discuss how their features are appropriate for their purpose and intended audience.

Adapting text conventions

Learning objective

- To understand how conventions can be adapted to appeal to different audiences.

What does adapting conventions mean?

Conventions are the features we usually expect to find in a particular form of text (for instance, a headline in a newspaper article, or a series of steps to follow in an instruction manual). The way writers adapt these features varies according to the audience and purpose of the individual text.

Focus for development:
News report conventions

Read this report from a **broadsheet** newspaper.

ACTIVITY

What is a typical news report like? Think about how journalists use

- the opening paragraph
- presentational features like pictures and headings
- quotations
- text boxes
- the conclusion.

THE TIMES Wednesday November 25 2009

Flood victims will suffer trauma of a war zone, says GP

Russell Jenkins

People in Cumbria may suffer depression and health problems as bad as if they were in a war zone, according to an expert in disaster medicine who practises in Cockermouth.

John Howarth, who has worked in Angola, Rwanda and Chechnya, said: "It is difficult mentally and physically for the victims of the floods. They have to pick themselves up off the ground. We have to be careful that no one else dies as a result of this major catastrophe. Depression is a major issue in these situations."

Heavy rain was forecast in the area last night, and the Environment Agency said that flooding was very likely in Cockermouth, Workington and Keswick. If the Calva bridge over the Derwent, declared unsafe by Cumbria County Council, collapses, it will cut the telephone lines to 1,000 households north of the river.

In Wales, the body of a young woman believed to have been swept away by the River Usk in Brecon has been identified. Kirsty Jones, 21, was found more than six miles downstream in Talybont-on-Usk.

Dr Howarth, who worked for Médecins sans Fron-

> 'We have to be careful that no one else dies as a result of this major catastrophe'

tières and now works in a practice in Cockermouth, said: "I have worked in war zones and flood disasters before, but I did not think I would need those skills here. These floods are going to make a large part of the county poorer and it will have a significant impact on the health of people living here."

Letters, page 33
Weather, page 78

BRITISH GEOLOGICAL SURVEY

Cockermouth pictured from 2,000ft on Sunday. The flooding of the Derwent and Cocker rivers has cut people off from health services

ACTIVITY

What typical textual and presentational features of a news report can you find here?

Now read this report from a **tabloid** newspaper.

AFTER THE RAIN, HERE COMES THE Sun

Drenched . . clear-up in Cockermouth yesterday

THE Sun joined the Cumbrian relief effort yesterday by helping people cut off by the devastating floods.

We took food to residents stranded when a raging river smashed the only bridge linking hundreds of locals with Workington.

The vulnerable and elderly like Agnes Bell have been particularly hard hit, so she was thrilled when we arrived with goodies from Asda. Great-gran Agnes, 84, said: "I am so pleased The Sun is helping us. When I heard that the bridge had gone I felt so alone.

"So many kind people have offered help. It makes you realise we have a great community."

Five hundred homes in Northside were cut off when the bridge over the Derwent collapsed on Friday, killing cop Bill Barker, 44.

It has turned a two-minute trip to town into a 20-mile detour.

Locals can collect food and toiletries from a supermarket-supported emergency aid station in the community centre.

Council officials have set up a Job Centre, GPs' surgery and a creche upstairs. Housing

By ROBIN PERRIE

officer Estelle Kent, 44, said: "People have been cut off, so we're bringing services to them."

Engineers fear the town's sinking Calva Bridge may collapse. If it goes, 1,000 homes will lose their phoneline.

Tory leader David Cameron described the damage as "biblical" yesterday on a visit to flood-ravaged Cockermouth.

Warnings

Asked if his party would help people in the county if elected next year, he said: "Of course we will. They're going to need help."

Residents and business owners, meanwhile, continued to return. Alison Watson, 37, of Al's Toys, said: "This couldn't have come at a worse time."

Locals were hoping the floods would not return after up to **FOUR INCHES** of rain in Cumbria yesterday. Eight roads and 21 bridges remained closed.

Across Britain, there were 15 flood warnings in place last night – ten in North West England, three in Wales and one each in the Midlands and the North East.

r.perrie@the-sun.co.uk

The Sun Says — Page Eight

Visit . . . Cameron in Cockermouth

Supplies . . The Sun's Perrie with Agnes Bell

Glossary

broadsheet: one of the larger-format newspapers (traditionally), such as *The Times* or the *Guardian*. They report national and international news in detail and offer in-depth coverage of 'serious' issues. They are also called **quality** newspapers.

tabloid: a smaller newspaper (traditionally), such as *The Sun* and *The Mirror*. They often cover less serious stories, for example, scare stories and celebrity news. They are also called **popular** newspapers.

In what ways are the broadsheet and the tabloid reports different? Copy and complete the table below.

Typical features	Broadsheet	Tabloid
pictures		
how the pictures are used		
captions		
other features to catch reader's eye		
language		
detail included		
opening		
ending		

Finally, look at this webpage:

ACTIVITY

What main differences can you find between this text and the paper-based news reports above?

EXAM TASK

How does the use of conventions in each of these three texts appeal to their likely audiences? Consider:

- **presentation and layout:** images, captions, headlines, subheadings
- **structure:** length of paragraph, order of argument, any organisational features
- **language and style:** vocabulary chosen, tone, difficulty or ease of reading, sentence length and structure.

Remember

- **Look at how conventions are used in different ways in similar texts.**
- **Decide how writers use conventions to match their purpose and audience.**

Purpose

Learning objectives

- *To explore writers' purposes.*
- *To read and analyse different kinds of travel writing.*

What does purpose mean?

Whenever anyone writes a text, they have an **aim** or **purpose**. For example, they could be writing to entertain the reader or to inform them about an important issue. Or both.

Checklist for success

You need to identify

- the **purpose** of every text you read (**why** it has been written)
- which textual and presentational **features** make the text appropriate for that purpose
- how the writer tries to produce a particular **response from the reader**.

Travel writing for different purposes

Travel writing is a popular genre of non-fiction; typically, it deals with journeys, holidays, different places, customs and cultures. However, *how* an individual travel-writing text is written will depend upon its **purpose**.

Read this extract from a guidebook about New York.

GAZE AT THE STATUE OF LIBERTY & ELLIS ISLAND

The Statue of Liberty (p48), the gorgeous green woman, a gift from France, has welcomed millions of immigrants and inspires awe in all who see her. Sculptor Frederic Auguste Bartholdi built the 305-ft tall, 225-ton statue, but Gustave Eiffel contributed the skeleton.

Just next to Lady Liberty is Ellis Island (p48), formerly the holding tank, so to speak, for third-class passengers coming off immigrant ships from Europe. Ellis Island's exhibits include leftover trunks and bags from immigrants, pictures of gaunt, hollow-eyed arrivals (who might have left home in decent health but didn't always arrive that way after weeks crammed on a ship), and an interactive display that lets you search among a database of émigrés for your own relatives. It's well worth waiting in line for the ferry that takes you there.

New York: Encounter (Lonely Planet)

- With a partner, discuss and note down
  - the text's purpose or purposes
  - how the language supports this purpose (what does it make us think?)
  - who might read this text.

  Refer closely to the text in your answers.
- Imitate the style of the guidebook by writing about an interesting place to visit where you live. Use facts, interesting detail and vivid description.

Now look at this website about visiting New York.

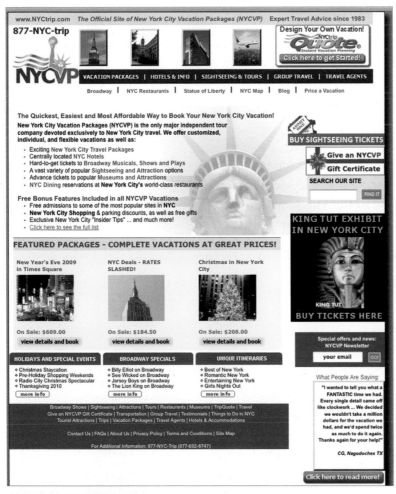

With your partner, discuss and note down

- the general purpose of the text
- its more specific purposes, for example, what the writer hopes we will do after reading it
- what impression of New York it creates, and how
- whether you would be influenced by this text. Explain why or why not.

Next, film star Richard E. Grant writes about his first visit to New York.

A gloved hand opens the door [of my cab] and is getting my holdall and me into the lobby of the Algonquin Hotel pronto! Inside, it's a wood-panelled Edwardian gentleman's club. The loose sexy style, you'd never encounter anywhere else. Punters are cocktailing and clinking glasses and fur-coating up for the short walk to the theatres.

Up in the old elevator with the bell-boy and holdall […]. Tip here, tip there, tip every-bloody-where. […] Put on the thermals and bound down the stairwell and into 44th Street and *run* to Times Square on Broadway. GUYS AND DOLLS FOR REAL. Bright, brash, busting with people and I feel about as *alive* as I think I ever *will* be.

A […] voice is coming from way back in my head saying, 'sssssSSSSSSSSEEEEEEXY!' And *yes* it is. *Sexy*. Get a grip, boy, you're talking about a *city*…

Withnails: The Film Diaries of Richard E. Grant

- How does the writer want us to see New York?
- How is the excitement of the city conveyed? Look in detail at the way he uses language: sentences, vocabulary, verbs and adjectives.

EXAM TASK

Compare the three travel-writing texts about New York.

Summarise the similarities and differences in their purposes in a grid like the one below.

	Guidebook	NYCVP website	Film Diaries of Richard E. Grant
Similarities in purposes			
Differences in purposes			

Write a paragraph discussing these similarities and differences, making reference to the three texts.

Remember

- Identifying purpose will help you interpret a text.
- A text can have more than one simple purpose.

Audience

Learning objective

- To understand how texts are designed to target particular audiences.

Why is it important to think about the audience of non-fiction texts?

Writers always keep their **audience** in mind, and write in a style appropriate for them. For example, an article from a broadsheet newspaper would mean nothing to a five-year-old.

An awareness of the target audience helps you read texts more effectively: you know why things are there and the effect they are intended to have.

Read this short report from *The Times*.

Birth of Asian elephant is trumpeted by zoo

Whipsnade The first Asian elephant to be born at Whipsnade Zoo in Bedfordshire makes her public debut at the age of six days under the watchful trunk of her mother Kaylee, 27. The 3ft-tall female calf, yet to be given a name by keepers at the zoo, weighs 126kg (278lb). The zoo's elephant population has declined this year after two of its animals died from a herpes virus. David Field, Whipsnade's director, said that the calf's birth was important for its endangered species programme. The calf's sire, Emmett, is the only adult male in the zoo's herd of eight elephants.

ACTIVITY

With a partner, discuss these questions.

- What about this article might appeal to a young child (aged 6 or 7)?
- Which words and phrases would not be suitable for a young child?
- If some of the language here is not suitable for children, who, do you suppose, is the target audience for the report?

Working on your own, rewrite the article using language and ideas suitable for a young child. Make sure you use words and ideas that will be understood and sentences that are simple enough for your audience.

Focus for development:
Identifying target audiences

Advertisers usually have a clear target audience in mind for a product, and design advertisements specifically for that group. So, for example, television adverts for toys are likely to feature happy children, and adverts for zit-busting face washes show teenagers' lives transformed by clearer skin.

Looking closely at the language and presentational features of an advert can provide clues about the target audience.

Look at these two adverts for holidays. The first is from a hotel chain's publicity brochure.

Escape!™ Romance package by Marriott

Rediscover each other

Secluded walks, breathtaking sunsets, crackling fires and romantic dinners. Or perhaps it's simply champagne and room service. Whatever the time of year, whatever the reason, the perfect setting awaits those treasured times together.

For Valentines, anniversaries, honeymoons or just a spontaneous weekend getaway, nothing kindles the magic quite like an Escape! Romance package by Marriott. We'll even add extra sparkle with champagne and breakfast for two included or for something extra special book a fairytale romance package at Dalmahoy, A Marriott Hotel & Country Club.

To book | Call the hotel of your choice *(see page 29)*, *call* 0800 328 3528 *or visit* MarriottEscape.co.uk   09

The second advert is from the travel section of a newspaper.

ACTIVITY

Discuss these questions with a partner.

- What sort of people might be the target audience for each advert?
- How does each advert try to appeal to its audience?
- What does each writer want the audience to think about the holiday?

Copy and complete the grid below to answer these questions.
Support your explanations with evidence from the text.

	Rediscover each other advert	**Arctic Spirit advert**
Target audience		
Effect of...	In each case, say what the target audience might think	
Pictures	• *Happy couple – implies holiday will provoke this reaction.* •	• •
Headings and subheadings	• • •	• *colours used make holiday seem beautiful, like the lights* • *'Greatest spectacle' sounds unmissable*
Language	• • •	• • •

Grade B responses tend to **explain** effects:

> The advertisement is aimed at people who love to travel and have experiences: the night sky is there to show the wonders you encounter. The colours are reflected in the word 'spirit', as if this is showing the spirit of adventure and discovery. The 'experience' is made to seem amazing...

Here is an extract from a **Grade A★** response.

> 'Search for the elusive Northern Lights' is intended to appeal to readers who like an adventure. The verb 'search' makes it seem a hard task and exciting – and, perhaps, as if you could be the first one to achieve it. The fact that the Lights are 'elusive' suggests it could be a long search, challenging and difficult, because the Lights are not easily seen. It flatters the target audience that they would be the ones to succeed in this challenge.

— ideas extended and developed

more than one interpretation offered

A student writes...

We are always told to analyse if we can, rather than explain. What's the difference?

Answer...

If you can explore layers of meaning, for example by writing that 'this feature suggests... but also makes us think of... and links with...', then you are analysing and so demonstrating more advanced skills.

EXAM TASK

Write an analytical response to the 'Rediscover each other' advert, explaining

- who it is appealing to
- how it appeals to its target audience.

Remember

- Focus on how the text is intended to affect the target audience.
- Be prepared to consider the presentational features and the language.
- Make connections in your analysis between different text features, to develop your points.

Focusing on language

Learning objectives

- *To practise analysing the language of non-fiction texts.*

- *To learn how to compare writers' use of language.*

Glossary

Simile: a comparison using 'like' or 'as'

Metaphor: a comparison which is not literally true ('My head is exploding')

Alliteration: when words close together begin with the same letter

Onomatopoeia: when words sound like what they are describing

Baracques: French word for barracks

⭐ Examiner's tip

Always consider the **effect** *the language has on the reader: that is why the vocabulary has been chosen. Deal with the words as you would when examining poetry.*

What do we need to know about language?

In the exam, you will have to compare the use of language and its effects in two texts. Being able to identify more than one simple meaning will bring more marks. So, instead of just saying 'it makes us think…', you might say 'it makes us think… and suggests… and makes us remember…'. One explanation has now developed into three ideas.

Checklist for success

You need to compare how writers use language. This might be

- imagery: similes or metaphors
- alliteration, onomatopoeia and other language devices
- sentence length and structure
- vocabulary choices, repetition, exaggeration.

How incidents are presented gives an insight into writers' feelings, as we interpret the words used.

Here is an extract from an autobiography written by a First World War nurse about her experiences of looking after injured men close to the battlefields.

> Outside the guns roar and inside the *baracques* shake, and again and again the stretcher bearers come into the ward, carrying dying men from the high tables in the operating room. They are all that stand between us and the guns, these wrecks upon the beds. Others like them are standing between us and the guns, others like them, who will reach us before morning. Wrecks like these. They are old men, most of them. The old troops, grey and bearded.
>
> There is an attack going on. That does not mean that the Germans are advancing. It just means that the ambulances are busy, for these old troops, these old wrecks upon the beds, are holding up the Germans. Otherwise, we should be swept out of existence. Our hospital, ourselves, would be swept out of existence, were it not for these old wrecks upon the beds. These filthy, bearded, dying men upon the beds, who are holding back the Germans. More like them, in the trenches, are holding back the Germans. By tomorrow these others, too, will be with us, bleeding, dying. But there will be others like them in the trenches, to hold back the Germans. […]
>
> They seem very weak and frail and thin. How can they do it, these old men? Last summer the young boys did it. Now it is the turn of these old men.
>
> *The Backwash of War*, Ellen la Motte

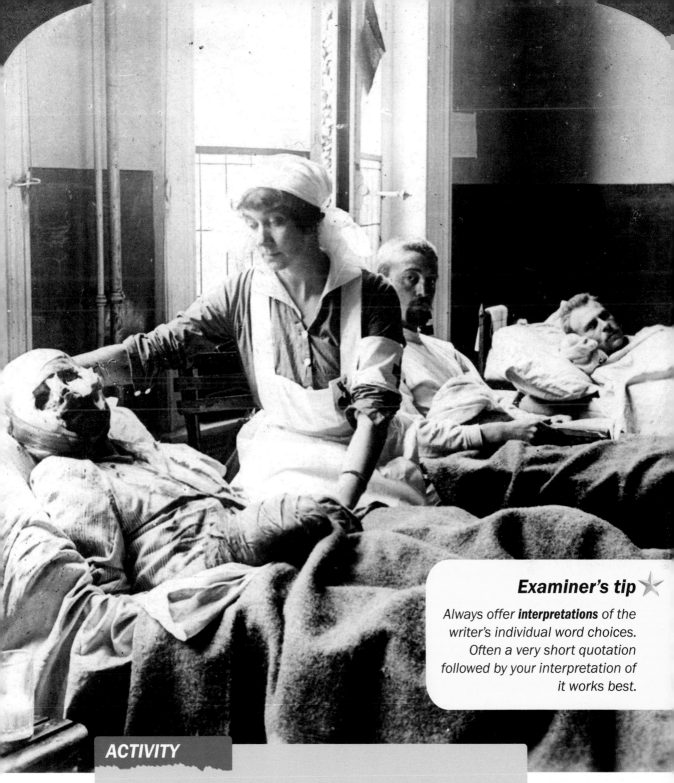

Examiner's tip ⭐

*Always offer **interpretations** of the writer's individual word choices. Often a very short quotation followed by your interpretation of it works best.*

ACTIVITY

- How does the nurse feel about what is happening?
- What do these phrases tell us about the writer's attitude?
  - 'They are all that stand between us and the guns'
  - 'these filthy bearded men'
  - 'others, too, will be with us, bleeding, dying'
- Decide and comment on how the writer uses other linguistic features, such as repetition, emotive language, powerful adjectives and verbs.

Glossary
emotive language: language designed to affect our emotions

Here is an extract from a Grade A response to the text.

offers interpretation ——

The fact that the nurse keeps repeating 'old' and mentioning the frailties of the men perhaps suggests that she is appalled that they are having to fight. At the

extends the analysis ——▶ *same time, it suggests her amazement that they are able to perform so heroically when they are so unsuited to fight a war...*

shows engagement with the text ——

Focus for development:
Different view, different language

Next, notice how another nurse in the same war presents what is happening rather differently. In her diary, an American volunteer nurse is describing a typical day. In the afternoon, she changes the dressings and bandages of the injured soldiers.

what picture is she creating? ——

… Dressings all the afternoon until it is time for temperatures; then soup for the soldiers; and mine, which is soon finished; then the massage for those that need it, etc., after which I prepare my soothing drinks and give the injections. It is the sweetest time of the day, for then one puts off the nurse and becomes the mother; and we have such fun over the warm drinks. They are nice and sweet and hot, and the soldiers adore their 'American drinks'.

effect of these details? ——

When this is done, I go round and stuff cotton under weary backs and plastered limbs, bid all the children goodnight, polish my instruments, clean out the surgical dressings room, and hurry home through the frosty night.

This is the rough outline of an ordinary day, and into that let your fancy weave all that is too holy or terrible, too touching or humorous to put into words: the last kiss a soldier gives you for his family he will never see; the watches with the priest when all is still and dark, but for the light of my little electric lamp and a bit of moonlight through the window; the agonies and heroisms; the wit and affection that play like varied lights and darks along the days.

what is suggested? ——

Mademoiselle Miss

what is suggested? ——

ACTIVITY

- What is the difference in this nurse's attitude to what is happening?
- Comment on how we react to these phrases or images:
  - 'It is the sweetest time of the day'
  - 'one puts off the nurse and becomes the mother'
  - 'bid all the children goodnight'
  - 'the wit and affection that play like varied lights and darks along the days'.

Read this extract from a **Grade A★** response to the use of language in the text.

gives overview

extends
comments
on this,
analysing
the language

... The nurse wants us to see her as brave, as if she is a heroine in a story. Even the horror is more romantic than brutal, so she takes time to describe 'the light of my little lamp...' rather than the soldiers' convulsions. 'Little lamp' makes us think that she is wonderful in such difficult conditions and the alliteration of 'l's seems childlike: it could even have been taken from a fairy story. It all seems unreal, so the soldiers die beautifully, with 'a last kiss' for the family and 'agonies and heroisms' are not detailed. It is all sanitised and heroic: 'polish', 'clean', 'frosty night'...

offers
related ideas,
using
embedded
quotations

perceptive final thought to round off the idea

EXAM TASK

Write a detailed analysis of the use of language in the first two paragraphs of the second nursing text.

Remember

- **Explain the effect of the language used.**
- **Make your analysis detailed – the more levels of interpretation and linked ideas you offer, the higher your mark will be.**
- **Choose short quotations and analyse what they add to the overall effect. It is better to write a lot about a little than to write a little about a lot.**

Presentational features

Learning objective

- To learn about the effects of layout and presentational features.

Glossary

pull-quote: a quotation lifted from the text and put in bold to stand out and alone - possibly in the middle of a column of text.

What is the difference between layout and presentation?

Layout is how a page is arranged. It is particularly important in non-fiction texts.

Presentational features are the elements that make up a non-fiction text: for example, pictures, text boxes, headlines, captions and pull-quotes.

Checklist for success

When reading any media text, you need to do the following.

- Consider **layout**. (What do I notice first and why? Where do my eyes go next? How have these features been arranged?)
- Decide if the use of **colour** is significant. (Is there more of one colour? For example: 'Does the yellow represent sunshine or…?', 'Is there red to suggest excitement or…?')
- Notice how **pictures** represent or add to what the text is saying.
- Ask yourself how any other presentational features are intended to affect the reader.

The use of pictures

Generally, pictures will be used to support the text.

ACTIVITY

Look at the article on the opposite page.

- List at least three possible reactions to this picture and explain your views.
- Working with a partner, decide how this picture reflects what the writer is saying.
- Consider why a close-up has been used.

The day of the vulture

Their feeding habits have not endowed vultures with the best public image, but conservation groups are trying to promote it anyway, declaring today International Vulture Awareness Day. This Cape vulture, which lives in a zoo in Johannesburg, is one of only 8,000 of its kind. Seven of South Africa's nine vulture species are under threat of extinction EPA

A student writes…

I just look at it and think: 'So... it's a picture ...?'
That won't get me far, will it?

Answer …

You need to think about what the picture suggests to you. So, does the vulture look fierce, as if it will tear you apart? Or does it look friendly, worried, sensitive, clean or dirty? What gives you that impression?

Daily Mail, Monday, July, 2009

Er, does this thing have a reverse gear?

The only way is down: Bradt at the top of the torrent

PERCHED on the brink of a 186ft drop, this was the moment when Tyler Bradt probably felt the urge to start frantically paddling backwards.

Less than four seconds later, he was celebrating a world record for kayak descents.

The 22-year-old American touched 100mph as he plummeted over Palouse Falls, in Washington State.

To complete the dramatic picture, birds circled the torrent while behind it a rainbow appeared right on cue.

After disappearing at the base of the falls, Bradt emerged with a broken paddle. His only physical damage was a sprained wrist.

The previous record was set only weeks earlier when a rival plunged 127ft over the Salto Bello falls in Brazil.

Bradt, from Montana, has been accused of encouraging others to endanger their lives in the extreme sport of kayak free-falling.

He responds: 'I hope it encourages people not to run huge waterfalls but to understand that the only limits that exist are the ones you create, no matter what you are doing.'

ACTIVITY

⭐ **Examiner's tip**

If you can analyse presentational features, giving more than one interpretation, and if you can link ideas about how features of the text build an effect, you will gain higher marks.

Look at the layout and presentation of this news report.
Using the grid below, decide how it has been designed to

- impact on the reader
- support and illustrate the text.

Feature	How it is used
Small (inset) picture	• •
Large picture	• •
Circle and arrow	• •
Headline	• •
Caption	• •

24

Give water
Give life
Give £2 a month

If you already support our work please pass this magazine on to friends and family who could help us reach more people without water.

Every day 5,000 children in the developing world die from water-related diseases. Yet a gift of just £2 a month from you today can help change this, bringing safe, clean water and sanitation to the world's poorest people.

Please call now on 0300 123 4341, visit www.wateraid.org/givelife or complete the form below and return it to:
Freepost RRRZ-YRRB-ELKE, WaterAid, MELKSHAM, SN12 6YY

Registered charity numbers 288701 (England and Wales) and SC039479 (Scotland)

WaterAid

FundRaising
Standards Board

EXAM TASK

Write about how layout and presentational features are used by this charity to persuade the reader to support their campaign.

In your answer, consider

- the picture and how it relates to the text
- the colours
- the use of the purple text box.

Remember

- Link your response to presentational features to the text's purpose(s).
- Consider the effects of layout, colour, pictures and any other features.

Learning objective

- To learn about how texts are constructed.

Glossary

anecdote: a short story which illustrates a point

What is structure?

Structure is how a text starts, develops and ends, and how the parts contribute to the overall purpose.

Checklist for success

- You need to pay particular attention to how texts begin and end.
- You need to decide on the purpose of any text, then on how the writing is structured to meet that purpose.
- You need to notice how writers develop their points with quotations, anecdotes, facts and figures or contrasts.

ACTIVITY

- Below are details from an article about Radio 1 DJ, Chris Moyles.
- Decide what description of Chris Moyles you could create from the details. Put the information into an effective and logical order.
- Be prepared to justify your decisions.

1 Moyles' success is the consequence of professionalism for which he is rarely given credit.

2 His job appeared under threat recently but whilst other presenters were sacked, he remained to rule the airwaves.

3 He first worked at a radio station as a schoolboy doing work experience.

4 'I find his continued presence on Radio 1 unacceptable,' said Oxford University's professor of broadcast media.

5 His programmes appear spontaneous but that cleverly disguises his acute attention to detail.

6 He has been criticised for being racist, homophobic, anti-semitic and 'laddish'.

7 He is Radio 1's longest-serving breakfast DJ.

8 Comedy and film writer Richard Curtis is one of his admirers.

Focus for development: Developing ideas

A text might be structured so that the writer's viewpoint emerges right at the end, or it could be apparent throughout.

Read this newspaper report.

'It's wonderful to see you all': Winton reunited with the evacuees he saved

By Chris Green

reader is taken back in time →

SEVENTY YEARS ago, a 29-year-old stockbroker called Nicholas Winton stood nervously on a platform at Liverpool Street station in central London.

gives factual background →

The train that eventually pulled to a stop in front of him was one of eight he had arranged to carry hundreds of young children, most of whom were Jewish, on a treacherous 642-mile journey across Nazi Germany from Prague to London.

comes back to the present day →

His actions were to save 669 of them from almost certain death in Hitler's concentration camps.

Yesterday, Sir Nicholas – who was knighted in 2003 and is now 100 years old – met 22 of the people he helped to safety, after they recreated the journey to mark the 70th anniversary of their escape.

provides historical background →

The centenarian, from Maidenhead in Berkshire, masterminded their removal to Britain shortly after the outbreak of the Second World War.

summarises what happened yesterday and shows his sense of humour →

Yesterday, a steam train from Prague bearing his name arrived at Liverpool Street, and Sir Nicholas was standing on the platform once more, greeting the surviving evacuees with the words: "It's wonderful to see you all after 70 years. Don't leave it quite so long until we meet here again."

Surrounded by a crowd of several hundred people who had gathered to witness the reunion, he gave an emotional speech on the platform where he had stood seven decades earlier.

uses quotation to show his self-effacing attitude →

Describing the scene at the station in 1939, he said: "It was a question of getting a lot of little children together with the families that were going to look after them. It was quite difficult to get them together and, of course, every child needed to be signed for.

includes stirring and emotive detail →

"Anyway, it all worked out very well and it's wonderful that it did work out so well because, after all, history could have made it very different."

Sir Nicholas Winton at Liverpool Street station yesterday with one of the 22 people he helped flee Prague during the Second World War, and her granddaughter IAN LLOYD

Sir Nicholas's grandson, Laurence Watson, 21, spoke with pride about his grandfather's actions. "It's very strange when someone you know as a relative turns out to be a hero," he said.

"There have always been bad things going on in the world and there have always been wars and conflicts. You see it everyday in the newspapers. Very occasionally you meet someone who has read those same articles but who decides to do something about it. That's what my granddad did. He said 'Something needs doing and I am going to do it.'"

'witness' portrays Sir Nicholas as hero ←

ACTIVITY

- With a partner, discuss the writer's purpose in writing the report. How does the structure help to achieve this purpose? (Think about how it opens, develops and ends.)
- Imagine the report had been written for a Prague newspaper.
  - How might the focus of the report have been different?
  - In note form, produce an appropriate structure for this different audience.

EXAM TASK

Read the report about Sir Nicholas Winton again.

- What impression of Sir Nicholas does the report set out to produce?
- How has the report been structured to fulfil the purpose?

Write a brief response, using evidence from the report.

Remember

- Identify how the structure of a text supports its purpose.
- Examine the structure closely, giving a stage-by-stage analysis.

Perspective and point of view

Learning objective

- To learn to identify and analyse the writer's perspective.

What does perspective mean?

A text will usually have a point of view, a perspective or 'angle', on its subject. This influences how we react to the content.

Checklist for success

When reading a text, you need to ask yourself: What does the writer think about this subject and how does he or she want me to react? Does the writer

- balance the argument
- give a one-sided viewpoint, perhaps using a first-person voice
- use a range of points, building a singular effect
- make clear points into which you might read extra meaning
- add persuasive touches (rhetorical questions, emotive language, persuasive connectives, for example, 'Surely', 'What is more')
- include ambiguities, where one thing is said, but another thing suggested, for example, 'What a convincing idea that is!'?

Read this problem page from a women's magazine from the 1930s.

"Around the Editor's Tea Table"

How can I prevent my father from making a slave of mother?

I SHOULD suggest most emphatically, "Norah," that you don't do anything! You say that mother waits on your father constantly, wearing herself out in his service, and that he takes it all for granted and does not realise her self-sacrifice. But isn't it possible – I should say highly probable – that mother *loves* this service? You call it "slavery," but that is not a word which has any connection with love's work. Your parents have been happily married for twenty years and you are perhaps looking at them with romantic young eyes when you think your father should fuss more over mother and turn the tables by starting to "slave" after her. Leave them to their own way is my advice. If they have covered a score of years peacefully together it is more than likely that mother revels in her service and father appreciates it more than you can realise. I have yet to find the really good wife who does not love "wearing herself out" over her husband's welfare!

from the *Woman's Magazine Annual, 1935*

ACTIVITY

- What is the writer's point of view here? How do you know?
- Look closely at the language. What techniques does the writer use to persuade us that she is right? Find examples of
  - forceful language that allows for no alternative viewpoint
  - questions and exclamations
  - words that are emphasised, for example by the use of inverted commas
  - imperatives (where Norah is told directly what to do)
  - how the marriage is presented in positive terms.
- List the ideas the writer uses to persuade Norah.
- What is your opinion of her perspective?

ACTIVITY

An **Grade A★** student was asked what the writer thought of Norah's parents' relationship. Here is part of her response.

> The writer (the magazine's editor) is totally convinced that the marriage is fine. She believes that women are happy to slave over their husbands.
>
> She opens with an exclamation, telling Norah exactly what to do and does so very definitely: 'emphatically'. We can immediately hear that she is a strong woman with firm views who is used to telling others how to behave. In the same tone, she challenges Norah with a rhetorical question: 'isn't it possible... that mother loves this service?' She presents the role of a wife as being like a servant 'in service', suggesting that wives should wait on their husbands. The italicising of 'loves' emphasises the word, stresses the bond of marriage and implies that this kind of life represents true love...

Notice how

- a clear overview is supported by perceptive comments
- apt quotations are used
- a range of points is interpreted
- there is a convincing final point.

Continue and complete this response.

Focus for development: Examining a different perspective

Here is a more recent article.

headline includes pun

subhead includes the phrase 'might injure vandals' in speech marks, mocking the idea

first sentence stresses 'fury' and uses another pun

For breaking news, go to: RELATED LINKS
www.mirror.co.uk/news

Daily Mirror
SATURDAY 05.09.2009   M 29

BARBED IRE

Allotment fence 'might injure vandals'

BY **EUAN STRETCH**
euan.stretch@mirror.co.uk

GARDENERS are so furious with their council they feel like throwing in their trowels.

The growers have been banned from using barbed wire to deter allotment vandals – in case they hurt themselves.

Property at the Muddy Bottom East Allotment is being damaged up to three times a week. In one attack 15 sheds were smashed, water butts were overturned and taps were left running.

But when allotment holders asked Southampton council to put up the wire, it said no for fear of being sued.

Grandfather Mervyn Hobden, 67, who rents several spaces there, blasted the decision as "absolutely crazy". He said: The fences are easy to climb over. We asked for four lines of barbed wire to be added to the top, but the council said they have a liability towards the trespasser.

"Some of the sheds cost £500. And we have to pay to repair them. Some people have packed in because of the vandals."

Lib Dem environment spokesman Tim Farron said the decision was "ridiculous".

Bizarrely, the council has allowed the old barbed wire around the allotment's entrance to stay, because it is "historic".

A council spokesman said: "A member of the public who falls on the barbed wire can prosecute – that includes thieves."

This week, the Mirror told how angry gardeners in Torquay planned to patrol their allotment after vandals wrecked grower Tony Mason's prize pumpkins.

▲ **FURIOUS** Grower Mervyn Hobden

next paragraphs add information

quotations add subjective views to story

Adverb gives editorial comment

quotation marks show sarcasm

offers 'expert' to support view

picture personalises report: stance looks strong

What is the reporter Euan Stretch's point of view?

Here are some ideas you might include in your answer.

picture suggests Mervyn Hobson is …

tone of headline: pun and words in speech marks

imbalance in opinions

emotive language

jokey approach implies that the writer thinks …

effect of detail included

effect of quotations

'Bizarrely'

Write your own ideas in two paragraphs, in response to the article.

Remember

- The writer's perspective affects how we respond to the subject of the text.
- In the exam, you will have to answer one question on inference – what you think is being *suggested* in the text. The more you practise analysing perspective in a range of texts, the better you will be able to answer this type of question.

Grade Booster

Extended Exam Task

Choose a lead story or article from a newspaper.

Keeping in mind the text's purpose and audience and answering in detail, analyse the text by responding to these questions.

1 What is the writer's point of view?
2 How has language been used to influence, interest or inform the reader?
3 How has the text been structured?
4 What is the effect of the presentational features?

Evaluation: What have you learned?

With a partner, use the grade checklist below to evaluate your work on the Extended Exam Task.

- I can make a perceptive analysis of a writer's viewpoint and the language, structure and presentational features in a non-fiction text.
- I can use quotations and evidence which are perfect for the context.
- I can interpret the ideas in the text in a detailed and persuasive way.
- I can offer originality in what I write.

- I can make a detailed interpretation of a writers' viewpoint and the language, structure and presentational features in a non-fiction text.
- I can make points persuasively and use valid quotations and evidence which supports and clarifies them.

- I can begin to analyse viewpoint and the use of language, structure and presentational features in a non-fiction text.
- I can make effective points and show an ability to see layers of meaning in the text.
- I can use quotations and evidence to support my points.

- I can make clear and relevant comments on a writer's viewpoint and on the use of language, structure and presentational features in a non-fiction text.
- I can offer relevant quotations and evidence in support of my ideas.

- I can identify a writer's viewpoint.
- I can understand how language and presentational features are used in a non-fiction text and comment on how they have been used.
- I can use some appropriate evidence.

You may need to go back and look at the relevant pages from this section again.

Close Reading in the Exam

Introduction

This section of Chapter 1 helps you to

- focus on the reading skills you will have to demonstrate in the exam
- develop and practise the necessary skills by analysing different non-fiction texts in detail
- understand the requirements of the exam by offering advice.

What will 'close reading' mean in the exam?

You will have to select the right material to answer the **four questions** on the Higher tier paper. These will require the following skills:

Question 1: Finding information in the text

Question 2: Dealing with inference – what the text is suggesting

Question 3: Analysing presentational features

Question 4: Comparing the use of language in two texts.

A **Grade C** candidate will

- understand and demonstrate how meaning and information are conveyed in a range of texts
- make personal and critical responses, referring to specific aspects of language, grammar, structure and presentational devices to justify their views.

C

A **Grade A/A★** candidate will

- develop perceptive interpretations of texts
- respond personally and persuasively to texts
- employ apt quotations to support detailed understanding
- comment perceptively on thoughts, feelings and ideas in texts.

A **A★**

Prior learning

Before you begin this unit, think about

- what you have already learnt about language, structure and presentational features such as pictures and headlines
- the different kinds of non-fiction texts you read every day.

Consider the use of colour, font size and why a particular illustration has been used. How do these features add to the text?

How can reading these more analytically help you to prepare for the exam?

Retrieving and collating information

What does retrieving and collating information mean?

To respond to questions with authority, you first need to be able to **select** and **retrieve** the details from the text that are most appropriate to answer the question. Then you analyse and **collate** (put together) information from different parts of the text so you can comment on the overall impact.

Checklist for success

Whenever you write about texts, you need to

- make sure the information you select answers the question
- ensure any reference or quotation actually supports the point you are making
- be selective when retrieving information so that you are not putting random points together.

ACTIVITY

Look at the two different adverts on pages 35 and 36.
With a partner:

- decide how each product appeals to the reader
- retrieve one piece of appropriate information from each advert.

Completing the entries in a grid format like this will help.

Harley-Davidson	Fiat
Relaxation/open road/freedom suggested by …	A car for a particular season suggested by …
Bike and rider's overall image captured in one word: …	One specific attraction of car captured in one phrase: …

BRIGHTSUN BIGSMILE
SHADESON SOUNDSUP
ROOFDOWN HAIRLOOSE
CAREFREE COOLBREEZE
ICECREAM TANNEDSKIN

500C
NOW OPEN

FIAT
fiat.co.uk

Fiat, the car brand with the lowest average CO_2 emissions in Europe.* Fuel consumption figures for the Fiat 500 C range mpg (l/100km) and CO_2 emissions: Urban 53.3 (5.3) - 36.7 (7.7) Extra Urban 78.5 (3.6) - 55.4 (5.1) Combined 67.3 (4.2) - 46.3 (6.1). CO_2 emissions 110 - 140 g/km. *Source: JATO Dynamics. Volume-weighted average CO_2 emissions g/km among European top 10 selling brands 2008.

The Harley-Davidson® XL883 Sportster®...

A cool £4995.

Motorcycle shown has been fitted with Genuine Harley-Davidson® Accessories at additional cost.

To locate your nearest dealer and book your free test ride call 0870 901 0883 or log onto www.harley-davidson.co.uk
IT'S OPEN HOUSE WEEKEND AT ALL HARLEY-DAVIDSON STORES, APRIL 1st & 2nd. EVERYONE'S WELCOME.

★ **Examiner's tip**

When you are collating information, you need to decide on the most effective order for it. You could put the points in order of priority, perhaps starting with the most important, or you might write about related points together.

Focus for development: Putting ideas together

Here is a Grade A★ response to this question:

> *What impression of the Harley Davidson is produced in the advertisement?*

provides an overview →

This motorbike, as shown in the advertisement, seems to be offering all the freedom a young person in America could ever want. It stretches across the page, just like the country seems to stretch out all around the rider. Putting it all in black and white takes us back many decades, as if we can go back in time to when there was still some of America to be discovered. The Harley Davidson badge looks like something from an era now gone too. However, it is also saying this is a bike for the young and 'hip', as summed up in the price: 'A cool £4995'. The guy looks cool, even in the desert – just like people used to be cool in the old movies.

← selects details to support overview

selects another feature to develop the point →

← gives sensible detail to link with previous point

makes additional point but with appropriate quotation/comment as supporting evidence and linking back to a previous point at the end

Here is a Grade B response to this question:

> **How does the Fiat advertisement try to appeal to the reader?**

The words across the top of the advert are in different colours, making the car seem exciting and modern – this is also shown by all the words running together as they do. The car is open-topped and seems to be the sort of car that would attract young people. It might attract the ones who want – or who have – 'tanned skin'. Maybe it is suggesting it is a British version of the sort of car we imagine them cruising around in in America...

ACTIVITY

- Which details from the Fiat advert are well selected in the Grade B response?
- What further analysis might have been added and about what?

EXAM TASK

The analysis of the Fiat advert could be improved by giving an overview, then selecting and collating information to support that overview.

Write an improved version by

- offering a brief overview to begin with
- adding appropriate details which, together, support your overview.

Remember

- Make sure you retrieve evidence that is appropriate to the task and to the point you are making.
- Be prepared to offer a general overview, then collate your points carefully so that they work together.

Using quotations and examples effectively

Learning objective

- To understand how to use evidence to support the points you make.

What do we mean by evidence?

How you support points will depend on the question you are asked and the nature of the text, but you are likely to be using direct quotation or mentioning detail from the text to back up your ideas.

Checklist for success

You need to

- remember that any analytical points you make require proof from the text
- select brief quotations – usually no longer than two lines
- refer to detail and make your examples precise, rather than offering generalised thoughts.

⭐ Examiner's tip

*Most responses include PEE (point, evidence, explanation); better responses include PEA (point, evidence, **analysis**). Writing about what words suggest or imply – giving different **interpretations** – will bring more marks.*

ACTIVITY

In the Grade A response below, a student begins to analyse this estate agent's house advert to explain how this property is made attractive to potential buyers.

Read and then complete the response.

includes a quotation to support →

makes a point →

Despite the positive description of the property (for example, it is 'attractive' and 'conveniently placed'), and the fact that a family would benefit from having schools such as Ripon Grammar nearby, it is obviously not perfect: it would 'benefit from some modernising and refurbishment'. This suggests that the interior state of the property is out of date and in poor condition. That would effectively increase the amount of money any potential purchaser would have to commit ...

← gives appropriate detail

← follows with evidence – a quotation embedded in the sentence

└ offers analysis, looking at layers of meaning

THORNTON HOUSE, RIPON, NORTH YORKSHIRE
PRICE: £500,000

This attractive home offers generous living space and is conveniently placed within walking distance from Ripon city centre. Dating from 1865, Thornton House has belonged to the same family for the past 100 years, so this is a real opportunity. The six bedrooms, family bathroom and four reception rooms would benefit from some modernising and refurbishment, while the basement, with wine cellar and four rooms, offers plenty of storage. Schools such as Ripon Grammar and Cathedral Choir School are close by, and Leeds, York and the Yorkshire Dales are within easy driving distance. Best offers need to be received in writing by 12 noon on Monday, September 14.

Call Peters and White Estate Agents on 01597 111523 or visit www.peters&white.co.uk.

Focus for development: Making interpretations

This letter was sent to a local newspaper in Oldham.

Academies are the only way forward

EDITOR – We are proud that Oldham's academy programme has this week been advertised to bidders.

This means that over the next few months we will be choosing the construction partner to build our three state-of-the-art new schools.

Considerable work remains to be done to make these projects successful, however that should not detract attention from our fundamental aspiration: to provide every student in Oldham with a new or nearly new secondary school by 2014.

This brave and ambitious aspiration is the only way forward for Oldham.

Our children are growing up in enormously challenging times - not just in terms of the credit crunch - but also the changes in the global economy. Jobs and skill requirements are transforming and so is the market of people competing for them.

The position for young people in Oldham has many positives. Greater Manchester's economy is still bigger than that of Beijing, for example, and is projected to grow, despite the current financial crises, to 2020.

This will give local children real opportunities, but they will

The Orb Mill site, which will be transformed into one of Oldham's three academies. Inset: Cllr Kay Knox

only be able to capitalise if they acquire high level skills. Education is key to helping them achieve this. Set against these aspirations, Stuart Paulley's criticisms of academy schools (Advertiser letters, September 10) seem out of touch.

He selectively uses evidence to try and sustain his case that academies are selective and failing. Yet we have made it clear that the model for Oldham means all of our academies will have the same admissions criteria as the local authority.

The picture on academies' performance nationally is, on the whole, encouraging and we

have always maintained that ours will be introduced into a local context which is favourable to their success.

Mr Paulley repeatedly criticises, but never proposes a realistic alternative to these plans.

I want the very best opportunities for all our children in order that they, their families, and this borough can prosper.

I refuse to have a two-tier system where some children have the best opportunities but others are left behind.

**Cllr Kay Knox
Cabinet member for
children, young people
and families**

To help examine how convincing the letter is, complete your own copy of the grid below, adding evidence and analysis for Points 2–4. Follow the example for Point 1.

Point	Evidence	Analysis
Cllr Knox says the academies will be totally up-to-date	'our state of the art new schools'	• comes at the start of the letter so has immediate impact • suggests nothing could be more advanced • contrasts with what we might imagine the old schools are like
Cllr Knox believes Greater Manchester is big enough to provide these expensive academies		• • •
Cllr Knox claims that Mr Paulley has no alternative plan		• • •
Cllr Knox claims the decision is not just brave		• • •

EXAM TASK

Write a response to this question.

> *How successful is the Councillor's attempt to convince readers that Academies are necessary?*

In your answer, try to
- begin with an overview of the letter's viewpoint
- select the main points the councillor makes
- offer point, evidence and analysis for each of these.

Remember

- **Find evidence from the text, then explain or analyse it.**
- **Analysing will bring greater rewards than giving an explanation.**

Making inferences

Learning objective

- To understand how to identify implications and 'read between the lines'.

 Examiner's tip

A detailed response might give an overview first, showing the writer's attitude, then work through relevant points in the text, explaining what they say and analysing what they imply. (For example: 'He uses the example of ripping out the hearts of altar maidens to show what happens when a country is hot, implying that we would all go mad and lose all civilised behaviour. This exaggeration makes us think…').

What does reading between the lines involve?

In the exam, you will have to interpret the writer's feelings or attitudes towards their subject.

So, if someone writes, 'This could be the most money ever spent on something so small', it might suggest the price is far too high, or that it is really precious, or that those paying are fools…

To write about what is being suggested, it helps to have a strategy.

- Identify the relevant parts of the text (underlining them in the exam).
- Open with an overview of the content.
- Write about each point in turn, saying what it suggests about the subject.

ACTIVITY

With a partner, read the article below about weather patterns and discuss these two questions.

- Why does the writer think a wet country is better? Find three reasons and explain why he suggests they are valid.
- What is the writer's opinion of British weather and what does he think of hot climates?

Let's rejoice in the rain

by Andrew Grimes

The suspension of global warming over Britain this summer has spared us all a lot of grief. Why some people are complaining about it is beyond my understanding.

This is not a hell-hot country, and with any luck it never will be. We are a group of islands off the northerly side of Europe. It rains a lot. The rain keeps us resourceful, resilient and glossily-wet.

No good ever comes of a country that is perpetually hot. I have just been reading about the Incas of Peru who got on perfectly well until, around AD1100, they were overcome by a cyclic heatwave that lasted 400 years.

The new-fangled sun went to their heads, causing them to build an empire, start wars and found a religion that demanded a constant flow of altar maidens to have their hearts ripped out. They also, poor devils, found tons of gold.

The Incas, who may have been half-way barmy to start with, reacted to their hot sun with manic hyperactivity, and the Spanish wanted their gold. When the conquistadores arrived to destroy them they were too worn out to fight.

Is there, in the Incan tragedy, a moral for those Brits who hanker for a permanency of hot suns?

Focus for development: Inferring from written text and presentational features

WHAT A HE ROW

Boat lad Will, 12, helps cops nab drowning fugitive

Oarsome . . . Will rows his boat with PC Mike Dawber

A BOY of 12 was hailed a hero yesterday for rowing two policemen out to save a drowning drugs suspect.

Will Abbotts — who uses his small boat to fish from his family's lakeside mansion — went into action after cops in riot gear raided a neighbouring home.

Officers arrested one man and found 1,000 cannabis plants. But a second men leapt from a balcony at the rented house, fracturing at least one leg, and then tried to escape by swimming the lake.

Will heard shouts as he stepped off his school bus and saw the fugitive's head bobbing in the water.

The lad — who was still in his public school uniform — said: "I shouted across that I had a boat. I was shaking a bit because I didn't know what this suspect was capable of.

"And when we picked him up there were four people on the boat and it is only meant for two adults at most. We were very pleased to get back to shore."

PC Mike Dawber — one

By BEN ASHFORD

of the officers he helped on a millionaire's row in Mere, near Knutsford, Cheshire — said: "Will's action was brilliant.

"His expert rowing got us across very quickly."

Chief Supt Mick Garrihy said: "He contributed to a police operation against organised crime and saved a man from drowning. He showed speed of thought, bravery and calmness under pressure."

Will's father Gordon, 63, said: "We're very proud, although his mother would have preferred he took the time to put on a life jacket."

Two suspects are facing trial.

b.ashford@the-sun.co.uk

EXAM TASK

Write a response to this question about the news article **above**.

> *How does this article suggest Will is a hero?*

Refer to
- the photograph
- the headings
- the main text.

Remember

- Interpret the text, don't just repeat sections of it.
- Support the points you make with examples or short quotations.
- Read between the lines by thinking about what is implied or suggested, but not directly stated.
- Comment on the writer's attitude to his/her subject, where appropriate.

Learning objective

- *To learn how to write effectively about presentational features.*

What does writing about presentational features involve?

The presentational features – pictures, headings, text boxes and so on – are there to create an effect: to make the reader react or think in a certain way. By focusing on why the text has been produced, you can link your ideas to its purpose and audience. This will give your writing more focus.

Checklist for success

- You need to make sure you understand and can use a range of **technical terms**: for example, headline, subhead, caption, banner.
- Rather than just describing or identifying features, you need to write about their **intended effect** on the reader.

ACTIVITY

- In groups of four, pool your knowledge and draw up a list of all the media terms linked to layout and presentation you know. (For more about presentational features see pages 22–25.)
- Produce a brief definition of each term.

Analysing presentational features and layout

"It's all there with a filmic slickness."
Sunday Express

"I am Dracula. I bid you welcome."

Imagine a world where you can only go out after dark, where you feel a constant hunger for human blood but where for all eternity you will appear young and beautiful. Welcome to the world of Dracula.

A creature who should inspire repulsion in every living thing but who has seduced countless generations, Dracula is possessed of a mesmerising sexuality which fascinates us all.

Choreographed by David Nixon, this dramatic ballet reveals the tormented world of the immortal Count. Images and moments from Bram Stoker's legendary novel are brought alive in sensuous and sinister dance and theatre uncovering our most basic desires and fears.

Features music by Schnittke, Rachmaninov, Pärt and Daugherty.

WY PLAY HOUSE

Thu 10 – Sat 19 September
Evenings: 7.30pm (No Sunday performance)
Matinees: Sat 12 & Sat 19 at 2pm
Box Office: 0113 213 7700
Book Online: www.wyp.org.uk
Prices £27, £22 and £17

Discounts
Discounts available Monday to Friday in areas A and B
Usual concessions and groups of 10+: £3 off per ticket
Groups of 20+: £4 off per ticket
Groups of 40+: £5 off per ticket
School groups: all tickets £10

Get Closer to NBT
Learn more about the production and the Company with their exciting series of talks and workshops. Including a Pre-Performance Talk, Open Adult Workshop, Touch Tour and Audio Described Performance there's something for everyone. For further details and to book please contact the Box Office.

Photos: HANSON, Brian Slater

ACTIVITY

- In your group of four, discuss the following questions about the leaflet above.
  - Why are two such different pictures used? How do we react in each case?
  - Are the colours used significant? How are they used?
  - Does the layout grab our attention?
  - Why have the fonts been used in this way?
  - Do the publicity quotation in white and strapline question in red work?
- Write your own response to the following question:

How have presentational features been used to attract the reader in this text?

Examiner's tip ⭐

*Look at the texts you are given and **be critical**. Consider purpose and audience, and weigh up how some techniques have more impact than others.*

Focus for development: Presentation and layout in web pages

Web pages often offer a range of presentational devices and the layout is carefully designed to

- appeal to readers
- help them to navigate the site easily to find what they want.

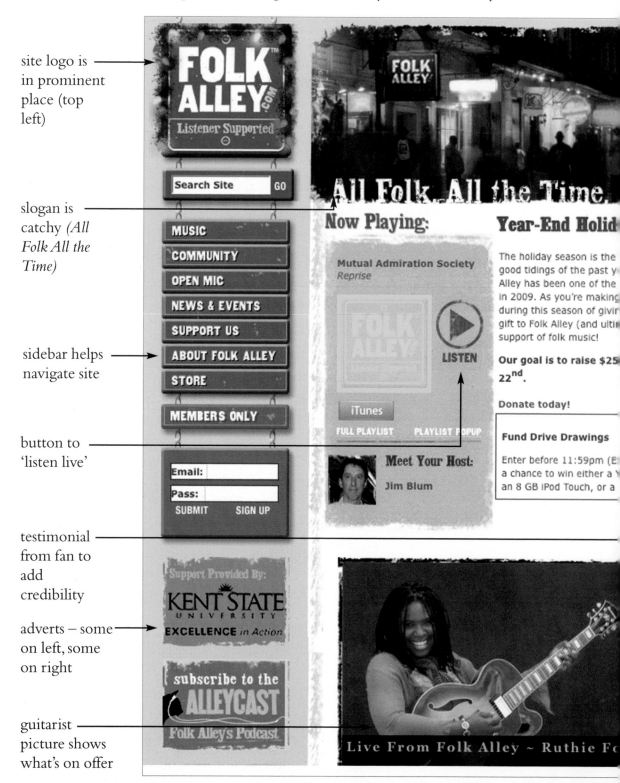

site logo is in prominent place (top left)

slogan is catchy *(All Folk All the Time)*

sidebar helps navigate site

button to 'listen live'

testimonial from fan to add credibility

adverts – some on left, some on right

guitarist picture shows what's on offer

competition
offer
highlighted

picture at top
adds atmosphere

Support Provided By:

text in small
digestible bites

ve

...lect on the
...e hope Folk
... in your life
...ay list
...consider a
...ourself) in

...ecember

...: 22th for
...325 guitar,
...Folk CDS.

$25,000
HELP US MEET
OUR GOAL!

CURRENT TOTAL
$10,380

KEEP THE MUSIC
PLAYING.

SAM BUSH
CIRCLES AROUND ME

THE NEW RECORD
AVAILABLE NOW

Testimonials

Lisa Meissner: Lisa is a Folk Alley supporter from Tupper Lake, New York. She's a life-long folk music fan and a musician in the duo the Rustic Riders. She says she listens AND contributes to Folk Alley because of the quality and range of folk genres and the mix of old and new artists that she hears.

dave
rawlings
machine
a friend of a friend

Available Now

EXAM TASK

- In a group, decide how successful this text is in appealing to its audience.
- Then, working on your own, write about the layout and presentational features.

Remember

- Link your comments about presentational features and layout to your understanding of the text's purpose and audience. It makes things easier.

- Move beyond description to analysis of significant features.

47

Comparing language

Comparing language

Learning objective

- To understand how language comparison questions work in the exam.

 Examiner's tip

It is vital to compare things that are actually comparable, for example sentence length or how particular words are used in the texts. 'Comparing' metaphors with alliteration, for example, is unlikely to bring the best marks.

Will there definitely be a comparison question in the exam?

You will always have to compare language. You will be writing about the impression created by the language in each text. You need to compare the effectiveness of the language used.

Checklist for success

- You need as much practice in comparing texts as possible. Try to find texts to compare at home. You could
  - examine two football reports of the same match, perhaps from a tabloid and a broadsheet newspaper
  - analyse how two 'Agony Aunts' respond to their correspondents in different styles.
- You need to focus on similarities, where they exist, and on differences, using examples from the text to support your ideas. That is the key to success.

ACTIVITY

Read the two extracts on the following page. They deal with the same subject but in different ways.

Complete a grid like this one to compare the extracts.

	Extract 1	Extract 2
General style or tone		
Opening sentence		
Punctuation		
Sentence length		
Similes and metaphors		
Illustrations/vocabulary		
Use of repetition		

Extract 1

Frankly, who cares about endangered species? Environmentalists rush around like demented wombats telling the rest of the known world to give money to save the lesser-spotted iguana or the Siberian toad. But why? If the world's last white rhino were to pass away tomorrow, would it make the slightest difference to my beans on toast? Would the beans be more expensive? I don't think so, because they already cost too much: and that is what worries me, not the fate of the Great White Shark. I'll be dead in fifty years, so who cares about the climate? What matters is my life now…

Examiner's tip ★

It becomes easier to write about the effects of language when you bear in mind the writer's purpose and, where relevant, audience. The language and style fulfil that purpose and aim to engage that audience.

Extract 2

We are living in desperately difficult times. With the massive expansion of the human race, animals are the last thing on most people's minds; yet once rare species have gone, they will never come back. If we look at the situation of the wild salmon, where stocks are rapidly diminishing; if we look at the Mediterranean, which used to teem with fish but now laps emptily against so many shores; if we think about the fall in the number of sharks and the effect that has on the entire eco-system; if we think about how similar situations are happening on land too – we must see that mankind has to change…

ACTIVITY

Write a summary of how the writers use language to put their message across, taking some of the information from your grid.

You are likely to reach a higher grade if you offer more

- detail
- layers of analysis
- points of comparison.

Glossary
Obituary: an account of a person's life, published after their death

Focus for development: Analysing how language creates a style

The viewpoint of the writer affects the approach to his or her subject. This viewpoint will be reflected in the language used.

Read these two obituaries for the writer, Keith Waterhouse.

Text 1

Farewell Keith, king of Fleet Street

by Sam Greenhill

Keith Waterhouse, acclaimed journalist, novelist, dramatist, raconteur and *Daily Mail* columnist, died in his sleep yesterday.

A legend of the golden age of Fleet Street and a man whose plays have filled theatres around the world, he was at his home in London when he passed away. He was 80.

His former wife, journalist Stella Bingham, said: 'He died peacefully at home.'

They had divorced in 1989 but remained friends and in recent times she was a crucial figure in his life, looking after him in his final weeks.

Waterhouse had been unwell since earlier this year.

The revered writer, whose extraordinary career spanned 60 years, came from humble beginnings in Leeds and rose to become a luminary in the worlds of literature, theatre and film.   *Daily Mail*

Text 2

Glossary
Pantechnicon: a large van used for furniture removals

Keith Waterhouse Daily Mirror legend, 1929–2009
Champion of the Word

by Anton Antonowicz

Keith Waterhouse, one of Britain's greatest journalists, novelists and dramatists, died before lunch yesterday.

Which would have annoyed him, given that his hobby listed in *Who's Who* was simply, 'Lunch'.

He could afford to enjoy that mid-day break because he rose early and wrote quickly, knowing that 'summat to eat' and the regular bottle of champagne beckoned at the end of that noontide full-stop.

But what he could write in those few hours before dawn and drink-time was marvellous.

In his distinctly northern way, this lad from Leeds – to whom he contritely returned library books 25 years overdue in a pantechnicon – was a constant child.

His finest work, whether writing those sparkling columns for the *Mirror* (and later the *Daily Mail*), harked back to more innocent times.

He was at his best summoning childhood memories of kids 'falling into ponds, eating poisonous berries, contracting stomach-ache from under-ripe stolen apples, getting lost, being bitten by dogs, fighting and starting fires, sitting in cow-pats and acquiring bumps the size of a duck egg on their heads'.   *Daily Mirror*

Discuss these questions with a partner.

- What is similar about the two headlines?
- What other similarities can you find in the two texts?
- What is the major difference in the way these two writers remember Keith Waterhouse?
- How does the language used reflect their attitudes towards him? For example, write about
  - 'king' and 'champion' in the headlines
  - how Text 1 uses words like 'acclaimed', 'legend' and 'luminary', whilst Text 2 also uses 'summat to eat' and 'lad'.

Here is an extract from a student's response comparing the articles.

Grade A★ response

> Whilst Greenhill uses predictable praise for Waterhouse ('king' and 'revered' making him seem a hero) Antonowicz uses language to show us the real Waterhouse, behind the writing. You feel he knew the man, is able to capture his northern speech ('summat to eat' – he was a 'northern lad'), and pick out the words Waterhouse probably liked best: 'lunch' and 'champagne'. We sense Waterhouse was a man of appetite and there was fun in him: his articles were 'sparkling' – presumably funny, enjoyable and as bubbly as the champagne he loved...

Notice how this Grade A★ response

- actively makes comparisons between the texts, using appropriate evidence
- captures the tone of the obituaries
- collates or groups ideas ('summat to eat' and 'northern lad')
- offers layers of analysis
- shows an understanding of **why** and **how** the texts were written.

Write a full comparison of how language is used in the two obituaries to capture the memory of Keith Waterhouse.

Remember

- **Make your comparison detailed.**
- **Start from your understanding of the writer's purposes, and build your analysis of the language around that.**

Grade Booster

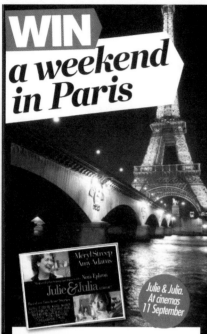

WIN a weekend in Paris

Meryl Streep
Amy Adams
Nora Ephron
Julie & Julia

Julie & Julia.
At cinemas
11 September

There's always an excuse to visit Paris. Whether you're drawn there by your love of food, fashion, architecture, romance or just a well-earned weekend away, you'll always find what you're looking for.

That's why we're offering one reader and a friend a fabulous weekend in the French capital.

You'll fly to Paris where a glass of chilled champagne will await you at the Hugo Hotel – your accommodation for the next two nights. You'll have £200 spending money, plus an evening dinner for two where you can sample true French cuisine.

Julie & Julia, starring Meryl Streep and Amy Adams, will be in cinemas on 11 September. It brings together the true stories of two women, a generation apart, who find the answer to their dreams through their experiments with French cookery.

For your chance to win, complete the film title:

MERYL STREEP STARRED IN THE FILM: THE DEVIL WEARS _____ ?

Extended Exam Task

Write a response to this question.

How does the text attempt to interest the reader?

Comment on

- its purpose and audience
- its layout and presentational features
- the main messages in the text
- the language techniques used.

Evaluation: What have you learned?

With a partner, use the grade checklist below to evaluate your work on the Extended Exam Task.

- I can make a perceptive appreciation and analysis of the presentational features, messages and language techniques, demonstrating how they combine to create their effects.

- I can make a detailed interpretation of the presentational features, messages and language techniques, incorporating them into a unified analysis.

- I can begin to analyse how the presentational features, messages and language techniques have been used.

- I can make clear and relevant comments on the presentational features, messages and language techniques.

- I can understand how the presentational features, messages and language techniques are used but my comments are not developed.

You may need to go back and look at the relevant pages from this section again.

Introduction

In this section you will

- practise the reading skills you have been learning about in this chapter
- read, analyse and respond to sample answers by different candidates
- write your own answers to sample questions
- evaluate and assess your answers and the progress you have made.

Why is exam preparation like this important?

- You need to be able to work under timed conditions
- Looking at sample answers by other students will help you see what you need to do to improve your own work.

Key Information

Unit 1 is Understanding and Producing Non-Fiction Texts.

- It has an exam of **2 hours**, worth **80 marks.**
- It is worth **40%** of your overall English GCSE mark.
- Section A of the exam is on Reading and Section B of the exam is on Writing.

Section A Reading

- This section is **1 hour long**, and is worth **40 marks** or 20% of your English GCSE.
- You will be asked to read three non-fiction texts and to answer four questions on the texts:
  - **Q1**: finding information in a text (**8 marks**)
  - **Q2**: analysing presentational features (**8 marks**)
  - **Q3**: examining what is inferred (suggested) in a text (**8 marks**)
  - **Q4**: comparing the language used in two texts (**16 marks**)

Examples of the different question types can be found on pages 55–57.

The Assessment

The assessment objective for reading (AO2) states that you must be able to do the following:

- Read and understand texts, selecting material appropriate to purpose, collating from different sources and making comparisons and cross-references as appropriate.
- Develop and sustain interpretations of writers' ideas and perspectives.
- Explain and evaluate how writers use linguistic, grammatical, structural and presentational features to achieve effects and engage and influence the reader.

Targeting Grade A

Some of the key differences between Grade C and Grade A/A★ answers are as follows:

Grade C candidates	See examples on page 59.
<ul><li>show clearly that the texts are understood</li><li>use appropriate evidence to support their views</li><li>offer relevant interpretations of the texts</li><li>make clear connections and comparisons.</li></ul>	

Grade A/A★ candidates	See examples on pages 58 and 60
<ul><li>develop perceptive interpretations of texts</li><li>respond personally and persuasively to texts</li><li>employ apt quotations to support detailed understanding</li><li>comment perceptively on thoughts, feelings and ideas in texts.</li></ul>	

EXTENDED TASK/PRACTICE

Complete the sample exam paper on the next pages.

Item 1

Grizzly bears starve as fish stocks collapse

Calls grow to suspend hunting season in Canada after wildlife guides sound alarm at lack of cubs

by Tracy McVeigh

Chief Reporter

First it was the giant panda, then the polar bear, now it seems that the grizzly bear is the latest species to face impending disaster.

A furious row has erupted in Canada with conservationists desperately lobbying the government to suspend the annual bear-hunting season following reports of a sudden drop in the numbers of wild bears spotted on salmon streams and key coastal areas where they would normally be feeding.

The government has promised to order a count of bears, but not until after this year's autumn trophy hunts have taken place. It has enraged ecology groups which say that a dearth of salmon stocks may be responsible for many bears starving in their dens during hibernation. The female grizzlies have their cubs during winter after gorging themselves in September on the fish fats that sustain them through the following months.

"I've never seen bears hungry in the fall before, but last year they were starving," said British Columbian wildlife guide and photographer Doug Neasloss. "I noticed in the spring there weren't as many bears coming out, but I felt it was premature to jump to conclusions." But now, he said, "there just aren't any bears. It's scary."

It was the same story, he said, from other guides over 16 rivers where once they would have been encountering dozens of grizzly bears. "There has been a huge drop in numbers. I've never experienced anything this bad." Reports from stream walkers, who monitor salmon streams across the vast territories, have been consistent, according to the conservation group Pacific Wild – no bears, and more worryingly, no bear cubs.

Grizzlies once roamed across most of North America and the Great Plains until European settlers gradually pushed them back. Only 1,000 remain in the contiguous US, where they are protected, but the number is less clear in the vast wilds of Canada and Alaska, where they are prized by hunters who shoot hundreds of the 350kg giants every year, providing a lucrative income for provincial governments that license the hunts. "It's appalling wildlife management, considering the widespread concern for coastal bears at the moment," said McAllister.

A report released last week showed species numbers to have fallen dramatically in the province of Alberta, where local officials have decided to suspend the annual hunting season despite intense lobbying from hunters. "There's no question that bears are worse off now than 20 years ago – both in numbers and range," said Jim Pissot, of the group Defenders of Wildlife.

The few grizzlies spotted this year in their usual haunts are said to be starving.
Corbis

Item 2

EIGHT PAGES OF THE
BEST TV SHOWS ON
SKY THIS MONTH

skymag
this month

Siberian tigers
are under threat
from poaching

FROM RUSSIA WITH LOVE

The beauty of the Russian wilderness is revealed – in stunning high definition

HD WILD RUSSIA
Sun 4, 8pm, National Geographic Channel **HD**/
National Geographic Channel **(543/526)**

This scene of Siberian tigers sparring in the snow is breathtaking, but for the crew of National Geographic's new series *Wild Russia* it was just one of the many jaw-dropping moments captured in HD during an epic 1,200 days' filming. "From the frozen forests of Siberia to the geysers of Kamchatka, the territory where we filmed is unknown even to many Russians," explains executive producer Amanda Theunissen.

Wild Russia reveals the secrets of the world's largest wilderness – almost 70 times the size of the UK – including many animals that, sadly, may soon be extinct. "Siberian tigers are under threat from poaching," says Amanda. "There are around 40 Amur leopards left, just 440 European bison and 1,500 breeding pairs of Siberian crane – a tiny amount."

Amanda points out that *Wild Russia* isn't purely an animal behaviour show. "It's also about the area – more than 60,000 miles of land between Moscow and Vladivostok where hardly anyone

ventures. There aren't many roads or places to land a helicopter. In high definition, the scenery is gobsmacking!" However, the remoteness did cause problems... "One of the crew was bitten by a snake and had to be stretchered for two days to get to a road," says Amanda.

The harsh landscape is a backdrop to scenes of beauty, including a surprising bear ritual. "Their mating is usually rough and ready," smiles Amanda. "So it was touching when we saw a pair being tender, before ambling off into the forest together. It was like a fairy tale."

**Love this?
Watch these!** ↘ ● *After the Attack,* Thu 1, 9pm, Animal Planet (525) ● *Secret Life of Elephants,* Wed 7, 9pm, Eden (532) ● *Orca Killing School,* Thu 15, 9pm, Nat Geo Wild **HD**/Nat Geo Wild (544/528) ● *Hooked: Monster Fishing,* Mon19, 8pm, National Geographic Channel (526)

october 2009 **skymag** 11

Item 3

The Deaths of Animals

In America, thirty species of large animals – some very large indeed – disappeared practically at a stroke after the arrival of modern humans on the continent between ten and twenty thousand years ago. Altogether North and South America between them lost about three-quarters of their big animals once man the hunter arrived with his flint-headed spears and keen organisational capabilities. Europe and Asia, where the animals had had longer to evolve a useful wariness of humans, lost between a third and a half of their big creatures. Australia, for exactly the opposite reasons, lost no less than 90 per cent.

Because the early hunter populations were comparatively small and the animal populations truly monumental – as many as ten million mammoth carcasses are thought to be frozen in the tundra of northern Siberia alone – some authorities think there must be other explanations, possibly involving climate change or some kind of pandemic. As Rose MacPhee of the American Museum of Natural History put it: 'There's no material benefit to hunting dangerous animals more often than you need to – there are only so many mammoth steaks you can eat.' Others believe it may have been almost criminally easy to catch and clobber prey. 'In Australia and the Americas,' says Tim Flannery, 'the animals probably didn't know enough to run away.'

Some of the creatures that were lost were singularly spectacular and would take a little managing if they were still around. Imagine giant sloths that could look into an upstairs window, tortoises nearly the size of a small Fiat, monitor lizards 6 metres long basking beside desert highways in Western Australia. Alas, they are gone, and we live on a much diminished planet. Today, across the whole world, only four types of really hefty (a tonne or more) land animals survive: elephants, rhinos, hippos and giraffes. Not for tens of millions of years has life on Earth been so diminutive and tame.

From *A Short History of Nearly Everything*, Bill Bryson

Answer these questions:

1. Read **Item 1**, the newspaper article entitled 'Grizzly bears starve as fish stocks collapse' by Tracy McVeigh

   What are the problems for bears in Canada, according to Tracy McVeigh?   **8 marks**

2. Now read **Item 2**, from a Sky television magazine, headed 'From Russia with Love'.

   How do the heading and the picture add to the effectiveness of the text?   **8 marks**

3. Now read **Item 3**, 'The Deaths of Animals' by Bill Bryson.

   What does Bryson think about the fact that so many animals disappeared?   **8 marks**

4. Now you need to refer to **Item 2**, 'From Russia with Love', and **either** Item 1 **or** Item 3. You are going to compare the two texts, one of which you have chosen.

   Compare the ways in which language is used for effect in the two texts. Give some examples and explain what the effects are.   **16 marks**

Exploring Sample Responses

Read the following response, judging how well you have done against the quality of these answers, bearing in mind the Examiner feedback.

1 What are the problems for bears in Canada, according to Tracy McVeigh?

Example 1

McVeigh shows grizzly bears in a dreadful situation. The headline sets out her basic message ('Grizzly bears starve as fish stocks collapse') and the subheading adds the idea of 'alarm'. Clearly something needs to be done, and quickly. — *first paragraph summarises / personal interpretation*

She adds weight to that impression, explaining that there has been a 'sudden drop' in the number of bears spotted on salmon streams, probably because there have been fewer fish on which they could feed. Conservationists point out that bears are likely to starve in their dens during hibernation because there are not enough fish to fatten them to survive. Cubs are usually born in winter, but will not be born to starving mothers. — *range of details used to support ideas*

We learn that, unusually, bears were starving last fall and there were fewer bears in the spring. McVeigh quotes photographer Doug Neasloss to emphasise what has happened: 'Now... there just aren't any bears. It's scary.' He adds that others have found the same over 16 rivers – no bears and no bear cubs. — *selective use of quotation*

We are given a brief history, to show how things have changed: bears once roamed freely across North America but now there are only 1000 in the US and no one knows how few are in Canada and Alaska. Provincial governments allow the hunting of hundreds of bears each year. — *good use of facts*

There is some hope offered towards the end of the article, though, as fewer numbers of bears in Alberta has brought a hunting ban, despite hunters' complaints. — *balance: introduces hope*

However, the final quotation from Defenders of Wildlife leaves us with the seriousness of the problem: 'bears are worse off now than 20 years ago.' It takes us back to the headline and the problem. — *effective quotation to conclude*

Examiner feedback

It is sometimes a temptation to just copy out relevant sections of the text. In this case, the student has given the ideas a framework. There is an overview, then the different sections are introduced, before being supported by detailed analysis of what is happening. The student includes everything that is important whilst making perceptive comments on how McVeigh has structured her article. We get the impression the student knows exactly what McVeigh is telling us and how she is putting across her message.

Suggested grade: A/A★

ACTIVITY

Read this next response, judging how well you have done against the quality of this answer, bearing in mind the Examiner feedback.

2 How do the heading and the picture add to the effectiveness of 'From Russia with Love?'

Example 2

> The title makes us think of the James Bond film, which is about beautiful spies and fighting, but really it is about many of the good and beautiful things in wild Russia. The tigers in the picture might be starting to fight or to mate but they also look beautiful to attract us to the programme. Their colours look amazing to show how lovely they can be and it is as if they might hold hands soon, or paws. The text is saying these creatures are becoming rare but they are lovely and that is what the picture shows.

Examiner feedback

The candidate has dealt with both the picture and the headline and offered some interpretation of each. Importantly, they are linked to the text, to show why they have been used. The points made have been explained.

To get a higher grade, the candidate needed to write about

- the headline with more clarity – saying why it is appropriate and interpreting it more precisely, in relation to the rest of the text
- the picture in more detail – perhaps mentioning the snow and its relevance, whether they appear to be rushing together or play fighting or whatever. Again, interpretations would need to be linked directly to words and phrases from the text (for example, 'jaw-dropping moments').

Suggested grade: C

ACTIVITY

Discuss with a partner. Based on the bullet points in the examiner's comments, how would you improve this response?

Read this next response, judging how well you have done against the quality of these answers, bearing in mind the Examiner feedback.

3 In 'The Death of Animals', what does Bryson think about the fact that so many animals disappeared?

Example 3

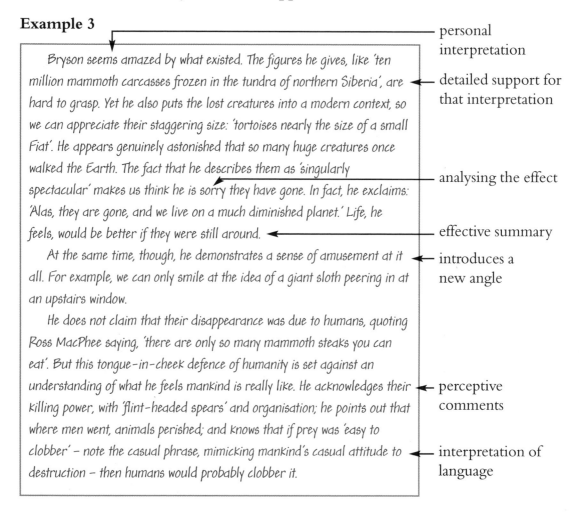

personal interpretation

    Bryson seems amazed by what existed. The figures he gives, like 'ten million mammoth carcasses frozen in the tundra of northern Siberia', are hard to grasp. Yet he also puts the lost creatures into a modern context, so we can appreciate their staggering size: 'tortoises nearly the size of a small Fiat'. He appears genuinely astonished that so many huge creatures once walked the Earth. The fact that he describes them as 'singularly spectacular' makes us think he is sorry they have gone. In fact, he exclaims: 'Alas, they are gone, and we live on a much diminished planet.' Life, he feels, would be better if they were still around.

    At the same time, though, he demonstrates a sense of amusement at it all. For example, we can only smile at the idea of a giant sloth peering in at an upstairs window.

    He does not claim that their disappearance was due to humans, quoting Ross MacPhee saying, 'there are only so many mammoth steaks you can eat'. But this tongue-in-cheek defence of humanity is set against an understanding of what he feels mankind is really like. He acknowledges their killing power, with 'flint-headed spears' and organisation; he points out that where men went, animals perished; and knows that if prey was 'easy to clobber' – note the casual phrase, mimicking mankind's casual attitude to destruction – then humans would probably clobber it.

detailed support for that interpretation

analysing the effect

effective summary

introduces a new angle

perceptive comments

interpretation of language

Examiner feedback

This answer shows a full understanding of what Bryson thinks and how he puts it across to the reader. There are perceptive comments about his attitudes (for example, 'tongue-in-cheek defence') and how he puts them across, and the quotations are all well chosen, supporting the interpretations being offered. The focus is always upon what Bryson says, how he says it and the thoughts behind the words.

Suggested Grade: A★

Read this final response, judging how well you have done against the quality of these answers, bearing in mind the Examiner feedback.

4 **Compare the ways in which language is used for effect in 'From Russia with Love' and one of the other texts. Give some examples and explain what the effects are.**

Example 4

'From Russia with Love' sets out to attract viewers, so there are many positive opinions about the programme: 'stunning', 'breathtaking' and 'gobsmacking'. It is obviously trying to attract a younger audience by using that last word. In contrast, 'Grizzly bears' is an article full of less appealing reality, which talks of 'impending disaster'. The vocabulary is depressing. In places, the bears' situation seems dreadful: 'It's scary'. The words are as if from a horror novel. We are expected to be shocked by the scale of what is happening, as reflected in the facts given. Whilst the animals in 'From Russia' are 'sparring' and 'ambling off into the forest together' sounding like playmates, the bears are starving. The language used is bleak: 'I've never experienced anything this bad...'

Examiner feedback

This response demonstrates clear understanding and analysis. The vocabulary is examined and compared and comments on the effects are included. Effective quotations support the points made and there are some quite sensitive comments (for example, 'The language used is bleak').

To gain a higher grade, the candidate needed to

- offer more detail and interpretation (for example, 'facts' are mentioned, but without any analysis)
- make further more perceptive comments (for example, the phrase 'impending disaster' is quoted but there is no significant comment on the actual words)
- extend the comparison through the remainder of the response.

Suggested Grade: B

If you only do five things...

1 Read as many different kinds of non-fiction texts as possible. Try to read at least one text each day.
2 Decide what the purpose and audience are for each text you read. Work out what the writer wants the reader to think.
3 Spot the techniques the writer uses to convince the reader: focus on how the writers use presentational features, and find elements of the language you could comment on, such as similes and metaphors.
4 Always try to analyse rather than explain, looking to interpret features in different ways, rather than making just one comment.
5 When writing about texts, always try to structure your answer so that ideas link and develop.

Unit 1B **Writing Non-fiction Texts**

What's it all about?

Writing non-fiction texts means you have a chance to write a fantastic variety of texts, many of which will be really useful for life outside school. What is more, a good letter, exciting news article or snappy web text can be just as creative as a story or poem.

How will I be assessed?

You will get **20% of your English marks** for your ability to write non-fiction texts. You will have to complete **two** written tasks in an exam lasting **one hour**.

You will be marked on your writing of two responses – one **short**, one **long** – to two set tasks.

What is being tested?

You are being examined on your ability to

- write for specific audiences and purposes
- communicate clearly, effectively and imaginatively
- organise information in a structured way, using a range of paragraphs
- use a variety of sentence structures and styles
- use a range of linguistic features for impact and effect
- write with accuracy in punctuation, spelling and grammar.

Purposeful Writing

Introduction

This section of Chapter 2 shows you how to

- understand what a written response question is asking you to do
- understand the meaning of the words 'task', 'audience', 'purpose' and 'form'
- generate ideas and plan your writing
- explore different approaches to planning the structure of your work.

Why is planning for purpose important?

- To complete any written task – either in class or in the exam – you need to **understand what you have to do** and, once you have done that, **focus on how you get there**.
- The **plan and the structure** for your writing are like a **'road map'** to make sure you get where you want to go.
- This gives you the **big picture**, not just the details, so that you understand the overall effect of particular choices you make.

A **Grade C** candidate will

- plan so that the organisation of his/her writing is effective, for example in using clear and coherent paragraphing to sequence ideas
- successfully adapt form and style to different purposes.

C

A **Grade A/A★** candidate will

- plan so that the organisation of his / her writing is effective, skilful and coherent with a logical structure
- exploit the chosen form fully, in an assured, confident and controlled way
- where, appropriate, engage and delight the reader.

A

A★

Prior learning

Before you begin this unit, reflect on

- what you already know about **audience**, **purpose** and **form**

  Could you jot down what you understand by these terms?

- previous occasions when you have had to **come up with ideas** for a written task

  What did you do? What techniques did you use?

  Do you find others can follow your ideas easily? Why? Why not?

- how confident you are about the **structure and organisation** of your written work.

  Do you use **paragraphs**, **headings** or other **organisational features** effectively?

Understanding task, purpose, audience and form

Learning objective

- To understand how task, purpose, audience and form shape your written response in the exam.

What do these terms mean?

The **task** is the question or problem you have been set: for example, to write a letter to an employer applying for a job, or an article for a travel magazine describing an exciting trip.

The **purpose** is the reason for writing the letter or article: for example, to persuade or to explain and describe.

The **audience** means the reader or readers: the people who will receive your letter, or read your article.

The **form** is the type and category of writing: letter, article, report, etc.

Checklist for success

- You need to identify the purpose, audience and form in the writing task you have been set.
- You need to consider how these things will shape your writing plan.

In the writing exam, **purpose, audience** and **form** are all present in the **task**.

ACTIVITY

Read these three sample questions and then, with a partner, note down for each case

- the audience
- the purpose
- the form.

The first has been done for you. Of course, the task and purpose are tied up together, so don't worry if you can't separate them.

Then, compare your answers with another pair. Did you agree? Which one of these would you consider the most difficult task? Why?

form ⟶   audience ⟶   task/purpose ⟶

Sample question 1: Write a **report** for your **headteacher advising** him or her about **whether it would be a good idea to lengthen the school day** by an hour and a half.

Sample question 2: Some people believe our country's energy needs will be solved by us taking responsibility at home. They advise us to save energy by turning off lights, unplugging phone-chargers, heating only the rooms we are in, and so on. Write a letter to your local newspaper either persuading readers to follow this advice, or arguing against it.

Sample question 3: A website called 'Classic Kids' Films' has asked users to suggest one classic film they would recommend to parents for their children. Review the film you would choose, saying why you would recommend it.

Focus for development: Audiences and purposes

Now read this email from a student to a revision website:

Can't texts have lots of purposes? If I send an email to a friend about him coming to visit me, I could be giving him information, persuading him – if he's not sure – even making him laugh, cos we're good friends…

Discuss this issue with a partner:

Can texts have more than one purpose? Think about the autobiography of a celebrity: what purposes might that text have?

CHRIS EVANS
LiTTLE BiGSHOT

Coleen
welcome to my world x x

Look at this extract from a student's answer in the exam. Can you work out what the task, audience, purpose and form were?

The production of Romeo and Juliet by Year 10 and 11 last night was one of the best performances to grace the school stage in a long, long time. With atmospheric lighting, moody music and fantastic sound effects, the whole production was a credit to the students, and I thoroughly recommend that you come along to see your sons and daughters performing. Don't miss out – tickets for the remaining nights are selling quickly.

Remember

- Identifying task, purpose, audience and form in the exam question will help shape your answer.
- Texts can have more than one purpose and more than one audience.

Planning an answer

Learning objectives

- To understand how important the plan is to a successful answer.

- To write a basic plan for an exam-style question.

 Examiner's tip

You can use other ways of generating ideas – for example, a list or flowchart or whatever works for you. The main thing is to get ideas down on paper!

You don't have to use everything you write down initially: you can always leave out ideas that you later decide don't fit what you want to say.

What does it mean to plan?

When you plan an answer you are thinking ahead. Your plan is an outline of the main ideas and content you are going to include. It may also be the stage where you decide which points to analyse in greater detail.

Checklist for success

A successful plan is one that

- answers the **main purpose** of the task
- covers the **main points**
- provides **a structure**, with a **clear sequence** of steps and sharp detail
- sometimes includes **key words**, **phrases** or **sentences** you intend to use.

You will have **one hour** to answer **two questions**. Spend **five minutes** planning each answer – but before you write the plan, you need to **generate ideas**.

ACTIVITY

Generating ideas

Read **Sample question 1** on page 64 again.

A student has started to **generate ideas** for this answer using a spider diagram. Complete it by adding main points of your own. Then include detail for each main point.

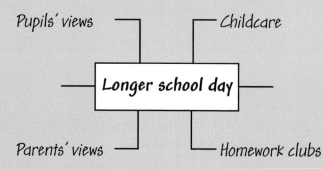

REPORT – lengthening school day, good or bad?

Pupils' views — Childcare

Longer school day

Parents' views — Homework clubs

Focus for development: What makes a good plan?

The plan

Now read this plan based on the spider diagram.

Look at the plan with a friend and discuss:

- whether you would be able to write an answer to the task based on this plan

- if there is another way the answer might have been structured.

Plan

1   Intro: thank him for asking me to report for him

2   Advantages of lengthening school day:
   - less childcare for parents
   - could have tea provided
   - homework done in school so equal for everyone

3   Disadvantages:
   - pupils want to go home, may be problems
   - clubs outside school will have to change times
   - buses, trains?

4   Conclusion: good idea if problems dealt with first; parents kept informed.

Now look at a second sample question.

A website called 'Classic Kids' Films' has asked users to suggest one classic film they would recommend to parents to show their children. Write a description of your suggestion, explaining why you would recommend it.

Generate ideas and then write a plan for this question. Take no more than five minutes to do so.

1   Start by reading the question and identifying the purpose, audience and form.

2   Next, generate ideas: use a spider diagram, list of points or notes.

3   Then write your plan. Use numbers or letters for each section (these could be your paragraphs in the final answer).

Examiner's tip

When you've done your plan, jot down a variety of suitable words and phrases ready to use in your answer: for example, some good connectives ('firstly', 'however', 'moreover') or impressive phrases you might use ('spectacular experience', 'thrill-a-minute adventure').

Remember

- **A good, detailed plan will help you to write a high level response.**

- **A plan will keep you focused and give you a clear sequence to follow as you write your answer.**

Structuring your text

Learning objective

- To understand how basic structure can change meaning and effect.

What is structure?

The **structure** of a text is the way it is **organised**, particularly the order of the content.

Checklist for success

Successful structure is achieved by

- including the **key conventions** of a particular form of text, such as the opening to a letter
- **sequencing** the content appropriately: for example, deciding whether to state your main point at the start of a text
- **organising** content effectively (for example, deciding whether to group certain ideas together)
- making sure the reader can **follow your argument**, viewpoint or explanation.

Check the key conventions of non-fiction forms on pages 4–5.

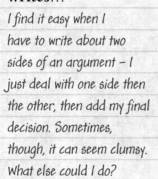

A student writes…

I find it easy when I have to write about two sides of an argument – I just deal with one side then the other, then add my final decision. Sometimes, though, it can seem clumsy. What else could I do?

Answer…

You could deal with each issue or topic in turn. It does mean, though, that you will need to use comparative language well ('on the other hand', 'in contrast').

ACTIVITY

Here is a Grade A/A★ example in which a student has written about the advantages and disadvantages of a beach holiday and a city break.

> The weather! That's what blights beach holidays. If it's sunny – fine, but what do you do if the sand is as soggy as a marshmallow? On the other hand, bad weather in a city is actually quite welcome. No one needs an excuse to sit in some trendy café sipping a hot chocolate, do they?
>
> When it comes to chilling out, the beach holiday wins hands down: you can't beat the mix of fresh air and warm sea. City breaks might be relaxing, but you can never escape the traffic, the fumes and the people.

Which structure has the student used from the two options given above in the 'A student writes…' section?

Focus for development: Sequence and organisation

Similar decisions about organisation – what you deal with and in what order – occur even in texts in which you are not comparing things. For example, what is the best way to **start** a text: to get straight to the point, or to be more subtle?

ACTIVITY

Write two plans for this task.

For each plan, jot down what you are going to include over five paragraphs.

- In the first plan, use the first paragraph for stating your point of view and then deal with all the pros and then all the cons.

- In the second plan, deal with each point in turn, looking at the pros and cons of each.

Work with a partner and give an improvised talk based on each plan. Discuss which structure worked better, and why.

Task:

Your form teacher has asked you whether having a 'whole school litter pick' at the end of each day is a good idea. Advise him or her on what is the best course of action.

ACTIVITY

Approaches to structure

You can use structure to affect tone and style, for example by having an unusual opening.

Look at these two emails students have written in response to a question about inviting an old friend to meet up. Which one do you think uses a more original and engaging opening? Why?

A *Hiya. Would you like to meet up some time? It's been ages since I've been in touch. It'd be great to hear all your news, and share a coffee. We could meet in Princes Park if you like?*

B *A sunny afternoon – Princes Park – veggie burgers, diet coke and a good laugh. Sound like fun? I haven't been in touch for ages, so it'd be great to meet up next week if you're around…*

Remember

- **Changing the order or sequence of information you give changes the effect. Sometimes it is best to be direct, but don't be afraid to experiment with structure.**

Grade Booster

Extended Exam Task

Generate ideas, plan a task and decide on a structure for this question:

> *Write an article for your school magazine in which you attempt to persuade your year group to volunteer to work for local charities.*

If you feel ready, write the opening two paragraphs of your article.

Remember to follow this process:

Generate ideas Plan Decide on structure or sequence

Evaluation – What have you learned?

With a partner, use the grade checklist below to evaluate your work on the Extended Exam Task.

- I can quickly and efficiently compose a plan which shows my immediate grasp of the full potential of the task.
- I can demonstrate my creative flair by using a wide range of language choices and techniques.

- I can quickly and efficiently compose a plan which shows the most effective organisation and structure for the task, audience, purpose and form.
- I can plan how to show a wide range of ambitious language choices and techniques.

- I can write a plan which allows me to develop and organise ideas for task, purpose, audience and form, with a clear sense of the effect they will have on the reader.
- I can consider things such as alternative beginnings and endings, and variety of paragraphs.

- I can write plans with a view to interesting the reader and my organisation is clear.
- I can choose language that is appropriate, linked to the purpose and form.

- I can write plans but they are not always detailed or properly focused on purpose, audience, form and the task set.
- I can use language that is mostly appropriate.

You may need to go back and look at the relevant pages from this section again.

Communicating Clearly, Effectively and Imaginatively

Introduction

This section of Chapter 2 shows you how to

- focus on the aspects of your writing which help you communicate successfully
- explore the importance of selecting appropriate vocabulary
- craft impressive, rich sentences and structure paragraphs coherently
- improve your use of punctuation for effect and impact, as well as accuracy.

Why is it important to communicate clearly, effectively and imaginatively?

- Your ideas may be wonderful, but you need to convey what you have in your head to the reader so that they 'get' your meaning.
- Good communication, however, is not just about clarity but about engaging the reader in what you have to say.

A **Grade C** candidate will

- use a wider range of sentences
- use generally accurate punctuation and carefully chosen and varied vocabulary
- use clear and logical paragraphing.

C

A **Grade A/A★** candidate will

- use varied and sophisticated sentence structures
- use a wide range of punctuation for deliberate effect
- demonstrate an ambitious and varied vocabulary
- vary the style and length of paragraphs to fully support the main thrust and purpose of the text.

A **A★**

Prior learning

Before you begin this unit

- jot down what you already know about the four main areas addressed here: **vocabulary**, **punctuation**, **sentences** and **paragraphs**

- reflect on any particular areas which have **caused you concern** in your general written work or, more specifically, in timed or assessed pieces of work.

Do you already have ideas about how to use each of these successfully? Do you understand how to use the main punctuation points?

Paragraphing – cohesion and coherence

Learning objective

- To understand how linking ideas within and between paragraphs improves writing.

What is cohesion and coherence in paragraphs?

Coherence means that the parts of a text link together and have a logical order. For example, an opening paragraph may introduce ideas and the second paragraph may then build on them.

Connectives (such as 'and', 'so' and 'however') and **pronouns** ('he', 'she', 'it', etc.) are the words and phrases that 'glue' sentences and paragraphs together to create a flowing, **cohesive** text. For example, the first paragraph may use the name of an object or person, but subsequent paragraphs may refer back to them as 'it', 'he' or 'she' to avoid repetition.

Checklist for success

- You need to make sure that sentences in individual paragraphs link well and make sense.
- You need to compose paragraphs which are structured for a particular impact or effect: for example, a long descriptive one, followed by a short one which shows someone's startled reaction.

ACTIVITY

Read these opening paragraphs to a review of a school production.

> The school's production of West Side Story was fantastic and had everything you could wish for. It had good acting. It had good dancing. The music was great. Amy Fisher was brilliant in her role playing Maria.
>
> The wonderful set design made us all sit up and take notice. It was colourful and snazzy and really fitted the story. The art department should be thanked for all their work.

This is a **C grade** response because

- the paragraphs are reasonably clear and fit the purpose (to review a school performance)
- the paragraphs are organised by content (the second one is about the set design).

However, complex ideas need to be presented in a **coherent** way for higher grades. How could the **cohesion** within the two paragraphs be improved to **enhance** meaning?

Rewrite the paragraphs

- removing unnecessary repetition
- making them 'flow better' (for example, could you use connectives to join short sentences together?)
- re-organising any ideas that should perhaps be linked.

Focus for development: Making paragraphs coherent

ACTIVITY

Now look at this student's **Grade A★** response to a design task on eco-friendly cars.

Make brief notes on the purpose and effect of the first short paragraph, and the reasons why the second two paragraphs are longer.

Then add another long paragraph in which you describe the interior of the car.

Finish by adding a one- or two-sentence paragraph in which you sum up the ideal car's qualities. This final paragraph could

- use a pattern of three adjectives to sum up its qualities ('the ideal car would be…,… and…')
- finish with a short sentence emphasising its importance.

EXAM TASK

Write four or five paragraphs describing the ideal eco-home. Make sure you

- link ideas within paragraphs by using connectives and pronouns
- use a short opening paragraph to set up your ideas
- use some longer paragraphs to develop the ideas
- end with a short, punchy paragraph to sum up your ideas.

The ideal eco-friendly car would have radical features related to outer appearance, engine and interior design. These three factors combined could revolutionise driving.

As far as external appearance is concerned, the car would blend into its environment: no gaudy colours, nor huge tyres or box-like shapes. It would be sleek, small and perfectly formed. Shifting through the air like a silent bird it would encounter little or no wind resistance, and merge almost seamlessly into the landscape.

Its engine would be capable of at least 60 mpg, use either electric power or clean fuels to ensure minimal damage to the atmosphere, and, in an ideal world, would be virtually silent, avoiding so-called 'noise pollution', thus satisfying the driver's need to save the world and save hard-earned cash.

Remember

- **Good cohesion and coherence brings clarity to your writing.**
- **Varying your paragraphs creates impact and effect.**

Using a range and variety of sentences

What does using a range and variety of sentences mean?

It is the ability to select, combine and organise simple, compound and complex sentence types in different ways, for effect.

> **Glossary**
>
> A **simple sentence** contains only one clause: *The cat miaowed loudly*.
>
> A **compound sentence** contains two clauses linked by 'and' 'or' or 'but': *The cat miaowed loudly **and** it went back to sleep.*
>
> A **complex sentence** contains two or more connected clauses: ***When** I laughed, the cat miaowed loudly **and** went back to sleep.*

Checklist for success

To write **successful sentences** you need to

- **create inventive combinations**
- select the **right sentence type** for **effect** and **impact**
- be **clear**.

ACTIVITY

Read this opening to an article in which an adult recalls her childhood.

Discuss with a partner:

- What is the effect of the two **short sentences** at the start of the article?
- How does the sentence beginning 'A little table' add to the effect created? (Is it a sentence?)
- How does the use of the **present tense** ('I am five years old') add to the effect?

I am five years old. I'm being naughty about food. I am sent to eat alone at a table in the hall. A little table, a little chair, a ticking clock (I can't tell the time, but I know I must finish my food before the big hand gets to the top) and something on my plate that I don't want to eat: an omelette whose edges taste burnt.

Julie Myerson, The Observer

⭐ **Examiner's tip**

Julie Myerson uses sentences to get 'inside the head' of a character (in this case imitating a child's thought-processes). A technique like this will really target Grade A/A★.

Focus for development: Making sentence choices

You need to decide on the right structure, length or combination of sentences for the task.

ACTIVITY

Consider this task.

Some people believe it would be better if clothing wasn't made in poorer countries and we produced more in the UK, even if that meant higher prices. Write an article for a magazine in which you argue for or against this idea.

You probably need longer sentences to explain and develop a point here.

Discuss with a partner:

Why is the Example 1 sentence effective? Think about its length and how the different parts are linked.

To target **Grade A/A★**, you need a **variety and range of sentences**. Look at Example 2 by the same student.

Now write briefly about

- the different types of sentences used and the effect each one creates
- the effect of using this variety of sentence types.

Example 1

Over-population means that in many poor countries people are desperate for work, despite the low wages and the terrible conditions they often have to endure to feed their families.

Example 2

The poor need work. That's a fact. Work is in short supply. That is also a fact. Within the sweatshops and the teeming factories that can be found in third-world cities, there are nameless thousands who rarely see the light of day – but if you gave them the chance to leave, would they take it? Not likely!

EXAM TASK

Write the first two paragraphs in response to this task. Use a variety of sentence types for effect.

'The biggest problem young people face today is older people's attitudes towards them.'

Write an article for *SAGA Magazine* (for the over 50s) in which you argue for or against this view.

★ **Examiner's tip**

Include some short sentences for effect, but use them sparingly.

Remember

- **Choose the right sentence type and length for the purpose.**
- **Vary sentences for impact and effect.**

Using punctuation for accuracy and impact

Learning objective

- To understand that punctuation can be creative and help to shape meaning.

What does punctuating for accuracy and impact mean?

When you punctuate **accurately**, you use the main punctuation marks – full-stops, capital letters, speech marks, commas, colons, semicolons, apostrophes – correctly.

When you punctuate for **impact** and **effect**, you are also using punctuation to convey a particular meaning, or to create a particular effect on the reader.

Checklist for success

- For Grade C you need to try and use all punctuation correctly.
- For Grade B you need to use a wide variety of punctuation accurately.
- For Grade A/A★ you need to select the right punctuation for the effect you want to create.

ACTIVITY

Read this extract. It is from a response to a task asking students to argue for or against raising the school leaving age to 19.

With a partner, consider how the use of punctuation has

- helped to organise the writer's ideas
- created specific effects and impact.

> The proposed age of 19 is clearly a bad idea for a number of reasons: firstly, everyone needs a break from education (I certainly did!); secondly, it would be very 'un-cool' to wear a uniform at that age; thirdly, teachers would certainly object.

Use the glossary below to help you.

Glossary

A **colon (:)** introduces a quotation or, following a general statement, a list.

A **semicolon (;)** is used to divide items in a long, complicated list, or to contrast or relate two ideas.

Brackets ( ) are used around extra information to highlight it or keep it separate.

An **ellipsis (...)** shows speech that trails off or shows that text or information is missing.

Focus for development: Sophisticated punctuation

ACTIVITY

Try these more sophisticated uses of punctuation to target a Grade A/A★. They are all from a piece about the perils of going out shopping.

1 Add the **bracketed text** to this sentence.

   Shopping in a crowded high street is clearly a dangerous activity if you're in a hurry (which I ....) and should be banned.

2 Add a **short rhetorical question** before this sentence.

   Go out ....?
   It's much safer just to stay at home and order what you need from the internet.

3 Use a **semicolon** to **juxtapose** two related ideas.

   Shopping or sleeping? There's a difficult one. On the one hand shopping is tiring, costs money and you have to leave your warm house on the other, sleep refreshes you, allows you to escape your boring life, and you don't even have to leave your bed!

4 Add a **colon** to introduce the list, and **semicolons** to separate the items in the list.

   So here's just a few reasons to avoid a busy shopping centre tripping over prams and buggies shops with narrow aisles and too much stock queues for fitting rooms overwrought shop assistants – to name but a few.

Share your ideas with a partner.

EXAM TASK

Write the opening two paragraphs to this exam question.

For a Grade A/A★, think how you could use a variety of sentences and punctuation for effect. For example, you could

- start with a question ('Remember when … ?')
- juxtapose two ideas with a semicolon
- make a point and add bracketed text as an aside
- use a colon to introduce a list.

> Write a light-hearted article for a magazine in which you argue that snowballing is *not* a fun activity.

Remember

- Accurate punctuation is vital for a Grade C (avoid using commas where there should be full-stops!).
- To target Grade A/A★, use sophisticated forms of punctuation in creative ways.

Selecting effective vocabulary

Learning objective

- To understand how the vocabulary you choose can improve your writing.

What does selecting effective vocabulary mean?

Vocabulary is your **choice** of **individual words** and **phrases**: for example, using 'thrilling' rather than 'good' to describe a book in a review.

Checklist for success

You need to **choose vocabulary** that

- fits the **subject** or **context**
- is **ambitious** and **imaginative** – but also **correct**.

ACTIVITY

Read this extract from a student's response to a request by her local council to suggest a location in her town for a new war memorial, and to describe what the memorial should look like.

> I reckon the best place would be the seafront by the old café. It is a good place because it's quiet but many people pass by taking in the view. The memorial should be big so people can see it and it will stick up or stand out and it should be made of something hard to stop the weather from getting in and ruining it.

This is a **Grade C** answer because

- the student has met the purpose – up to a point
- there is some appropriate description
- she has chosen a particular tone for her audience.

However, it could be improved, especially the vocabulary.

Look at the weaknesses and discuss the questions with a partner.

The vocabulary…	Questions
is often rather **general or vague**	What other details could she add? What word or phrase would be better than 'something hard to stop the weather'?
lacks **impact**	Is there a more effective word than 'quiet'?
lacks **detail** and terms suitable for the context or purpose.	Could she describe the memorial's appearance better?

Besides these vocabulary weaknesses, what else would you improve?

Focus for development:
Ambitious content and vocabulary

Examiner's tip ★

*For a Grade A, get the **register** right. For example, you wouldn't call a war memorial 'stunning' or 'glamorous'. These words may not actually be wrong, but they are inappropriate.*

ACTIVITY

Read this question:

> *A holiday website aimed at teenagers has asked for contributions to its section on 'The Perfect Beach' and wants to know what makes an ideal beach. Write your views on what such a beach would be like.*

Most students would probably write about a beautiful beach in summer. However, would that be an **ambitious** and **imaginative** response?

Read this Grade A★ response:

> My perfect beach: rain lashing the concrete promenade, a scrawny terrier cocking its leg against the rotten hulk of an old dinghy, and not a person to be seen. On the horizon, grey, angry clusters of clouds would gather over breakers like mountains, and the oil-tankers would be shrouded in choking fog and mist. This is perfection for me – the cold easterly wind flattening my hair against my cheeks, red and smarting from the icy rain, clearing my mind of all worries.

Discuss with a partner why this response is effective.

Consider

- the impact of the language (adjectives such as 'scrawny', nouns such as 'promenade', and imagery in the form of similes and metaphors)
- the general approach taken.

EXAM TASK

Continue the response above by adding two or three more paragraphs in a similar style. Alternatively, write your own response to the task.

Remember

- **Consider alternative approaches to the task; these can help your vocabulary stand out.**
- **Create impact and be ambitious with your vocabulary choices – use imagery to paint a picture in the reader's mind!**

Grade Booster

Extended Exam Task

Write at least three or four paragraphs in answer to the task on the right.

Make sure your focus is on communicating two or three ideas clearly and imaginatively. Use

- coherent paragraphing
- effective and meaningful punctuation

- a variety of sentences
- appropriate and well-chosen vocabulary.

> *Some people believe that teenagers have only themselves to blame for the negative ways they are represented by the media. Write a letter to a national newspaper in which you respond to this statement, agreeing or disagreeing with the viewpoint expressed.*

Evaluation – What have you learned?

With a partner, use the checklist below to evaluate your work on the Extended Exam Task.

- I can cleverly and clearly express my viewpoint with a real sense of organisation and development, using a wide range of sentences and paragraphs to affect the reader's response.
- I can use vocabulary which is rich, ambitious and well-chosen – yet always appropriate.

- I can state my purpose and viewpoint clearly and effectively; my ideas are very well expressed in clear sentences and a range of paragraphs which develop and sustain my argument.
- I can use vocabulary which is always appropriate and well-chosen and is often ambitious and rich.

- I can use effective paragraphs supporting each point made; my ideas are well-thought out in a range of sentences that have an impact on the reader.
- I can use vocabulary which is accurate and occasionally ambitious.

- I can use an increasing variety of sentence forms, accurately punctuated; my paragraphs are logical and I clearly present main ideas.
- I can use well-chosen, but not especially varied, vocabulary.
- I can ensure my viewpoint comes through and is supported by some good ideas.

- I can use simple sentences (and occasionally complex ones).
- I can sometimes use more varied vocabulary, but it is still rather limited.
- I can use paragraphs but they lack thought and variety and my point of view is rather undeveloped.

You may need to go back and look at the relevant pages from this section again.

Writing to Engage the Reader

Introduction

This section of Chapter 2 shows you how to

- engage the interest of your reader
- adapt form and style to meet your reader's needs
- use some particular literary devices, such as hyperbole, to create a real impact on your reader
- develop the skill of sustaining your point of view over the whole text so that the reader remains 'on track'.

Why is engaging your reader's interest important?

- Texts that work best create a relationship with the reader.
- You tend to enjoy writing more if you set out with this purpose in mind.
- You are more likely to be persuasive, appear knowledgeable and interesting, and be understood if your writing creates impact.
- The highest grades at GCSE are reserved for students whose writing is not just efficient but really makes the reader sit up and take notice.

A **Grade C** candidate will

- have a clear sense of purpose and audience, communicating ideas clearly and appropriately and with a conscious attempt to engage the reader
- use linguistic devices appropriately and make a clear attempt to sustain and develop ideas.

A **Grade A/A★** candidate will

- communicate in a convincing and compelling way
- engage the reader through subtle, well-judged and original language and ideas, including abstract concepts brought alive for the reader
- ensure all structure features, including varied and linked sentences and paragraphs, come together to serve the purpose of the text.

Prior learning

Before you begin this unit, reflect on

- any particularly **impressive** texts, or parts of texts, you have written where your writing has really 'shone' and made an impact on your teacher (it could be an opening to a story or the end to a report)
- any non-fiction texts that have made an impression on you

> What keeps *you* interested in texts or **engaged** in what the writer has to say?

- the **techniques** or **approaches** you already know that help your writing create an **impact** on the reader, or **sustain** their attention.

Engaging the reader

What does engaging the reader mean?

Engaging the reader means **capturing his or her attention**, and then **sustaining** it throughout the text.

Checklist for success

- For a Grade C you need to use the right form and style for the task.
- To target a Grade A/A★ you need to show originality to hold your reader's attention throughout. Your style and tone need to be fitting and totally engaging. Even in the most functional tasks there are choices you can make to help your writing stand out.

ACTIVITY

Read how two different students have responded to the same task: to persuade a Dragon's Den-style business man or woman to invest in their new gadget.

Student 1: Grade A

I appreciate you taking the time to read this letter. You must get a lot of crackpot inventors and slightly unhinged 'mad professor' types who want you to invest millions in some unlikely scheme or new product. I hope I am different. I have ...

- *carefully and methodically developed my idea with my own money*
- *tested it with clients, organisations and members of the public*
- *worked out exactly what I need in terms of finance.*

Student 2: Grade C

Thank you for reading this letter. I am writing to you in order to explain a really well-thought out idea which I think will appeal to you, and is worth investing in. I can assure you any money you spend will not go to waste. I have worked hard on the product and can be relied on to deliver success if you lend me what I want.

Discuss with a partner what makes the first letter more effective.

- How does the writer get on the right side of the reader?
- Look at the vocabulary and imagery used.
- Are there any structural or organisational features of writing to persuade?

Focus for development:
Being creative with form and style

ACTIVITY

Could you go even further? **Grade A★ writing** shows creative flair and style.

Student 3

> Some years ago, a young man sold his house and invested his money in a secret product he was developing. In a small factory he sweated for hours at an old workbench to get the product ready for the outside world. I was that young man, and now I am ready to present it, ask for your help, and for you to place your faith in me.

Student 4

> 'Unique. Brilliant. Ingenious.' Three words used by renowned business guru Professor Thorpwell of Imperial College to describe my product. I hope you will feel the same way as I outline its features, capabilities and potential to change the world...

Discuss with a partner:

- What is successful about these two openings?
- What different techniques do they use to appeal to the reader?
- What do you notice about the change in tense in each?

ACTIVITY

A charity is trying to raise money to help communities in Africa build their own schools. Write the first two or three paragraphs of an email to send out to local business people. Try at least two of the more effective approaches you have seen here.

★ Examiner's tip

Switching between **abstract concepts** such as 'faith' and 'hope' (things you cannot picture but which represent larger ideas) and **vivid detail** ('sweated for hours at an old workbench') will show the examiner you can control your language in a sophisticated way.

Remember

- **Stick to the task: just because you are engaging the reader, don't forget the purpose.**
- **Try out alternative openings and original strategies to draw the reader in.**

Matching your language to the task

What does matching language to task mean?

Quite subtle changes of language can have a profound impact on the effect of a text. Different forms, different purposes and different audiences will require different language and approaches to writing.

Checklist for success

- Focus on the small things: types of sentence, organisation of paragraphs, simple structural features to shape the meaning of what you want to say.
- Make sure your language and tone are appropriate to the form and audience.

ACTIVITY

Read this extract from a **Grade B** response to the following task:

> *Write an article for a magazine advising people on ways they can improve their lives through sport.*

> *Sport can improve all our lives. It makes us fitter so we think better; it offers us different ways of spending our leisure time; and it needn't be expensive. You can spend time with other people and you feel better in yourself.*
> *Of course, joining a club can be a good starting point. It can encourage you to be competitive...*

Here are some reasons why this response does not receive a higher grade.

- The points in each paragraph are relevant but **not developed enough**.
- It lacks **facts or figures** that would help it sound convincing.
- It does not use **cause and effect language** (such as 'thus', 'consequently') that would make this clearer and more coherent.
- The **vocabulary is repetitive and uninspiring**. Using technical sports or health-related vocabulary would help.
- It could sound more authoritative by using appropriate **imperative verbs**.

Glossary
Imperative verbs tell you what to do: '**Run** up the stairs instead of walking!'

Focus for development:
Improving the language of advice

Read this extract from another response to the same task.

> The first, **and main**, benefit to **participating** in sport – at whatever level – is that it enhances and maintains your fitness. **Moreover** it allows for the intake of **oxygen** into the lungs and bloodstream, with its consequent effect on one's body, and forces you to exercise muscles and reduce the body's fat content.
>
> I recommend that you begin by initiating a full health check at your local GP surgery. In this way, you can identify which elements need attention, and develop strategies to improve your health...

Note down at least three ways in which this Grade A text improves on the Grade B text opposite.

Now write a further paragraph focusing on a new topic, for example socialising through sport. Add statistics (you can make them up if you wish) and advice as to what to do.

> A key additional benefit of sport is that it allows me to socialise with a wide range of people...

Next, read this public-health advice leaflet found in libraries and post-offices.

Discuss with a partner what subtle differences you notice in the style, tone, and organisation of this leaflet, compared with the article on the same subject on the previous page.

Consider

- the immediate impact the text needs to make
- the audience and the source of the leaflet.

THINK SPORT'S A WASTE OF TIME? THINK AGAIN!

Playing sport:

★ Enhances and maintains fitness

★ Allows for better respiration

★ Exercises the muscles you never use

★ Is fun, friendly and sociable.

You may feel you're not the sporty type. Or that sport is only for the young. Equally, you might feel it's over-competitive, aggressive and all about winning. The fact is that doctors see thousands of people every year whose best medicine would be half-an-hour throwing a tennis ball to their children. Statistics back up these findings, with nearly 1 in 3 people reporting improved well-being from exercise.

It's simple. Pop into see your GP for a quick check-up, find out what health issues you need to address, and then explore the sporting possibilities in your area. Use the Yellow Pages, the internet or visit our website…

http://www.nhs.uk/LiveWell/ fitness/Pages/Fitnesshome.aspx

Many people say that there are health benefits to cooking and preparing food for yourself, rather than buying fast-food takeaways or ready-meals. Write the text for a two-sided leaflet for a doctor's surgery, which explains these benefits.

Remember

- **Use professional language for informative or advisory texts that have a public readership.**
- **Adjust your tone and language subtly according to your audience.**

Language for power and impact

What does power and impact mean?

Texts can convey certain information or particular messages, but the ones that affect how the reader thinks and responds have something extra. This comes from the language choices made.

Checklist for success

- For a **Grade C** you will need to use some basic literary techniques in your writing.
- To target a **Grade A/A★** you will need to use a wide range of literary techniques and select the appropriate techniques to make an impact on the reader.

ACTIVITY

Read the start of Review 1 about a wildlife documentary.

There is nothing exactly wrong with this piece.

- It is clear and gives reasons why the programme was bad.
- It gives some idea of the writer's viewpoint but is a little anonymous.
- It uses a reasonable, if not exactly rich vocabulary.

Now read Review 2 of the same programme. How does the writer engage the reader and create real impact?

You could consider the use of

- hyperbole
- repetition for effect
- adverbs to add power to adjectives (for example, 'wonderfully entertaining')
- metaphors related to the subject (for example, 'nature and the sea').

Now write your own paragraph in which you review or comment on either your football team's recent worst performance or a terrible TV programme you have seen.

Use at least two of AA Gill's techniques.

Review 1

It was clear from the start how poor the presenters were, but much worse was what they were given to say. It was full of clichés and things you had heard before. In fact, really embarrassing, even childish. It had the same old message about looking after the world, and even used really obvious pictures of Indians collecting shells.

Review 2

Worse than the empty Sea of Cortez, worse than the horrible presenters, was the utterly bereft script. A sea of intellectual plankton, an ocean of clichés, truisms, non-sequiturs and the mood music of happy-feely words, it was chronically embarrassing. The hug-a-halibut environmental message was depressingly childish; the anthropological element, showing us happy Indians collecting clams by hand then wagging a finger, telling us this was a model of sustainability for the world, was cretinously idiotic. Altogether, it was dispiriting and depressing.

AA Gill, The Times

> **Glossary**
> **Hyperbole**: deliberate exaggeration to make a point. 'He is simply the greatest, most gifted and charismatic tennis player of his or any other generation.'

Focus for development: Entertaining the reader

This sort of writing is clearly entertaining – we enjoy AA Gill's insults and criticisms. Here, Kathy Lette uses similar techniques to describe applying fake tan before a holiday.

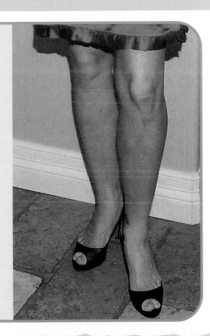

It said 'rich Mediterranean' on the bottle, but I was beginning to look more tandoori than tanning salon. My so-called 'tan' pulsated. It radiated. I looked as if I was wearing a tangerine wet suit, with darker elbow patches and kneepads. I was like a distress flare. People could employ me at the scene of a boating accident.

Good Housekeeping

Jot down two ways in which Kathy Lette has used hyperbole.

Consider her use of strong verbs to describe how the fake tan felt and her use of vivid similes (and how she develops her similes into a ridiculous idea).

Write a full account of a recent personal experience: for example, a shopping trip, a night out, a family visit or a sports event you took part in. Use as many of the techniques you have learnt here as you can.

Remember

- **Use literary techniques to give your work power and impact, and to entertain and have an effect on the reader.**
- **These techniques are particularly useful in reviews, accounts of personal events or experiences, and discursive articles about issues of the day.**

Using irony

Learning objective

- To understand how irony, used appropriately, can add to the impact of your writing.

What does irony mean?

Writers use irony to point out ridiculous or challenging ideas, or to draw attention to events, issues or situations.

For example, in a humorous text, a writer might place together two images for ironic effect:

> I had locked myself out. Through the window I could see the note I had left on the table. 'Don't forget door key,' it said.

This is **situational irony**.

Checklist for success

You need to use irony appropriately and selectively to help you get an A/A★ grade.

ACTIVITY

Discuss with a partner how this Grade A answer uses irony in at least two ways in response to the task:

> Write an article in which you describe how holidays don't always work out as they should.

> Most airports have 'meeting points' in case you get lost. The problem is that if you get lost, you usually can't find the meeting point. Or, if you're abroad, the words 'meeting point' are in a language you can't understand. In fact, it's a good idea to keep your mobile phone on at all times, although doing so will probably run down your battery so that when your friends finally get your message, you can't read their reply!

★ Examiner's tip

Note how the linking words and phrases ('the problem is', 'although') help set up the ironic situations. Phrases like this help link the text and ideas together coherently.

ACTIVITY

Complete the contrasting 'ends' to these two ideas taken from the same response.

> Often, you are told your hotel's beach is a 'short drive' away. However, in my experience, the drive may be short in distance but...

> Every year when I go to a holiday destination with 'guaranteed sun all year round' I make sure I take...

Focus for development: Judging when to use irony

ACTIVITY

The same student has been asked to write a charity leaflet in which he appeals for more help for the homeless. How **appropriate** is his use of irony and sarcasm here?

Identify the uses of **irony** (where the writer has juxtaposed Tam's world and life at the Ritz), then the **sarcasm** (where the writer means the opposite of what he says).

- Which do you think is more effective?
- Is one likely to alienate the reader? Why?

> Only yards from the Ritz Hotel, where tourists pay up to £100 for afternoon cream teas and cakes, a shabby figure sits in Green Park and holds a paper cup full of lukewarm coffee. A few pence are scattered on a mat next to him. Tonight, while the same tourists sleep in cotton sheets in air-conditioned hotel rooms, Tam will sleep on the streets. He'll have a wonderful night in the fresh air, enjoying the sweet smell of urine, the violence of passing strangers. Does he love his life? You bet he does! Please keep Tam on the streets by refusing to send money to us like the decent person you are. Instead, give money to any passing rich tourists you see. They deserve it!

⭐ Examiner's tip

It is easy to overuse sarcasm and irony. Whether you are using them for humorous or serious effect, include two or three examples at most, to have real impact.

EXAM TASK

Write your own charity text appealing for more help for the homeless. Try to use irony by juxtaposing different situations.

Remember

- **Use irony to contrast or juxtapose ideas or situations for comic or serious effect.**
- **Use irony sparingly and, if used with sarcasm, make sure it fits the context.**

Sustaining your style and tone

Learning objective

- To learn how to maintain and develop the ideas, style and approach throughout your response.

Examiner's tip

For questions like this, it is usually better to adopt a formal style, even if you think a chatty tone might connect with some readers. Remember this is a serious issue, so it would be best to make that clear throughout to ensure that readers are not shocked by shifts in your approach.

What does sustaining your ideas and tone mean?

Sustaining your ideas and tone means you keep to the task, follow what you have set out to say and use the same level of formality or informality throughout. Your style should be maintained, so that, for example, you do not suddenly switch from thoughtful advice to scathing sarcasm.

Checklist for success

- You need to be clear about your outcome: make clear your aim, then stick to it.
- Maintain one style throughout.

ACTIVITY

Read this response to the task:

> Are we truly a nation of animal lovers? Write a magazine article to support or argue against this statement.

> Do people really love animals? In this article, I wish to explore the idea that people shouldn't be allowed to keep pets unless they have proved they can look after them. Sadly, far too many pet owners are without consideration for animals and do not deserve to have pets in their charge. My mate Tony is a perfect example. If you met him in the street, you'd say: 'Great guy! Love him.' But, oh boy, has he got a history. He's had more dead pets than some people have had hot dinners…

1 Has the student set out clearly his aim in writing the article?

2 Is he answering the task set?

3 What effective techniques has he included so far?

4 How successful is he in maintaining his style and tone?

ACTIVITY

Rewrite the second paragraph so the style is more appropriate and develops from the opening. You can use the same ideas, but they need to be expressed more formally.

ACTIVITY

What might the editor want to change in this next extract if the article were for

a) the main section of a national newspaper

b) a supplement for 14–16 year olds in the newspaper?

> It is amazing that some people – old ladies in particular – treat their pets better than they treat themselves. Their moggy gets the steak and they live on pet food. Honestly. It's happened. Staggering, eh? Makes you think. The fortitude and resilience of some hardy souls can only make you wonder.

Focus for development:
Sustaining and extending your ideas

An effective plan will ensure you maintain your focus.

EXAM TASK

Produce a full and detailed plan in response to the task on page 92.
Try to include

- facts and figures supporting your view (search the Internet or invent any you need)
- relevant examples and, perhaps, an anecdote
- a consideration of people's different attitudes
- a conclusion suggesting what, if anything, should be done about the present situation.

Write the full article, for a broadsheet readership.

A student writes…

If we have to write for a younger audience, doesn't that lead to 'dumbing down'? Will we still be able to get good marks?

Answer…

Remember that you are being rewarded for the quality of your sentences and the breadth of your vocabulary. So, if writing for young people, show the range of your abilities but make the writing appropriate for that age group. However, don't ever use text language and avoid slang!

Remember

- **Your responses need to be consistent. Always read through to check that your ideas develop logically and your style has been sustained throughout.**

Writing to persuade and advise

Learning objectives

- *To learn how to persuade and advise effectively.*
- *To be aware of techniques which can be used to persuade and advise.*

What is the difference between persuading and advising?

When you **persuade**, you try to make someone accept your point of view, or do what you want.

Advising is similar, but you might offer alternatives and usually the focus will be on trying to help another person.

Checklist for success

- You need to examine persuasive writing critically: will it convince the reader?
- For advice, you need to ask yourself: is this detailed and logical enough, so someone can easily follow the advice?

ACTIVITY

Is this piece of advice persuasive?

Why/why not?

How could it be made more convincing?

> You must be less aggressive. Sooner or later, the police will arrest you and then it will mean more than just a telling-off. You should get a therapist. That's what I'd do.

Focus for development: Convincing the reader

Persuading

To be effective, you need to organise your ideas sensibly and use techniques to help persuade your audience that yours is the right point of view. You might

- focus on just one viewpoint
- offer both your view and the opposite point of view, as in an argument, but show that yours is the better viewpoint
- use emotive language to convince the reader
- include examples and anecdotes to illustrate your ideas
- employ rhetorical questions to hammer home what you say.

Glossary

emotive language is language which appeals to the emotions: Tiny starving babies, crying out for food...

anecdote: an extended example; a very short story

Notice how this Grade A/A★ extract uses persuasive techniques.

There can be no doubt that Rome is ← definite, allowing no challenge
the most beautiful of cities. It's a city ┐
full of life, history and love. Who can └ list of three to impress
fail to be impressed by the Colosseum? ← rhetorical question to engage
Who can wander through the narrow
streets to the Trevi fountain without ← repetition to 'browbeat' the reader, plus emotive touch
feeling the romance? It was there that ┐
once I sat beside a beautiful woman; └ anecdote
we talked and fell in love, and she has
been my wife for many years ...

 Examiner's tip

Be careful when using anecdotes. They need to be brief to be effective.

ACTIVITY

Write the opening paragraph of an article to persuade the reader that a city of your choice is the most beautiful in the world. Use persuasive techniques.

Advising

Here are the key techniques you can use to advise:

- setting out the problem, then delivering a solution
- working through different aspects of the problem and dealing with each in turn
- using imperative verbs ('**Do** this', '**Remember**')
- adopting a more sensitive approach ('Have you ever considered...?')
- using logic and evidence or experience to back up what you say.

ACTIVITY

Discuss with a friend how the advice in this **Grade C** response might be improved by

- adding detail
- adopting a more sensitive approach.

You must find yourself a new boyfriend, it's as simple as that. It's no good just hoping things will improve, because I can assure you it's not going to happen. It's down to you now: you could tell him straight that it's all over or you could let him down more gently. In either case, you need to get on with it.

EXAM TASK

Write a letter to a friend to advise them to work harder in the lead-up to their exams and to persuade them it will bring rewards. Use the language techniques you have learnt to persuade and advise.

Remember

- **People generally respond better to sensitive advice and persuasion.**
- **Using suitable techniques will make your writing more convincing.**

Writing to inform and explain

Learning objectives

- To learn how to inform effectively and explain appropriately.

- To understand what is involved in each form of writing and the differences between them.

What is the difference between informing and explaining?

The difference between these two types of text is important.

Information writing involves presenting facts – and perhaps offering a personal interpretation of them.

Explanation writing involves going behind a set of facts and explaining why things have happened or how they can be improved. It demands an **interpretation of the information**.

Checklist for success

You can improve your **writing to inform** by including relevant facts and details.

When writing to explain it is best to use a logical approach, moving from information to explanation. For instance, you might choose to say

- what the situation is (information)
- how it came about (information and explanation)
- how we might resolve it (explanation).

This extract from a **Grade A★** response, both **informs** about having to move home and **explains** the problems involved.

information about the change →

personal slant on the change →

more details →

introduction to the problem →

explains how he felt about it →

> *Until you have gone from living with your father in a four-bedroom house in a country town, to living with your mother in a tiny terraced house in the roughest of areas, you can have no idea how difficult such a transition can be.*
>
> *Life with my father had been idyllic. I had my own king-size bedroom, HD television and even a quad bike for the weekends. Leaving all that was shattering. Suddenly I had no space, no spending money and no easy way of visiting the friends I had come to rely on. My life was in pieces – and the pieces were all grimy and, apparently, paid for with bank loans...*

Focus for development: Clarity and effectiveness

Informing

Writing to inform usually contains facts and an interpretation of them. Be prepared to research the facts when you can. However, in an exam you will probably have to make up any you don't know.

Explaining

When you begin to give reasons for the facts you have put forward, you might be offering explanations of

- why something happened and the effect it had
- how someone feels about something.

ACTIVITY

Write a paragraph to inform the reader about what life is like where you live. Include facts or statistics and an interpretation of them. For example: 'So, it is obvious that there needs to be more services coming in to help the pensioners…'

ACTIVITY

Focusing on your own local area, complete a table like this.

Problem with area	Explanation: how it came about	Explanation: how it could be solved
Vandalism	Not enough for youngsters to do	More youth centres or evening activities

Now look at this **Grade C** response from a student explaining what his/her area is like.

Identify both the **information** and the **explanations** that are offered in this response.

Then decide how you would improve it towards Grade A standard. Think about

- additional information that would make it better
- extra explanation that might be added.

My town is not the sort of place anyone would choose to live. There is nothing for young people to do because the council is not prepared to spend any money on what we need. At the same time, the older people have to sit indoors and just watch television because since the college closed there aren't even night classes for them to go to…

EXAM TASK

Write a letter to a travel company to

- inform them about what happened on the holiday you booked through them
- explain what went wrong.

Remember

- Use detail wherever you can to make the events more credible.
- When you are explaining, give reasons.

Writing to analyse and review

Learning objectives

- To learn how to analyse.
- To be familiar with the conventions of reviews.

What does it mean to analyse or review?

An **analysis** looks in detail at an object, situation, reaction or event. It looks beyond the obvious and endeavours to pick out different ideas for comment.

A **review** looks back at something and examines it critically. It offers opinions.

Checklist for success

Learn from examples in newspapers and magazines. See how they

- analyse events, from political events to football matches
- review television programmes, films and theatrical performances.

EXAMPLE

Read these **Grade A** responses.

This **analysis** considers a range of ideas in examining one situation.

> There are three important factors that have played a part in the demise of the corner shop: the fact that supermarkets carry such a range of different brands; the financial situation (small shops are often more expensive than larger stores); and, ironically, convenience – although corner shops are closer, the supermarket offers everything you need in the same place...

This **review** looks back and criticises, offering detail, not just comment.

> It is easy to see why our fund-raising day was not as successful as we hoped. First, there was the weather, which dampened everybody's spirits. If only we had taken the plunge and booked the marquee we considered and rejected! Then, our advertising was disappointing, to say the least...

ACTIVITY

Think about the last TV drama you watched. What would you say in a review analysing its strengths and weaknesses? Complete a table like this.

Strength/weakness of TV drama	Analysis: comments to be made

Focus for development:
Sustaining an approach

Any analysis or review needs to be sustained. This means **structuring your ideas** and then **using the same style** throughout.

It also means **linking your opening and ending**.

A student writes…

I have trouble ending essays.
I can never decide what to put, because
I've moved on from my opening.

Answer…

Practise writing openings and endings: set your own titles and just write those parts. The more attempts you make, the easier it becomes.

ACTIVITY

This opening and ending are from a **Grade C** TV drama review.

> *I did not get excited about watching 'Dream On'. It sounded like one of those dramas my grandma used to watch on weekday afternoons. It starred John Gilbert and Francesca Prima, but since I had never heard of either of them, that was hardly a good recommendation. 'Give it a try,' said my friend Jo.*
>
> *[…]*
>
> *Jo was proved right. It had some really good episodes, like the one with the oil spillage and the hospital, but it was also about the wildest dreams of each main character, which tied in to the title, which I didn't expect. I really enjoyed it. So should you trust your friends' opinions? Yes, you should.*

With a partner, identify the writer's opinions. Are they clear?

- Which parts at the end link back to the beginning?
- What techniques has the writer used to try to interest the reader?

How might you improve this opening and ending. Think about

- including more interesting vocabulary and using connectives
- extending some of the ideas using more precise detail
- making sure you maintain the same style for both parts.

EXAM TASK

Write the review of your chosen TV drama, using the notes you made in the activity on page 98.

- use an effective opening and ending
- analyse what happened, including relevant detail
- make your opinions clear.

Remember

- **When writing to analyse or review, you need to include details to support your opinions.**
- **Try to move beyond simple points; considering different interpretations will lead to higher marks.**
- **Sustain your style and link your opening and ending.**

Arguing with sophistication

Learning objective

- To write a high-level text which argues a particular point of view.

What does arguing with sophistication mean?

Writing to argue has some key conventions that you know already – but how can you improve to a Grade A★ level?

Checklist for success

- You need to recognise the **conventions** (typical features) of writing to argue.
- You need to use further sophisticated language and techniques to engage the reader.

ACTIVITY

Read the opening to this article.

> **If I were to make a list of all the rights I would be willing to fight for, it would not include the 'right to die'.**
>
> I expect the right to free speech, the right to protest, the right to freedom of movement, the right to vote. Those key rights make us free and autonomous beings, allowing us to determine the course of our lives and to carry out our daily activities without having the state peering over our shoulders.
>
> But the right to die? The right to end it all?
>
> The right to stop existing entirely? I don't want that right.
>
> And yet that's the right that is being talked about and fought over most passionately these days. Elbowing aside even the ongoing battle for full freedom of speech, or the right to of migrants to travel freely to the UK, the 'right to die' has become the No.1 *cause célèbre* in contemporary Britain.
>
> *Brendan O'Neill,*
> *Big Issue*

Here, the writer's opinion is stated 'up front' and his viewpoint is clear. Jot down ways in which the writer uses some of the typical conventions of argument texts, such as

- repetition for effect
- rhetorical questions
- use of particular tenses
- patterns of three
- dealing with the other side of the argument
- imagery.

Focus for development: Choosing your approach

Read this opening to an article on the same topic.

> Approaching the staring glass doors of the hospital, I was struck by the faint odour of fading roses. A nurse wheeled someone past, and I caught a glimpse of a thin figure like a broken twig, staring right through me. Some would say this is a last resort for the desperate carer, others that it's a place where the old and unwanted come to die.

Note down:

- How has the writer tried to engage the reader with his/her use of language?
- What point of view emerges? Is it clear?
- How does the sequence of the sentences lead the reader into the detailed discussion?
- What might be the article's purpose (or purposes)?

A student writes…

I thought there were set ways of writing to argue, explain, etc.

Answer…

There are some typical features, but many texts have several purposes. For example, 'explain why it is a good idea to travel' is really arguing as much as it is explaining. So the key is to use a range of impressive skills.

Examiner's tip ★

Notice how the text uses literary language such as alliteration ('faint … fading') and simile ('like a broken twig'), even though this is a text that is arguing and/or persuading.

EXAM TASK

Look at this task.

To get the top grades, it is important to select your approach and the skills you will use independently. For this task, consider

> *Write an article for MAX SPEED bike magazine in which you argue for the right for young people to ride their bikes on the pavement.*

- whether you will begin with a direct viewpoint which you develop through the response (as in the extract on page 100), or using a vivid account or image to set up your response (like the article opening above)
- how you can integrate the 'typical' features of writing to argue (see page 100)
- whether you need to adjust your tone in any way for the different audience the task requires.

Remember

- **Texts can have a number of purposes – but will use the key conventions you know.**
- **Take the opportunity to show off your language skills, whatever the task or text type.**

Grade Booster

Extended Exam Task

Draw on what you have learned about engaging the reader's interest to respond to this task.

> *Write an article for a cycle magazine offering advice to cyclists on how to deal with aggressive car and van drivers.*

Make sure you

- consider how imperatives can make your advice hit home ('Avoid …', 'Make sure …', etc.)
- use irony, if you can, to juxtapose what cyclists think their rights should be in certain situations, and the different ways in which car or van drivers see the same situation.

You could consider playing with the conventions of an advice/guidance text, perhaps using exaggerated language or ideas in the way Kathy Lette and AA Gill do on pages 88 and 89.

Evaluation – What have you learned?

With a partner, use the grade checklist below to evaluate your work on the Extended Exam Task.

- I can write with a convincing, compelling tone and use detailed ideas which engage the reader from the start.
- I can use varied and carefully selected linguistic devices such as irony to create impact on the reader.

- I can provide succinct advice supported by developed evidence.
- I can use a wide range of linguistic devices, including irony, in an effective and appropriate way.
- I can sustain tone and ideas throughout.

- I can write well thought out, detailed, reasoned ideas showing consequences and implications.
- I can use linguistic devices including exaggeration and imperatives as well as a range of more subtle ones, such as irony.

- I can use more detailed ideas and support my advice with reasons.
- I can begin to use linguistic devices such as imperatives, exaggeration and rhetorical questions.

- I can engage the reader, developing some ideas, but the tone and linguistic devices I use are not always sustained or appropriate.

You may need to go back and look at the relevant pages from this section again.

Exam Preparation
Unit 1B: Writing Non-Fiction Texts

Introduction

In this section you will

- find out the exact facts about, and requirements of, the written element of Unit 1 of the exam
- read, analyse and respond to two sample answers by different candidates
- plan and write your own answer to a sample question
- evaluate and assess your answer and the progress you have made.

Why is exam preparation like this important?

- You need to know exactly what you need to do in order to feel confident when you sit the real thing.
- Looking at sample answers by other students will help you see what you need to do to improve your own work.
- Planning and writing a full sample written response after you have completed the whole chapter will give you a clear sense of what you have learned so far.

Key Information

Unit 1 is 'Understanding and Producing Non-Fiction Texts'.

- It has an exam of **2 hours**, worth **80 marks**.
- It is worth **40%** of your overall English GCSE mark.
- Section A of the exam is on 'Reading'.
- Section B of the exam is on 'Writing'.

Section B Writing

- The writing part of the exam is **1 hour long**, and is worth **40 marks**.
- It is worth **20%** of your overall English mark.
- In the exam you will be given **TWO** writing tasks.
- The first writing task is a **shorter task** worth **16 marks**. You should probably spend about **25 minutes** on this task, including reading and planning time.
- The second writing task is **slightly longer**, and worth **24 marks.** You should probably spend about **35 minutes** on this task, including reading and planning time.

The Two Writing Tasks – What's Different?

- The most obvious difference will be in how much you might write in response.
- The shorter task is likely to be more straightforward, perhaps a letter to a friend, or something in which the format is short and more easily controlled. Whatever you do, don't spend more time on this than the 'longer' second task.
- The longer task may ask you to consider different viewpoints or develop your ideas a little more.
- The tasks will change every year, but you have been working on some of the typical questions in this section so far. Here are two further examples.

Short question [16 marks]	*A family friend from abroad is coming to visit your home town or area. Write to them and describe what there is of interest to see and do.*
Longer question [24 marks]	*Some people think it is wrong that members of the public are allowed to be humiliated in talent shows by celebrity judges. Write an article for a magazine in which you argue for or against this idea.*

The Assessment

The assessment objective for Writing (AO3) states that you must be able to:

- Write to communicate clearly, effectively and imaginatively, using and adapting forms and selecting vocabulary appropriate to task and purpose in ways that engage the reader.
- Organise information and ideas into structured and sequenced sentences, paragraphs and whole texts, using a variety of linguistic and structural features to support cohesion and overall coherence.
- Use a range of sentence structures for clarity, purpose and effect, with accurate punctuation and spelling.

Targeting the top grades

Some of the key differences between a C and an A/A★ are as follows:

Grade C candidates	See example on page 106
• write with general accuracy in their sentences and punctuation and use a variety of sentence forms (short and long), although sometimes the effect has not been thought through (they just happen to be short and long) • occasionally, but not often, choose sentences and vocabulary which are bold and original • use paragraphing which is effective and helps make the meaning clear, but whereas the top candidates will skilfully change or adapt structure to create an effect on the reader, a C grade student will do this less often.	

Grade A/A★ candidates	See example on page 108
• confidently use language for creative delight: their language is sometimes surprising and original so that it doesn't feel like the marker has read it before – but it is still under control and is appropriate to the task and purpose • produce ambitious writing – which means students don't just stick to simple or not very interesting vocabulary or sentences, but use a wide range of different types and choices for particular effects (they have consciously thought how their sentences, for example, will affect the reader) • use convincing and compelling arguments, really making the reader *want* to read.	

Exploring sample responses

Read the following extract from a student's response to the second, longer question from page 104.

Consider the key elements a marker would look for:

- how clearly and effectively the writer has conveyed his/her ideas
- how appropriate and well-chosen the vocabulary is
- whether the structure and organisation fluently guide the reader through the ideas
- how much of an impact on the meaning the range of sentences and choice of language features have
- whether, overall, this text engages and interests the reader throughout.

Example one

Celebrity rudeness

We all love talent shows such as the 'X Factor' and 'Britain's Got Talent'. These shows show people making fools of themselves as well as showing off their talents, such as singing, dancing. My view is that it has all gone a bit too far and OTT. It's fine to have some criticism if you need to improve and you are not singing as well as you could, but if you are a poor person with some trashy job with no real talent, it's not fair to make you feel like a dummy.

Sometimes, what is even worse is that the person who is criticised doesn't even realise what is happening. That is terrible. It is like a private joke between the celebrities and the audience. I think it is like bullying in school behind someone's back when they don't notice. For example, calling children a horrible name but not to their face.

The thing is the shows would not work unless they had people making fools of themselves. If it was just people with talent it would be boring, and I admit that I am watching when these programmes come on. So I am as bad as the programme makers I suppose.

But you can't really stop people wanting to take part and no one really knows until someone opens their mouth whether they are going to be an idiot or a genius. I suppose you could choose not to show the really stupid ones, but probably some of them don't mind. Perhaps they would rather be on telly even if it's making themselves look stupid?

This leads me to my final point. You would need to be from a different planet not to know what goes on in these shows. Everyone knows what they are letting themselves in for – nobody is completely innocent are they? And perhaps they like being shouted at by Simon Cowell. In fact, it might be the highlight of their lives, which is pretty sad – but it's their choice. No one forced them to sing out of tune or dance clumsily!

So, as long as there are people willing to humiliate themselves, I guess it's OK. I will continue watching and may be one day I will be the daft one on stage making a fool of myself! Simon Cowell beware!

Examiner feedback

This is generally a clear, well-argued article with accurate sentences and organised paragraphs. There is a good beginning and ending, and the candidate uses some variety of sentences, sometimes to good effect. There is a sense of how the text might affect the reader but occasionally the article reads slightly informally. The language is generally clear but there is some unnecessary repetition of words, and a little more variety would be welcome.

Suggested grade: C

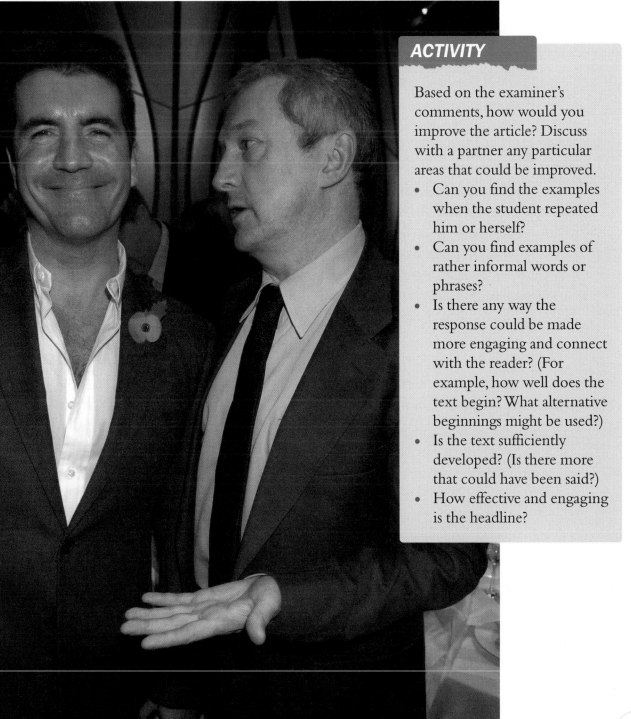

ACTIVITY

Based on the examiner's comments, how would you improve the article? Discuss with a partner any particular areas that could be improved.

- Can you find the examples when the student repeated him or herself?
- Can you find examples of rather informal words or phrases?
- Is there any way the response could be made more engaging and connect with the reader? (For example, how well does the text begin? What alternative beginnings might be used?)
- Is the text sufficiently developed? (Is there more that could have been said?)
- How effective and engaging is the headline?

Now read this response to the same question by a different candidate:

Example two

Clever headline engages reader

BRITAIN'S GOT IDIOTS

How we love humiliating ourselves and others on prime-time TV

By-line fits the form and adds information

Use of short, direct opening sentence speaks to reader

Prime-time television can be so cruel. It is a talent show: on comes a poor, unemployed middle-aged man with terrible fashion sense. He tries to sing and it is awful, and the crowd laugh, the judges rip him to shreds and he leaves the stage in tears.

Is this entertainment? Is this fun? If it is, then it is more like when the Romans used to throw the gladiators to the lions. In fact, perhaps we will only be satisfied when the singers are thrown to real lions! One day, hurtful comments will not be enough – perhaps the celebrity panel could press a button and the poor singer or dancer will drop through the stage into a bottomless pit. Perhaps that is a bit far-fetched, but to me it's not as unlikely as you might think.

Use of rhetorical questions support point

Range of punctuation used to emphasise point

New paragraph used to introduce counter argument

Some might argue that nobody forces people to audition for these shows, that no one forces them to apply, or to spend years preparing some terrible act no one wants to see. They would say, 'it's their own stupid fault'. Some might argue that these people have a right to do as they wish because it is a free country where people should be allowed to make a complete fool of themselves in front of millions. Well, I am not one of them.

Final short sentence of paragraph creates impact

This sort of talent (or 'lack of talent') show encourages the worst in you and me. They teach us to laugh at those who aren't naturally attractive, or who are different. Would this be allowed in my school? Of course not. The answer is 'no'. In fact, it would be seen as a form of bullying. Yes, people might lose their jobs for not being good enough, but rudeness, humiliation and spitefulness would not be acceptable.

Repeating questions engages reader

Pattern of three nouns in a list further support argument

In addition, I would like to know if there are any statistics which tell us whether people humiliated on talent shows suffer long-term problems. Imagine if you were made a complete fool of in front of millions. Imagine what it would be like walking down your street with people pointing at you and calling out, 'Hey! Look – there goes that idiot from the TV!'. Some people might be able to cope, and some (very sad) people might actually enjoy it because for them being famous for five minutes – even if it's for something humiliating – is better than not being famous at all.

Connective coherently links new paragraph and new point

Slight shift in emphasis loses the flow of argument

No – as far as I am concerned, I'm going to press the buzzer three times on these talent shows. It's X – X – X from me – and, I hope, from you too.

Cleverly structured ending links to title

Sense of personal engagement and 'voice' coming through

Before you read the examiner feedback, note down any improvements you think the student could make to his or her response. In particular, have a look at some of the literary techniques used: for example, types of imagery, sound effects, or a note of irony.

Examiner feedback

The candidate has shown a structured and well-argued response to the task. The argument is developed and sustained, and the organisation of ideas flows coherently; the beginning and end, in particular, are powerful and compelling, helping to convince the reader. The vocabulary is often ambitious, and overall the candidate engages the reader with some original ideas and expressive language.

Suggested grade: A/A★

EXAM PRACTICE TASK

You are helping to organise a charity day at school to raise money for a hostel for homeless youngsters.

> Write a letter which will be sent to all parents, persuading them to come along to the charity day. [**24 marks**]

Remember
- Read the task carefully, selecting the key information you need: what is the purpose, audience and form
- Plan very quickly what you are going to say.

If you only do five things...

1 Read a range of non-fiction texts and note the ways that the best writers interest and engage you. Draw on what you know about the conventions of different forms of writing, but don't let these be a straitjacket – be flexible in order to make an impact on the reader.

2 Where appropriate, plan for original ideas and different perspectives on the task set; this will make the reader sit up and take notice.

3 Develop detailed ideas so that any points you make will usually have a further stage, or other points within them can be drawn out.

4 Use a wide range of ambitious vocabulary – but keep it appropriate to the task and audience – and use powerful and original imagery – especially similes and metaphors – to make your writing come alive.

5 Use a variety of sentences, both in terms of length (short and long) and in terms of type (simple, compound and complex).

3 Unit 2 **Speaking and Listening**

What's it all about?

We can all speak and listen, but if we develop our skills, we can communicate much better throughout our lives. Speaking and listening involves many skills that can be used elsewhere in English work and offers an immensely enjoyable change from reading and writing.

How will I be assessed?

You will get **20% of your English marks** for your Speaking and Listening ability.

You will have to complete three Speaking and Listening Controlled Assessments.

You will be marked on your

- presenting
- discussing and listening
- role-playing.

What is being tested?

Your teacher will be judging your ability to

- speak clearly and purposefully
- organise your talk and sustain your ideas
- speak appropriately in different situations
- use standard English and a variety of techniques when speaking
- listen and respond to what others say and how they say it
- interact with others, shaping meanings through suggestions, comments and questions and drawing ideas together
- create and sustain different roles.

Presentations

Introduction

This section of Chapter 3 shows you how to

- give a presentation to an audience
- select a topic and structure your talk
- decide what content you might include
- use a range of techniques to boost your performance.

Why is it important to develop good presentational skills?

- We can all talk generally about topics, but to get top grades you need to demonstrate a range of presentation skills.
- Planning, structuring and enlivening your presentation makes success easier to achieve.
- You will use the same skills in other parts of the English course, for example when you write in the examination.
- It is likely you will have to use these presentational skills throughout your working life. Developing these skills now will help you succeed in whatever you choose to do.

A **Grade C** candidate will

- adapt their talk to the situation, using standard English confidently
- engage the listener through their use of language, so that information, ideas and feelings are communicated clearly.

C

A **Grade A/A*** candidate will

- use assured standard English
- vary sentence structures to help hold the attention of the listeners
- use a broad range of vocabulary employing a style and register suitable for the task
- maintain the listeners' interest throughout.

A **A***

Prior learning

Before you begin this unit, think about

- times when you have heard someone talk in a formal situation: which speakers have interested you most and why?
- how you have been taught to structure your formal essays.

When you watched someone on a news programme, listened in assembly or had an outside speaker in school, how did the speaker try to hold your attention? How did they begin and end their talk?

Which of their techniques might you be able to use?

Which essay techniques could you use when preparing and delivering a presentation?

Learning objective

- *To consider what an audience expects and how to address its needs.*

⭐ **Examiner's tip**

Remember – there are no marks for reading from prepared notes in Speaking and Listening assessment tasks.

What does understanding your audience mean?

Your **audience** is a vital consideration when making a presentation. You might be talking to a class, an individual, a group of people outside school or an assembly.

You need to **understand** what type of presentation is required. Should it be

- factual
- argumentative or persuasive (supporting a point of view)
- entertaining?

You also need to use an appropriate **speaking style**.

Checklist for success

- You need to be clear about who you will be addressing and what they expect.
- You need to adapt your language, content and style to suit your audience.

ACTIVITY

You are going to deliver a presentation on how your school's rules should be changed. With a partner, decide how you would vary your style and content for

- the headteacher
- your classmates
- a meeting of interested parents.

In each case, ask yourself:

- What will they already know?
- What do I need to tell them?
- How can I convince them to share my views?

Focus for development: Adapting vocabulary, content and style to audience

ACTIVITY

This **Grade A★** presentation has the right **tone** and **vocabulary** for the audience.

> 'In all my dreams, before my helpless sight, / He plunges at me, guttering, choking, drowning...'
> Few poems have this power: to affect our senses, to make us feel the suffering, to plunge us into the midst of horror and pain. Wilfred Owen's poetry still has this power to shock, even a century on, and, incredibly, the power to transform from a picture of a specific time to a universal image of war...

Who do you think the student is talking to? Give reasons.

If he were talking to Year 7s, what might he say instead of

- 'affect our senses'
- 'plunge us into the midst of horror and pain'
- 'transform'?

A student writes…

Do we have to use complex vocabulary all the time? Isn't it better to just say things clearly?

Answer…

You get marks for a wide vocabulary. However, always make it suitable for your listeners.

ACTIVITY

Read this extract from a **Grade C** presentation. The student struggled at times to find interesting vocabulary. Try to improve the

- choice of words (nouns, adjectives, verbs and adverbs)
- variety of sentence lengths and types (see pages 74 and 75)
- style (making it less chatty).

> I know many of you will laugh at me for having *Sharpe* as my favourite television programme because it's what your mum and dad used to watch. Well, I've seen it on satellite and although the programmes were made quite a long time ago they are still quite good. It's about soldiers from Britain fighting against Napoleon. The sorts of things that happen are fights to win forts and there is quite a lot of falling out amongst the men. Sharpe is always the hero. He wins all the battles and all the women too.

ASSESSMENT FOCUS

Prepare the opening of a presentation to your year group, describing your favourite place and explaining why you like it. Use an appropriate style.

You might include

- your earliest memories of the place
- a precise description of what it is like
- why it is special for you
- a story about it which would be suitable for your audience.

Remember

- **Use different styles and approaches for different audiences.**
- **Focus on your choice of tone and vocabulary.**

Choosing a topic

Learning objective

- *To understand why a sensible choice of topic increases your chance of success.*

Examiner's tip

Try to choose a subject you can talk about at length and will be confident to answer questions on.

Examiner's tip

Some speaking tasks are more difficult than others. For example, it is harder to persuade someone that your football team is the best than to describe what happened during a match. You gain more credit for completing a more complex task.

Why is choice of topic important?

If the **topic** is something you feel comfortable with because you know a good deal about it, your presentation will flow better and be richer in detail.

Checklist for success

- You need to choose your topic and approach carefully, thinking about how you can make it interesting for your audience.
- You need to know or find out as much as possible about your topic.
- When you are asked to give a presentation, you need to make sure the topic allows you to do your best. If not, negotiate a change of topic or emphasis if possible, or research enough information so that you can do yourself justice.

ACTIVITY

Which of these topics could you talk about most successfully? Why?

- Argue that knife crime is sensationalised in the press.
- Advise the parents of primary school students to send their children to your school.
- Explain why teenagers prefer technology to real life.

Focus for development: Successful topics

ACTIVITY

- If you could choose your presentation topic, what would it be? Give reasons why.
- How would you approach your topic? Would you want to describe, persuade your audience or put forward an argument, for example? Give reasons why.

Look at these two extracts, showing how different students approached the same topic.

With a partner, decide what is good about the first one and what advanced skills are demonstrated by the second.

Examiner's tip ★

*Your audience **will not** want to hear lists of facts, rambling stories or unconnected ideas. They **will** be interested by new ideas, touches of humour and facts that make them stop and think.*

Grade C

The trip was a huge success. We met at 6.45, which was really early for most of us, then the bus arrived at about seven. I rushed straight to the back, to sit with Jenny and Asma, and a whole gang of us were on the back seat. Mind you, we didn't feel like singing that early in the morning. I swear Lucy was still chewing her breakfast when she got on...

Grade A

I know what the reaction from most of you will be when I ask this but... how can anybody justify a trip to Alton Towers in school time? And before you start, yes, I know everyone enjoys it – but what in the world does it have to do with education? Wouldn't it be better to sit in lessons during the week and go to an amusement park at the weekend? Obviously, we all love the excitement of rushing on to a coach in the early hours of the morning with our hair just washed and still wet and our latest trainers dazzling our friends, yet...

ASSESSMENT FOCUS

You must make a 5–10 minute presentation to your class on the topic of 'The Trip'.

Decide

- which trip you will talk about
- how you will approach the topic, to best show your abilities
- what details you will use to support your points and interest your audience.

Remember

- **You must know about a topic to talk about it confidently.**
- **You will be rewarded for responding well to a more complex task.**

Researching and developing Content

Learning objective

- To understand the importance of selecting and using content wisely.

Why is a focus on content important?

- If your **content** is not interesting and relevant, you will not engage your audience.
- Listening is a different skill from reading. What you say must be understood and each point needs to be clear and precise. If the audience misses a point, they have no second chance to hear it.
- If you confuse your audience, you are likely to lose their attention.

Checklist for success

- You need to have enough information about your topic so that you avoid making irrelevant points or unconvincing claims.
- You need details and examples to support your main points.
- You need to be very clear about the purpose of your talk when selecting your content.

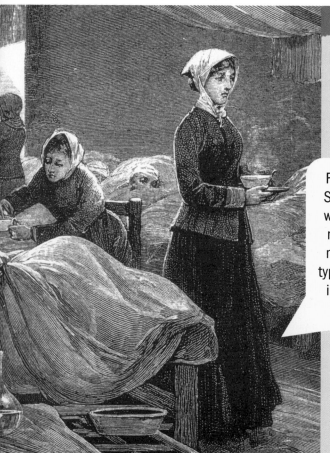

ACTIVITY

This extract is from an A★ Grade presentation. The student is clearly comfortable with her topic because she has researched it thoroughly. It is full of detail and uses a rich vocabulary and varied sentence structures.

> Florence Nightingale took a group of 38 nurses to the Scutari Barracks Hospital in October 1854, to care for wounded British soldiers in the Crimean War. Although many were in agonies because of their injuries, many more were dying of terrible diseases like typhus fever, typhoid and cholera. The nurses cared for these soldiers in a way we have come to expect nowadays, but back then it was a revolutionary move...

Discuss:

- How many facts does the student include?
- How does she use the facts?
- What is her main point?
- How does she try to make us interested in Florence Nightingale?

Examiner's tip

Even a fairly 'everyday' topic like 'School rules' can be made more interesting by including, for example,

- **statistics** – *how many rules are broken*
- **survey results** – *how students feel about particular rules*
- **comparisons** – *with other schools.*

Focus for development: Selecting effective content

Be selective in your choice of materials. Just because you find a detail interesting does not necessarily make it appropriate to your presentation.

So, for example, the talk on Florence Nightingale

- offers facts which give a clear picture of what was happening
- indicates the problems the nurses faced
- shows the number of nurses coping with them
- moves on to talk about how the care was revolutionary for its time.

It only includes facts relevant to the main topic – nursing.

ACTIVITY

You have been asked to present to your class a review of a film you have seen recently.

Decide which of the following points you would or would not include in your review, and why.

Character details	Your range of hobbies
When you saw it	Why you watched it
Your favourite forms of entertainment	Length
Storyline	Best/worst moments
Themes	The last production you saw before this one
Others' opinions of it	Alternative ways of spending your time
Comparison with other similar productions	

Of course you don't only get marks for your main points, but also for how you comment on them.

ACTIVITY

Compare these extracts from students' reviews.

- To what extent does the first review rely on description?
- How has the second student improved her review by making her comments more critical?

Grade C response

I think 'Boys will be Boys' is a programme that would appeal to anyone. I thought about my own brothers when I was watching it. I laugh at them, and I laughed at the boys on the screen. The show made fun of Steve, Imran and Ben, but I have to say the girls seemed ridiculous too: Maeve with her hair and Sammy with her turned-up nose. She tries to be <u>so</u> superior...

Grade A response

My sister loves 'Boys will be Boys'. Mind you, she loves boys full-stop, so maybe she's not the most reliable judge of the programme. She adores Steve because 'he's cute', but she has always reacted to Bambi in much the same way, so take that as you will.

Effective research

Before your presentation, you can **research** the facts you need. That does not mean finding out everything you can about a subject; you need to be selective, finding information which suits your purpose.

When you research, remember that finding the facts is just the start. What counts is how you use and develop your ideas around them.

The information you've found needs to be part of your central message or purpose: for example, to argue that Florence Nightingale changed nursing across the world. Your research findings need to support that message.

ACTIVITY

If you were researching the talk about Florence Nightingale and how she revolutionised nursing care, which of these websites do you think might be useful? Write notes to explain why.

- Florence Nightingale Museum: www.florence-nightingale.co.uk
- Jon Baines Tours – Florence Nightingale in Istanbul: www.jonbainestours.co.uk
- Florence Nightingale quotations: www.en.thinkexist.com/quotes/Florence_Nightingale/

Use the internet to find five relevant and interesting facts about Florence Nightingale.

Having found relevant material, you need to decide how to put it across effectively to your audience. For example, you might use

- diagrams or pictures
- PowerPoint slides
- anecdotes.

A PANORAMIC VIEW OF THE SEA OF AZOF, KERTCH, YENIKALE, ARABAT, &c.
SHEWING THE POSITION RECENTLY TAKEN BY THE ALLIES, LIKEWISE COMPRISING THE WHOLE OF THE CRIMEA.

Finishing well

Organise the facts below into a conclusion for a presentation which argues that Florence Nightingale is one of the greatest women to have lived.

Try to offer a conclusion which

- summarises your argument
- includes only relevant details
- leaves the audience with a positive impression of Florence Nightingale (and of you as a presenter!)

> Died 1910, aged 90
>
> 1907: International conference of Red Cross Societies listed her as a pioneer of the Red Cross Movement
>
> Was asked by US for advice on caring for the sick during their Civil War
>
> Called 'Lady of the Lamp' because of her hours tending the sick in the Crimea
>
> First woman to receive the British Order of Merit

ASSESSMENT FOCUS

You are preparing to talk to your class on your favourite hobby. Complete a table like the one below, which is about running.

Summarise:

- the points you would select
- why you would choose them
- how you would develop them – to show their effects or go into more detail.

Point	Why	Development
Running is healthy	Health issues important at any age	How much weight I lost / How my life changed as I became healthier
15 million British people run	Pleasure / Competition / Feeling of well-being	Age no barrier: Constantina Dita became world marathon champion at 38; Buster Martin ran in the London marathon aged 101

ACTIVITY

Look at this Grade C response.

> So, Florence Nightingale was famous all over the world. She was even respected in the United States and by the Red Cross Movement by the time she died in 1910. The Lady of the Lamp, as she was called, was the first woman to receive the British Order of Merit and she certainly deserved it.

Produce a better conclusion by

- organising the material more effectively so that the ideas develop more logically
- adding more detail and commenting appropriately
- rephrasing or totally rewriting where necessary.

Remember

- **Content needs to be appropriate for your purpose and audience.**
- **Research if necessary but be selective in what you use.**
- **Ensure all your content is relevant and supports your main points.**

Structuring your presentation

Learning objectives

- To focus on organising your ideas for maximum effect.
- To learn about the importance of effective openings and endings.

What does structuring your presentation mean?

In a **well-structured** presentation, the speaker knows what they are going to say, and in what order. Planning a strong opening and a memorable ending should be part of the structuring.

Checklist for success

- You need to prepare your presentation in detail.
- You need to consider the different ways you can begin, develop and end your presentation.

ACTIVITY

You have been asked to give a presentation about your favourite school subject.

- List the points you might make.
- Put them into a logical order.
- How would you begin your presentation?
- How might it end?

A student writes…

Surely planning a presentation is just like planning an essay.

Answer…

In many ways, they are alike. However, when you are talking, you can develop ideas further on the spot and interact with your audience using different tones of voice, facial expressions and gestures.

Focus for development:
Planning, openings and endings

A **bulleted plan** can contain all the relevant information you need whilst speaking.

ACTIVITY

Complete a table like the one here, developing your ideas. The right-hand column is where you can add more detailed information.

Main idea	Points to be included
Teachers	Miss Spivey (obsessed with Crimean War) Mr Jenkin (anecdote about haunted mansion)
Lessons	dramatic reenactments
Trips	

Using your plan, run through what you would say.

Examiner's tip

*Practise your delivery.
Powerful words are
wasted if they are not
delivered well.
You can present to a
friend or a mirror, or
you could record
yourself and then judge
your own performance.*

Openings

Your opening **sets the tone** for what follows. It should make it clear what you intend to talk about and immediately engage your audience.

Some possible openings:

- **rhetorical questions**: 'Have you ever had the wrong tooth extracted?'
- **relevant humour**: 'Have you heard the one about the dentist, the missing tooth and the court action for damages?'
- **powerful facts**: 'Last year in Britain, 57% of children under the age of 10 had at least one tooth extracted…'

Endings

A memorable ending can leave a powerful impression upon your audience. You could try

- a summary of your argument
- one final, convincing point
- a joke
- a rhetorical question.

Which of these you choose will depend on your topic, purpose and audience.

ACTIVITY

Use these techniques to write three interesting openings for your presentation about your favourite school subject.

ACTIVITY

Look at this Grade A★ ending and decide with a partner

- what the purpose of the talk is
- how the speaker hopes to impress the audience at the end.

Grade A★ ending

Inaction and ineptitude on the part of governments across the world have led us to this state. It's not too late to save the world but it's going to have to be last-minute stuff, because midnight is approaching. And if you think you can party through the night and all will be well tomorrow, you're wrong. There won't be a tomorrow… Fight to make things better, petition parliament… If we all use our grey matter, there might still be hope.

ASSESSMENT FOCUS

Plan in detail a presentation to persuade local business leaders to donate to a charity supported by your school.

- Bullet-point your plan.
- Prepare, in advance, what you are going to say to open and close your presentation.

Remember

- **A detailed plan is essential for success.**
- **Openings and endings are vital parts of any presentation.**

Using standard English, imagery and repetition for effect

Learning objectives

- To appreciate the importance of standard English in presentations.
- To understand how imagery and repetition for effect can add to the quality of performances.

Glossary

Standard English: the form of English which is grammatically correct – not the more casual, colloquial form you might use with friends.

imagery - the use of imaginative comparisons, such as similes and metaphors (see page 18).

What does using these techniques for effect mean?

Using **standard English** creates a more formal tone, which is expected as part of your assessment.

Including **imagery** and **repeating** words or phrases will help engage or evoke a response from your listeners and emphasise your key points.

Checklist for success

You need to understand the differences in grammar and vocabulary between talking informally to friends and speaking in more formal situations. Listen to news presenters on television, as a reminder of what standard English sounds like.

Planning imagery and repetition into your presentation can create more of an impact.

ACTIVITY

Read this extract from a formal presentation.

> See, it's clear, init? There's them that's got the cash, sitting on it like some big greedy thing, and them that 'asn't. You gotta find some guy with big wads – and I'm talking major league money now – and make 'im cough up his big wads. Then yer charity's got wads of stuff to work with...

- What is inappropriate about the use of English here?
- How effective is the imagery?
- Comment on the use of repetition. Is it effective?

Presenting in standard English means using correct grammar and avoiding informal language or **slang**.

- Generally use verbs in sentences, rather than offering half-completed thoughts.
- Speak in full sentences.
- Use conventional vocabulary rather than street language.

ACTIVITY

Rewrite the example above using more formal English.

Focus for development: Imagery and repetition

This extract is from a **Grade A★** presentation. It is in perfect standard English and has been enriched by using imagery and repetition.

ACTIVITY

Identify the imagery and repetition in the extract. Comment on the linked metaphors and the long final sentence and their effects.

Explain the effect of 'That chokes. That destroys.' These are not conventional sentences. How are they used?

Discuss with a partner:

- why each example you have found is appropriate for the purpose
- how these devices affect the listener.

> The years thunder on but there is no sign of a break in the darkness for so many in Africa. Darkness that oppresses. That chokes. That destroys. Support, for many, is just a gun pointing away from them rather than at them; relief is a bomb that fails to explode. Still, they are like shattered fragments in wars that know no boundaries and never seem to end, wars that rumble across the continent, wars that take lives indiscriminately, run by men who can have no heart and no soul...

Examiner's tip ★

Remember, using repetition because you have run out of ideas is not good. However, using it to hammer home a point is a strength and will earn you marks.

ACTIVITY

Improve this extract from a **Grade C** response by adding imagery and repetition.

> And in the evening there is nothing to do at all. Just because we live in a village, no one seems to remember we exist. There's nothing here and we can't even go into town because the bus service stops at seven o'clock. It's pathetic...

ASSESSMENT FOCUS

Produce the opening of a presentation about the job you would like to have when you are older.

Use standard English, some imagery and at least one example of repetition for effect.

Remember

- **You are expected to use standard English in most presentations.**
- **By including imagery and repetition for effect, you will make your presentation more impressive.**

Using rhetorical questions, humour and exaggeration for effect

Learning objective

- *To understand how rhetorical questions, humour and exaggeration can engage your listeners.*

Glossary

rhetorical question: a question asked of an audience to involve them, without expecting a reply – 'How could anyone ever think that?'

exaggeration: making things seem bigger to hammer home a point – 'I've told her a million times not to exaggerate.'

What does using these techniques for effect mean?

The careful use of **humour**, **rhetorical questions** and **exaggeration** will appeal to your listeners and bring variety of tone to your presentation.

Checklist for success

- You need to used rhetorical questions, humour and exaggeration sparingly and only when suitable for a topic or an audience.
- You need to plan in advance which of these techniques you will use.

ACTIVITY

Read this extract from a presentation to a group of university lecturers.

With a partner, decide which rhetorical questions, humour and exaggeration are inappropriate.

> So, how are you guys doing? I've got to say, you look pretty bored: I suppose you always do. Anyway, I've managed to cheer up thousands and thousands of conferences like this one, so it was worth your while turning up today. Actually, it's just as well you came today, because I don't suppose many of you will be around much longer. I bet your doctors are pretty busy, aren't they?

Focus for development: Making presentations more interesting

Rhetorical questions

Rhetorical questions will challenge the audience to think more actively about an issue. For example:

'Can this ever be acceptable?' – desired reaction: 'Probably not!'

'Why, then, have these changes been introduced?' – desired reaction: 'Tell me more.'

Add two rhetorical questions to this extract to add more interest.

> The royal family is an institution we should treasure. They stand above politics and give stability to our country. Without them, we might not have our current status in the world. It's not even as if they are so different from us any more: the princes are just ordinary young men, with ordinary interests and ordinary problems,

Humour

If you can add witty touches it may encourage the audience to warm to you. Try:

- a funny **anecdote** (or short story) to support your point, for example: 'I caught measles on holiday. Well, actually, measles caught me. What happened was…'
- an **aside** (a quick 'throw-away' comment) for example: 'I knew you wouldn't be interested in this photograph of a steam train. My dad said I'd do better with a picture of Lily Allen…'

ACTIVITY

Add a funny follow-on to each of these sentences.

- Anyone can dress well if they know where to shop.
- I try to help my cousin.

Exaggeration

Be careful not to over-use exaggeration, but used sparingly it can have considerable impact.
For example:

'Crack SAS commandoes couldn't track down and bring back my father when he's out for a night on the town.'

A student writes…

I always try to use a rhetorical question to begin my presentations. It seems to get everybody listening.

ASSESSMENT FOCUS

Prepare the opening of a speech about a person you admire.

- Use rhetorical questions, humour and exaggeration.
- Underline each example of these techniques.

Remember

- Using rhetorical questions, humour and exaggeration can help keep your audience listening.
- Only use these techniques occasionally, when appropriate for your audience.

Delivering your presentation

Learning objective

- To be prepared to deliver a presentation effectively.

⭐ **Examiner's tip**

Make sure any props that you might choose to pass around during your talk don't distract your audience. Use PowerPoint to identify the main points you will be developing or to illustrate your ideas (with a short video or photograph, perhaps). It can help guide you through your talk as well, but never read from the screen or from notes. You get no marks for reading!

⭐ **Examiner's tip**

Making regular eye contact with your listeners shows confidence. A smile helps too.

What is needed to deliver a presentation well?

To deliver a presentation successfully you must present the material with style. If you are not prepared, you could underperform.

Checklist for success

- You need to organise your presentation so that you know what to say and in what order.
- You need to know how to handle your audience: this is crucial for success.

Speakers deal with audiences in different ways: a stand-up comedian might move around and joke with the audience; a presenter at an awards ceremony will be more serious.

ACTIVITY

In a small group, discuss what you think will be your major problems when presenting to your class, and how you might overcome them. For example:

- students not being interested
- the way the room is set-up
- your nerves.

ACTIVITY

In a group of four, improvise two scenes where young people attend job interviews at a supermarket.

- One interviewee knows about the job, is prepared and enthusiastic.
- The other knows nothing about the job and shows no interest.

Talk about the different impressions created.

Focus for development: Establishing and maintaining a good impression

First impressions

First impressions count. If you appear calm and prepared, you will impress your audience. People notice body language, so try not to look nervous.

Sustaining your role

Having created a good impression, you need to maintain your confidence throughout. Remember:

- Listeners can get bored quickly, so vary your pace to sustain their interest.
- A strong opening is wasted if it's followed by a muddle of points.
- Move through your well-planned material towards a clear ending.

Dealing with questions

You will probably have to answer questions at the end and audiences will expect direct responses. Try to foresee questions you might be asked and have the information ready.

ACTIVITY

Discuss with a partner:

Which of these will make the worst impression on your audience?

- Losing track of where you are in your notes
- Messing up a funny line
- Speaking in a monotone and not making eye contact.

What could you do to remedy each of them?

Examiner's tip ★

Not being direct in answering questions – a politician's trick – might appear a clever tactic but can also make you seem evasive.

ACTIVITY

Look at these two answers to the question:

What more can we do to help old people?

Discuss with a partner why the Grade A answer is better.

Grade B answer

I have a friend who suggests we could carry them across the road! No, seriously, we need to take time to talk to them... that sort of stuff, they're much happier if they feel wanted.

Grade A/A★ answer

Obviously, it's never easy. Age Concern gives out leaflets like this one, with advice, but we can't just wave a magic wand to transform their lives. Nevertheless, to just give up on them isn't an option. And even little things matter. Last week, for instance...

ASSESSMENT FOCUS

Deliver an impressive opening to this presentation:

My life out of school

Then take questions and ask for feedback on how you performed.

Remember

- **Prepare thoroughly and be ready for questions.**
- **Impress your audience from the start.**
- **Sustain their interest to the end.**

Grade Booster

Extended Assessment task

> Produce a detailed plan for a presentation to your class, entitled:
> **What is the best sort of day out?**
> Persuade your audience to accept your view.

Or, you could choose one of the following topics:

- Argue that there is no such thing as a good day out.
- Argue that it would be better if people concentrated on making everyday life better rather than being obsessed with holidays.
- Offer advice on how to enjoy your time and avoid problems on holiday, or on how to enjoy yourself without going away on holiday.

Make notes in your plan of the techniques you will use at various stages to interest your audience.

Pay particular attention to your opening, how you develop your ideas and your ending.

Deliver the presentation and ask for feedback.

Evaluation – What have you learned?

With a partner, use the grade checklist below to evaluate your work on the Extended Assessment Task.

- I can organise and deliver a challenging and sophisticated presentation which impresses the audience from start to finish.

- I can organise and deliver an assured presentation which uses imaginative techniques for a desired effect on the audience.

- I can organise and deliver a confident presentation using techniques which affect the audience.

- I can organise and deliver a structured presentation, using some presentational techniques.

- I can plan and deliver a presentation as required.

You may need to go back and look at the relevant pages from this section again.

Discussing and Listening

Introduction

This section of Chapter 3 shows you how to

- prepare for a discussion with one or more people
- speak and listen effectively in group situations
- improve your discussion skills.

Why is it important to spend time improving speaking and listening?

- Although we all talk and listen each day in many different situations, many people do not understand how to take part effectively in group discussions.
- Discussion is not about simply making your point of view known; it is also about listening, responding and possibly adapting previously held views.
- Listening sensitively and accepting other views is a sign of maturity.
- We spend our lives having discussions with all kinds of people on all kinds of subjects; it benefits us if we can do it skilfully.

A **Grade C** candidate will

- communicate clearly, using language that is appropriate to the situation
- listen carefully, develop their own and others' ideas and make significant contributions to discussions.

C

A **Grade A/A*** candidate will

- communicate in a suitable style, depending on the situation, using language confidently in discussion
- begin, sustain and develop discussions
- listen well so they can respond effectively and sympathetically to what others say.

A **A***

Prior learning

Before you begin this unit, think about:

- discussions you have watched on television

> Who has appeared to be in control? How do they direct the conversation? Which people seem left out, and why?

- discussions you have taken part in at school

> How successful have they been? Why have they sometimes ground to a halt or not produced a conclusion? What can go wrong?

- discussions with friends.

> Who do you most like to talk with, and why? When do you find conversations with friends annoying?

Preparing for discussion

Learning objectives

- To appreciate how preparation can improve some types of discussion.
- To practise preparing for a discussion.

Examiner's tip

Notes are fine but you should never read directly from them.

What is there to prepare?

The type of preparation needed will depend on the topic. For example, if you are discussing teenage crime, you may **research facts, figures and opinions** from the Internet. If you are asked about what policies the government should change, you might **assess a range of options** and then **adopt a point of view**.

If you are working as a group, preparation might be done together; if you are speaking from a particular standpoint, you might prepare alone.

Checklist for success

- You need to know what you will be discussing and, if appropriate, what your role in the discussion will be.
- You need to prepare ideas and information and note them down.

ACTIVITY

What would you need to find out in advance to allow you to contribute successfully to this discussion?

> *With a group of friends, come to an agreement about who are or were the five greatest ever Britons.*

Focus for development:
Roles and research

Chairing the discussion

You might be asked to chair a discussion. As chair you need to have questions ready to ask and information ready to keep the discussion going. You will need to direct the discussion but must also be prepared to adapt to what others say.

You have been asked to chair a discussion about how £5 million should be spent to improve your school.

Draw up notes you might use. For example:

- How will you start? For example, you could offer a range of ideas to be discussed.
- Will each person speak in turn?
- Will there be summaries?
- How might you draw the group to a conclusion?

Examiner's tip ⭐

Make sure your notes are brief. They can be put into a possible running order but should not be developed into any form of script.

A student writes…

We did the £5 million discussion. I found some facts, figures and quotes from students and staff to use. It was the first time I've performed like a 'star' in English.

Adopting a point of view

You may be asked to take a particular point of view. If so, you need to be clear about what view you represent and prepare how you are going to support that viewpoint.

ACTIVITY

Imagine you are to be involved in the discussion about spending the £5 million.

You are supporting the view that half the money be spent on new sports facilities and half on new teachers. Prepare your notes.

Examiner's tip ⭐

Work as a group as you prepare, but avoid practice run-throughs. They can make your discussion sound stilted and you will not speak and listen as impressively as if it's fresh to you.

ASSESSMENT FOCUS

Your teacher has warned you that you will be involved in a group discussion about whether there is still time to save the world from climate change.

You can choose whether to agree or disagree.

Organise notes and details to support your opinion.

Remember

- **Prepare for discussions as much you can, to enrich the content of what you say.**
- **Don't over-prepare: reading from scripted notes is not acceptable.**
- **Be ready to adapt your notes as the discussion develops.**

Developing strategies for confident talk

Learning objective

- To understand how to appear more confident in discussion.

How can anyone become more confident?

Confidence is important in all speaking and listening activities, including group discussions. You will feel more confident if you are well prepared and can use strategies to help you feel more comfortable.

Checklist for success

- You need to stay in the discussion and not allow others to dominate.
- You need to make your points clearly, including detail to support them.
- You need to engage with what others say and make sensible responses.

ACTIVITY

Look at these titles for discussions.

> *Should we should bring back hanging?*
> *Who should be in charge of the world: men or women?*
> *'Everyone should be able to go to university.' Is this a realistic target?*

- Which topic would you feel most confident to participate in? Why? How could you increase your confidence about the other topics?

Focus for development:
Demonstrating confidence

Speaking with confidence does not just mean speaking clearly. You also need to sound as if you **believe** in what you are saying.

Some hesitation is natural, because we think as we speak, but hesitating all the time indicates a lack of confidence.

ACTIVITY

In this extract from a discussion, the students are analysing advertisements. They have not prepared their ideas.

What impression do Jenny and Abi create? Give your reasons.

Abi: So, this magazine cover balances the idea of men ruling the world – that's why he's standing on all that money – with the figure of the intelligent woman over here. It's a neat concept. But does it work for readers of this magazine?

Jenny: Well… the picture…

Abi: Yes. *(Raises her eyebrows to Jenny.)*

Jenny: Erm… The colours are good. I like them… Some of them…

Abi: Do they have any effect though? Do they make us think..?

Jenny: Yes. No… Some… I don't know really…

Asking questions

With her confident opening comment and then her questions to Jenny, Abi seems more in control in the discussion. Asking **appropriate questions** can also show you are listening carefully.

For example, you might be

- requesting extra information: 'So, if you think Pythagoras was the greatest mathematician ever, what did he do that has improved the quality of my life?'
- encouraging more reluctant speakers: 'James – can you add to that point?'
- challenging what someone else has said: 'Surely not! Have you forgotten Van Gogh?'

ACTIVITY

Use a table like the one below to note down the different types of question that Grade A student, Steph, uses in this discussion.

Question	Type of question and use
1	Steph is encouraging Anne to be clearer and make a point more simply
2	

A student writes…

I never feel I'm saying enough in discussions. Other people say a lot more than me. But I think what I am saying is important.

Answer…

Confidence is not just about talking at length. Careful listening, followed by a pertinent comment or question, can show your confidence just as well.

ASSESSMENT FOCUS

In a group of three, choose one of the topics from the first activity opposite. One of you needs to lead the discussion and

- introduce the discussion confidently
- allow others to do most of the talking, but try to use questions at different stages to prompt the discussion

Then choose another topic, with another person leading the discussion.

Steph:	So, can you just simplify what you've just said?
Anne:	OK. Shakespeare makes no sense because the stories are utterly stupid.
Steph:	Stupid?
Anne:	Yes, stupid. Come on, they could never happen in real life. None of them.
Steph:	Which means there is no point in studying his plays?
Anne:	Exactly.
Steph:	Mm. Why has he been popular for over 400 years then?
Anne:	No idea.
Steph:	So you really can't see why he's regarded as a genius?

Remember

- **A confident performance will gain you more marks.**
- **A confident performer knows when to speak and when to prompt or listen.**

Developing and supporting ideas

What does developing and supporting ideas mean?

In conversation, speakers often simply state an idea but then fail to **offer evidence** to support it or develop it.

Being able to **extend ideas** or **offer alternatives** to ideas put forward by others sustains the discussion and moves it on.

Checklist for success

- You need to know what you are talking about and to extend ideas in a discussion to be convincing.
- You need to listen carefully so that you can successfully challenge or support what others say.

ACTIVITY

If the points below were made in a discussion, how would you develop them (add information) and argue against them?

Statement	Development	Counter argument
'Football is a total waste of time.'		
'Nothing in life is more important than love.'		
'London gets a chance at everything. It's time for the rest of the country to be treated equally.'		

Focus for development:
Extending and opposing ideas

Extending ideas

Discussions are better if you can make your own ideas detailed and encourage others to clarify their ideas.

To improve your own ideas, you can add **supporting evidence**: for example, facts or statistics, examples, anecdotes or others' opinions.

To **encourage others to extend their ideas**, you can use phrases like

- 'True! What else?'
- 'And can you take that idea one stage further?'

To **develop an idea yourself**, you might use phrases like

- 'Yes. And that reminds me of when…'
- 'Yes, I agree. Not only that, but…'

Countering a viewpoint

To argue your point in a controlled way, you can

- support a viewpoint
- challenge an alternative viewpoint
- try to change other speakers' minds.

ACTIVITY

Discuss with a partner:

Why is Carl, the Grade A student, coming out on top in this argument with Grade C student, Amy?

Carl:	The advertisement is basically fine, but who actually buys the soup? Shouldn't they be targeting housewives?
Amy:	That's sexist!
Carl:	OK. Househusbands as well. We all know about appealing to target audiences. We did that in Year 9, didn't we? So… the target audience here is…?
Amy:	Everybody. Everybody eats soup, everybody can understand the ad and everybody's likely to buy it, aren't they?
Carl:	(*smiling*) Barristers? The royal family?
Amy:	Stupid! You know what I mean…

ACTIVITY

What evidence could you use to develop this point? Jot down some ideas.

> *Everyone should take more care to avoid sunburn.*

Add some **facts** and an **anecdote**. You can invent what you need.

Examiner's tip ★

*The key word when countering a viewpoint is **tact**. If you respond tactfully you just might make the other speaker reconsider their view.*

ASSESSMENT FOCUS

Write down what would you say in response to these statements made during a group discussion. How would you counter each point successfully?

> *There is only one good place to live: Australia. Australia has everything anyone could ever want. Only a fool would choose to live anywhere else.*

Remember

- **Extend your ideas to make them more convincing.**
- **Challenge other people's ideas tactfully and in detail to encourage them to change their minds.**

Responding to talk

Learning objectives

- *To understand the significance of physical and linguistic responses to talk.*
- *To understand how you can show you are listening closely.*

What does responding to talk mean?

You are assessed on your ability to **talk *and* listen**. Your **physical reactions** will indicate how well you are listening, and **linguistic responses** – what you say – will show how well you have understood the discussion.

Checklist for success

- You need to remember that both speaking and listening skills are vital in any discussion.
- You need to focus on listening carefully because what you hear affects how well you respond.

ACTIVITY

Discuss with a partner:
- how people respond to talk in lessons (both students and teachers)
- how you can tell if people are not listening.

⭐ Examiner's tip

Don't force a reaction – you aren't acting! If you are listening carefully, your face will reflect this naturally.

Focus for development: Responses

Physical responses

It is easy to identify who is not listening carefully. Try to avoid
- gazing out of the window or muttering to someone else
- messing around or, perhaps, doodling.

Facial expressions are revealing too. A careful listener is likely to
- raise eyebrows or open or narrow their eyes slightly
- smile, bite a lip or take an intake of breath.

Such signs are only slight, but they show the listener is reacting.

Linguistic responses

What you say reveals how well you are listening because you respond appropriately. Poor listeners are easily identified.

Effective listening allows you to absorb others' ideas and develop new ones.

Read this extract from a group discussion about whom we should respect.

Discuss with a partner:

- How are Lucy's listening skills limiting this discussion?
- How are the others better at listening?

doesn't answer/just another idea

Shabnam:	OK. So we're putting these people into order of importance. Lucy, you start.
Lucy:	Princess Diana.
Steve:	I think she was over-rated. No one talks about her now. When did she die?
Lucy:	There's Martin Luther King too. He was good.
Steve:	They all were, weren't they?
Shabnam:	My dad never liked Margaret Thatcher. What was she like?
Steve:	First woman Prime Minister…
Lucy:	President Kennedy… I don't know anything about him…
Shabnam:	He changed America, didn't he? He fought Russia or something and got shot.
Lucy:	Mohammed Ali…

forced to respond, rather than developing original idea

Decide:

- How well do Grade B students, Jermaine and Laura, collaborate here?
- How often do they take on board and develop each other's comments?
- What more will they need to do to get A/A★ grades?

Jermaine:	Why do people love fashion so much?
Laura:	Well, it's not everybody, is it?
Jermaine:	No. There's my dad for a start. Talk about bad taste. And he doesn't care…
Laura:	It's often girls, though, isn't it? I mean, boys too – but are they as obsessed?
Jermaine:	Some are. It's to do with friendship groups and how they want to be seen, very often: hip… Kind of in vogue. All that.
Laura:	Yes. I was just thinking about how you were dressed last year for that trip we went on…

ASSESSMENT FOCUS

Discuss this in a group. Record the discussion, then play it back.

> *Is fashion really important?*

How often did you

- 'disappear' from the discussion (Were you still listening?)
- argue effectively
- develop an idea?

Examiner's tip ★

It's all about focus. Pay attention to the task and you will be listening. It's simple.

Remember

- **In discussions, listening is as important as speaking.**
- **Your listening ability will be clear in how you react and what you say.**

Reacting to implications and summarising

What does reacting to implications and summarising mean?

Responding sensitively – not only to what people **say directly** but to what they **imply** – shows you are a good listener. People regularly say things which imply something else, for example: 'I love your new dress. It's so… different.'

A good listener picks out what is implied and comments on it.

Summarising briefly what has been said during a discussion proves that you have listened and understood well. It also helps to round off the discussion.

⭐ Examiner's tip

Look out for what other speakers are implying just as you try to spot things they say which are inconsistent. Challenge them if necessary

Checklist for success

- You need to listen sensitively and make perceptive responses.
- You need to show that you understand others' arguments and their implications.
- You need to be able to sum up what has been said.

Focus for development: Demonstrating listening skills

Reacting to implications

Responding to implications demonstrates good listening skills – but your response must be appropriate.

ACTIVITY

Look at this discussion.

- Which responses could have been challenged by a perceptive listener?
- What is implied in each response you have identified?

Daniel:	Geography's like RE: a total waste of time.
Jenny:	I agree. I've hated it since Year 7. I've had Mrs Bates every year and she's always had it in for me.
Daniel:	Too right. And I've had Mrs Cowen. How can she teach? She's too old to even know what's going on.
Maisie:	She said, 'An understanding of geography is vital if we are to understand the world around us.' You don't have to have a degree to know that's rubbish.
Daniel:	And she said, 'You've got to work hard to achieve anything.' That's like something my grandma would say.

ACTIVITY

What implication is B challenging here?

How might A respond?

A: I know you're right. You're always right.

B: So, are you saying I'm wrong?

A student writes...

You can't just write down everything that's said. Surely we're supposed to be talking, not writing?

Answer...

Group simple notes under headings, to make sense of the different arguments. For example:

Reducing the age of consent

For

Against

Summarising

If you listen closely, you will be able to

- sum up what has been said in a discussion so far
- explain the main points of view at the end of the discussion.

Making brief notes though the discussion will help, so nothing is missed. Notes are useful to

- group members, for weighing up different opinions
- the chair, for maintaining the balance between people with different views
- the summariser, for commenting at the end.

ACTIVITY

In groups of four prepare a discussion entitled:

> *'Space exploration is a waste of time. The money could be spent on more worthwhile things.'*

Two of you should take one viewpoint and two the opposite point of view.

- Note down the points made by each speaker taking the opposite view.
- Summarise what each speaker thinks.

Examiner's tip ★

To summarise, use phrases like 'On one hand... Whereas on the other hand...'. This shows you are balancing the views.

ASSESSMENT FOCUS

In a group of three, discuss this statement.

> *Out of school, most teenagers waste most of their time.*

- Look out for implications and challenge them.
- Afterwards, each member of the group should summarise the discussion.

Remember

- **Attentive listeners will identify implications and respond to them.**
- **If you can summarise accurately, you show you have been listening.**

139

Leading a group

Learning objective

- *To learn how to manage a discussion successfully.*

Why is the ability to lead important?

In assessments, high-achieving students are expected to support others in the group, responding to and showing understanding for their ideas, and to lead the group through a discussion to its conclusions.

Checklist for success

- You need to be able to employ all the discussion skills covered so far.
- You need to be prepared to direct discussions, help resolve disagreements and bring the discussion to a conclusion or outcome.

Notice the leadership qualities here:

- **initiating:** 'Right, to kick things off, why don't we like this story?'
- **prompting and supporting others:** 'Are you sure, Satish? Let's just look at…'
- **directing:** 'Well, that's a totally different point. For now, can we get back to…?'
- **summarising:** 'That's agreed, then. We think…'.

Focus for development:
Working on effective leadership skills

ACTIVITY

This extract shows the difference in performance between students working at Grade C, Sheri and Abdul, and a Grade A/A★ student, Jessica, who leads the discussion.

Discuss with a partner:

- What skills are being demonstrated by Jessica?
- How does she prompt and negotiate with Sheri and Abdul?
- How does she summarise?
- How will the others react to her suggestion at the end? Explain why.

Jessica:	So, are we in favour of single-sex education or against it? Abdul?
Abdul:	It's unnatural. Boys and girls are part of society, so why keep them apart at school?
Jessica:	Sheri?
Sheri:	We'd get more work done if the boys weren't there, messing about. Then there's the time wasted while they all explain why they've not done their homework.
Abdul:	That's a silly line to take. Often it's girls with their stupid questions who are the timewasters.
Jessica:	OK. So, if you're both saying the others waste time, could it be better if they were kept apart? Only half the time lost?
Abdul:	Maybe. But I work better with girls around…
Sheri:	We definitely don't need the boys…
Jessica:	Are we saying we need single-sex schools as an option, then? I mean, for those who want it. Or maybe single sex classes for subjects in the same school? Would that work for both of you?

Examiner's tip ★

Just because you are leading a discussion doesn't stop you agreeing with one point of view. However, you must make sure that all viewpoints are allowed and that all participants feel comfortable.

ACTIVITY

Here, a group is discussing where they would like to live. What might a leader in the group have said to

- make this discussion more positive?
- move the discussion forward?

Wayne:	This is the worst place to live.
Jane:	It's better than the middle of a slum.
Wayne:	This is a slum.
Jane:	It's not. Have you ever been to places with rubbish lying around and broken windows everywhere?
Wayne:	It's like that round here …

A student writes…

I like working in groups but I'm hopeless at leading the others. I always get swamped by their ideas.

Answer…

The ability to manage a group is expected from a top student. However, you can always try to guide the group through sections of the discussion. Taking brief notes might help you stay in touch.

ASSESSMENT FOCUS

In a group of three, have a discussion in which two take directly opposed viewpoints and the third is responsible for leading them to an amicable conclusion. Choose from:

- *Football is more important than anything.*
- *Exams should be banned.*

The important thing is that it must be a topic on which there is strong disagreement.

Repeat with a different topic and different roles.

Remember

- **When leading a discussion your priorities are to balance views, avoid conflict, encourage agreement and move to a resolution.**
- **Sensitive listening and the ability to encourage involvement and compromise are key leadership skills.**

Grade Booster

Extended Assessment task

> *Working as a group, prepare a discussion on the topic below. Then hold the discussion.*
> ***From the age of 14, young people should have much more freedom in every area of their lives.***

Each member of the group should
- decide on their initial viewpoint
- produce some bulleted notes and/or other materials for discussion
- come to the discussion with an otherwise open mind.

It is likely to help if
- one member of the group chairs the discussion
- at least one person takes each side of the argument
- one member summarises the discussion for the rest of the class.

Evaluation – What have you learned?

With a partner, use the grade checklist below to evaluate your work on the Extended Assessment Task.

- I can listen sensitively, showing empathy for others' views.
- I can probe opinions through searching questions, encourage interaction in groups and resolve outcomes.

- I can initiate discussions and perform with assurance in them.
- I can listen sensitively and sustain discussion in suitable ways.

- I can reflect on what is said, challenge others and build on their ideas.
- I can help structure and manage the discussion.

- I can communicate clearly and interest other members of the group.
- I can listen carefully, ask relevant questions, develop ideas with detail and make significant contributions that move the discussion on.

- I can sustain involvement and make effective contributions.
- I can show evidence of understanding and respond appropriately to what is said.

You may need to go back and look at the relevant pages from this section again.

Adopting a Role

Introduction

This section of Chapter 3 shows you how to

- approach the task when adopting a role
- develop a role successfully
- improve performances.

Why is the ability to adopt a role important?

- It is one of the three tasks you must complete for the Speaking and Listening Controlled Assessment.
- If you can adopt a role successfully, it demonstrates empathy with the character you portray. Adopting a role also help you understand how writers create characters and how actors can portray them.
- Adopting different roles is something everyone does in different situations in life, so this is good preparation.

A **Grade C** candidate will

- develop and sustain roles through appropriate language and effective gesture and movement
- engage watchers' interest by showing understanding for characters, ideas and situations.

C

A **Grade A/A*** candidate will

- create complex characters to fulfil the demands of challenging roles
- sustain the watchers' interest through the skilful use of a range of vocabulary and non-verbal techniques.

A **A***

Prior learning

Before you begin this unit, think about

- soap operas and/or television series or films you watch

What is distinctive about your favourite characters? How are facial expressions and gestures used? How are the most memorable lines delivered, and why?

- how the characters were portrayed in any live theatre you have seen

How were they made convincing?

- what the acting was like in any amateur drama you may have seen.

How might the characters have been made more realistic and engaging?

Getting into role

Learning objectives

- *To learn how to explore a role and what is required when improvising it.*
- *To think about what can be done to improve your performances.*

What does improvising a role mean?

In your Speaking and Listening assessment, you will be asked to **improvise a role** using drama techniques. You might have to play a character from literature or someone from real life such as a doctor or cleaner, or you might have to represent a viewpoint in a discussion – supporting a new leisure complex, for example.

You need to prepare in advance to create and develop a **convincing character**.

Checklist for success

In order to portray a character convincingly, you need to explore

- their **history**: what has happened to them
- their **attitudes**: what they think about different issues/people
- their **behaviour**: how they speak to and treat others
- their **relationships**: with people around them
- their **motivations**: why they behave as they do.

ACTIVITY

Choose a character from a novel/play/poem you have studied.

- Make notes about this character for each of the areas listed above.
- In a group of three, imagine your characters meet in heaven. Introduce yourselves, describing your life and what has happened to you.

Focus for development:
Planned improvisations

How well you perform can often depend on how well you work with others. Shared preparation and positive criticism will improve performances in most cases.

ACTIVITY

Look at this improvisation by two Grade C students.

Situation: a headteacher is meeting an angry parent whose child has been excluded for fighting.

⭐ **Examiner's tip**

Some improvisations are disappointing because they have no 'depth'. To succeed, you need to know as much as possible about your character, so that you can think and behave as they would.

Lisa:	(*sitting at her desk*) Hello, Mrs Garvey, please come in.
Katie:	Yes, well, I had to come. (*She sits down*)
Lisa:	I think I know why you're here.
Katie:	I'm not happy about what's happened to Susannah.
Lisa:	No, I thought that would be what has brought you in. Would you like a cup of tea?
Katie:	Er… No, I don't think so. I'm here to talk about Susie, not join in a tea party.
Lisa:	OK. So, what exactly would you like to happen? (*She sips a cup of tea*)
Katie:	That's obvious, isn't it? I want our little Susie back in school. She didn't do anything wrong (*hammering the desk*). We're tired of her being held responsible for everything that happens in this place. She's a good kid.
Lisa:	Well, let's not get over-excited, Mrs Garvey…

Discuss with a partner what advice you would give these performers to help them improve their marks. Consider:

- what they say
- their movements
- who is in control of the situation.

Improvise this situation yourselves, bearing in mind the improvements you have suggested.

ASSESSMENT FOCUS

- With a partner, act out your own headteacher/parent interview. Choose your own topic.
- First, make notes to help you play your role. Try to make your character distinctive – through gesture, movement or ways of speaking. Avoid exaggerating your character as your performance could turn into a caricature.

After performing, decide which were the most successful parts of your performance, and why.

Improve any details and try again. Ask yourselves:

- Do we need to know more background about the characters or the situation?
- Can we structure how the conversation will start – develop – finish?
- Could we change the mood to increase the interest for the audience, for example by building gradually to a climax?

Remember

- Careful planning for your characterisation is essential.
- Try to make your character convincing.
- Co-operating well with your group will help make your performance better.

Speaking in role

Learning objective

- To focus on developing a role through what you say.

What does speaking in role mean?

Sometimes, characters appear two-dimensional; the audience do not believe they could be real. Knowing your character's background will help create this credibility but, to be really convincing, you also need to pay attention to **how** your character speaks and **what** you say, so you reveal what you are thinking and feeling.

Checklist for success

Before your practise your performance, ask yourself:

- Have I prepared properly?
- Have I thought through what will happen and what I need to do at every stage?

After a practice run-through, ask yourself:

- Have I worked effectively as part of the group?
- What can I do to improve my performance?

Before the final performance, ask yourself:

- Do I know roughly what I will be saying at each stage?
- Am I secure in my character: how will I react?

A student writes...

How precise should we be about preparing our performance?

Answer...

You need to know enough before starting so that no one in the group will be surprised by the events and everyone is aware of roughly what will be said. Beyond that, you should feel free to improvise what you do and say.

ACTIVITY

In these extracts, a father, who is a single parent, is talking to his ex-wife.

Both students are convincing in this role, but the Grade A student has developed his part by adding more obvious emotion.

Write down what creates the emotional appeal of each sentence in the A Grade response.

Grade B response

They're not just my kids. They're yours too. I need you to help support them because you know I simply don't have enough money. My wages can't stretch far enough and it's hard to even feed them properly, never mind buy new clothes...

Grade A response

Look, you are going to have to help. <u>We</u> decided to have children; now <u>we</u> have the responsibility for feeding them and clothing them. I'm doing all I can – you know that – but I just can't manage. You have to understand what a mess we're in and you have to help: not for my sake – for theirs!

Focus for development: Speaking in character

Obviously you need to speak clearly, but you also need to speak in the way your character would. This means you won't always use standard English.

ACTIVITY

Look at this **Grade A★** improvisation in role as the Nurse in *Romeo and Juliet*.

Notice how the way she speaks gives the audience a clear impression of what the Nurse is like.

Discuss with a partner what features of her speech make this successful?

> Lordy, lordy, lordy. What a day I'm having! Rush here, rush there! It's been so hectic that every part about me quivers... Dust this! Shift that! I'm at everyone's beck and call and especially that Juliet... 'Course, she's a dear. Love her. Love her. But she's wanting this and needing that. Never a thought for poor old me...

The Nurse is a chatterbox who feels she has to look after the whole household.

Continue her speech, detailing what else she has had to do today and how she feels about it.

ASSESSMENT FOCUS

Work with a partner, each choosing two different characters from literature, the media or real life. One could be the character you chose on page 144.

Demonstrating clearly how they speak, make a 30-second speech by each character.

Ask a friend to criticise your performances, identifying:

- what was convincing
- what you said that was unconvincing, in terms of the characters' personalities and the words you used.

Remember

- **Focus clearly throughout your improvisation on what you say and how you say it in character.**

Developing a role through expression and movement

How can I develop a role through gesture and movement?

As well as thinking carefully about the words your character would use (see page 146), you can develop a character by adding physical actions. This might be a limp, a mannerism such as furrowed brows, or showing anger with the jab of a finger, for example.

However, to develop a role successfully though **gesture** and **movement**, you first need to understand the character's emotions. Then you can act accordingly.

Checklist for success

You need to observe people closely – their expressions, movements and peculiarities. Notice how they

- register emotions through facial expression
- stand
- move
- show feelings in their mannerisms (for example, scratch their head, play with their fingers).

Try imitating some of these mannerisms to develop your skills.

Focus for development:
Expression and movement

ACTIVITY

Your face usually shows what you are thinking. In groups of three, each produce three facial expressions your group would recognise. Decide what emotion each expression represents.

Read these statements.

- I'm happy here. There's nothing more I want from life than this.
- Things have got to change if we are going to get through this.
- Oh, yes. I'm just going from strength to strength.

Create very different characters by delivering each statement as

- an old person
- a confident business person.

Concentrate on giving your characters physical characteristics, such as a bad leg or a habit of smoothing their hair. Make your facial expressions convincing.

Gestures and movements add to the feelings you want to show. For example:

- Hugging someone shows affection.
- Hands to the mouth could show shock.
- Arms wide apart could show welcome.
- A waved fist demonstrates anger (or triumph).
- Sitting down suddenly could register dismay.
- Walking away could show a struggle to accept what has been said.

A student writes…

My father was an actor. When he was getting into role, he'd behave like the character around the house. He called it method acting. He said it helped him make the role convincing.

ACTIVITY

In pairs, decide what facial expressions, gestures and movements you might use when reacting to the following statements. Mime your response to each one.

- We have no money left. We will have to move away, I'm afraid.
- She simply stepped into the road without looking. It wasn't the driver's fault. He couldn't stop.
- There's news! The war is over. At last, life can go back to normal.

ASSESSMENT FOCUS

With a friend, act out the extract below, using expression and movements.

- The first time, A is drunk and B is confused.
- The second time, A is frustrated and B is happy.
- The third time, A is angry, B is relaxed.

A: When the guy walks in…

B: Yeah… What?

A: Make sure it's safe…

B: It's safe?

A: Yes, safe.

B: Then what?

A: Get him.

B: Get him?

A: Yes. Are you stupid? Get him!

Remember

- **Create an impression by how you react and move – but don't overdo it.**
- **Show your feelings even if you are not speaking.**
- **Support your words with appropriate expressions and movements.**

Maximising the impact

Learning objective

- *To learn how you can make the most of your role and gain high marks.*

What does maximising the impact mean?

Maximising the **impact** of your role means making every effort to engage your audience's attention throughout your performance. This means doing more than just showing aspects of your character and sustaining your role.

Checklist for success

- Plan exactly what you will do, what you will be talking about and how you will move and behave.
- Think seriously about how you will begin, maintain your role, and finish in a memorable way.

ACTIVITY

You are auditioning for a part in *Hollyoaks*. The part is a teenager who has just moved into the area and comes from a rich family but does not get on with their parents.

You have to walk into the café for the first time. How will you set about making an impact?

- What aspects of your character will you want to show?
- How will you behave towards the owner and other customers?

Focus for development: Making an impact

The opening

Performances can **start in different ways**. However, your opening section is likely to concentrate on establishing your character.

ACTIVITY

You are 24 and have just arrived on holiday with a friend from work. You know no one else in the hotel. Your friend has gone out to look around and you go down to the pool.

In a small group, you are going to act out your first entrance. Imagine the people by the pool all go silent as you arrive. What will you do? What will be the first thing you say and to whom?

You might want to

- tell them about yourself/what kind of person you are
- tell them about your journey
- ask about the resort.

★ Examiner's tip

To be impressive, you don't have to push yourself forward all the time. It's more about being confident and convincing in everything you do.

The middle

Stay focused on your role. Even if you are not playing a lead role, you can continue to impress if you

- react in a convincing way, using speech, expression and movement
- remain focused and do not become distracted by the audience
- do not allow yourself to be excluded from the main action.

Examiner's tip ★

Talk to the people around you, but remember the audience too. Sometimes, actors on stage talk directly out to the audience when they have something important to say.

ACTIVITY

On the same holiday, your friend has been bitten by a cat. Doctors fear she could have caught rabies. You go with her to the local hospital. In your groups, role play what happens. One of you will play the bitten girl, one the friend and another two, the hospital staff.

Make sure you are fully involved in what happens. Jot down some notes on

- what you will do in this section of the role-play
- the conversations you might initiate.

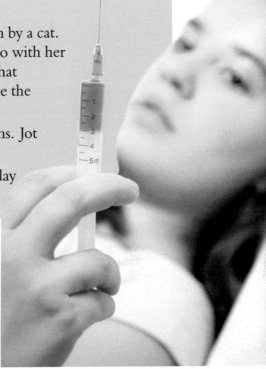

The ending

Your final appearance or your final speech will be your last chance to create an impact. It will help you if you can

- demonstrate that you have sustained and developed the role – for example, you could show how you have changed from the start or how you have been affected by the action
- end memorably, perhaps with a jokey line or a sad farewell, depending on the situation.

ASSESSMENT FOCUS

To end the improvisation, you phone your friend's mother to explain what has happened. Deliver your speech in the form of a monologue.

Ensure your performance is memorable.

Remember

- **Begin and end by making a strong impression.**
- **Make sure you sustain your character – you will be assessed throughout your performance.**

Interviews

Learning objectives

- To understand what is required in an interview situation.
- To understand how to act as an interviewer or interviewee.

When might I come across an interview situation?

You might have to take part in an interview as your presentation task – responding to questions – or when you adopt a role.

Many of the necessary skills are the same in each case.

Checklist for success

- You need to know how to be successful as an interviewer and interviewee, to ask probing questions and to give detailed answers.
- Watch interviews on television to see how it can be done.

ACTIVITY

Watch two different interviews on television, one involving a TV personality and one a politician.

Compare the two styles of interviewing:

- How do the interviewers ask questions differently?
- How and why is the style of answers different?
- What are your impressions of the interviewers and interviewees?
- What are the differences in language used, facial expressions and body language?

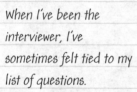

A student writes…

When I've been the interviewer, I've sometimes felt tied to my list of questions.

Answer…

It's fine to have a list of questions but only as a guide. You need to listen to the answers, ask for clarification, comment on what is said if appropriate and change your next question if necessary.

Focus for development:
Good questioning and good answers

Interviewing

ACTIVITY

In this extract, what does Sarah, the interviewer, do badly?

Sarah:	Tell us about your early life. ◄	standard opening
Beata:	I was brought up in Warsaw, then we moved to England.	
Sarah:	What did you first think of university? ◄	sudden switch
Beata:	I had a terrible time…	
Sarah:	Yes. I think we all know that story.	

Being the interviewee

Prepare fully for the interview so that you know your subject well.

If you are in role as a character from literature, research the following:

- what happens to you in the text
- how you are going to play this role and what you plan to say

Always try to extend answers with relevant details and opinions. An extended answer might even become a short monologue.

Examiner's tip ★

In a role-play interview, work though the detail as a pair before you start. Then the interviewer will know where to delve during the interview itself.

ACTIVITY

This is the start of an A★ performance where George, from the novel *Of Mice and Men,* is being interviewed.

> How do you remember Lennie, looking back over your time together?

> It was OK with Lennie. We had a lotta good times. He was a good guy. No, he really was. I remember once I was hungry an' he went an' found a chicken – don't ask me where he foun' it. He wouldn't eat none of it. He just sat there, an' he said, 'Ya do so much for me, George, an' I don't do nothin' for you, but this is for you, George.' See, he was like that, but people didn't see none of that. People didn't see none of that at all…

- short simple sentences capture character of George
- aware of audience
- anecdote appropriate to characters
- correct style of language
- effective, sad repetition

ASSESSMENT FOCUS

Imagine you are a famous person of your choice.

Prepare to answer these questions in role, inventing any necessary details:

- What are your earliest memories?
- Tell us about your time at school.
- How has fame affected your life?

A partner will ask the questions. Then analyse your performance:

- How interesting were you?
- What went well?
- What did you need to improve?

Remember

- **Interviewers must listen and respond appropriately and interviewees must engage the audience.**
- **You are assessed on your speaking and listening skills, so show both.**

Grade Booster

Extended Assessment Task

In a group of three or four, plan an improvisation set in a workplace. A valuable item has gone missing and one person is accused.

Work though these stages:

- Plan what will happen.
- Divide the improvisation into scenes and decide what will happen in each one (or, decide what will happen in one scene, if that is all there is).
- Make detailed notes on your own character.
- Decide how you will play your role.
- Practise as a group.
- Discuss improvements.
- Have a run-through.
- Perform for the rest of the teaching group.

Take feedback on the performance. Discuss it with your group, then improve your performance in the light of what you have learned.

Evaluation – What have you learned?

With a partner, use the grade checklist below to evaluate your work on the Extended Assessment Task.

- I can perform persuasively, sustaining the audience's interest and emotional investment throughout and fulfilling the demands of a challenging role.

- I can create a complex character skilfully, using verbal and non-verbal techniques to intensify the impact on the audience.

- I can create a complex and convincing character, shaping the audience's response through the use of different techniques.

- I can sustain and develop a role.
- I can use effective language, gestures and movement to show I understand how the character thinks and feels.

- I can prepare a performance, perform in role and use some appropriate language, gestures and movement.

You may need to go back and look at the relevant pages from this section again.

Controlled Assessment Preparation
Unit 2: Speaking and Listening

Introduction

In this section you will

- consider what is required of you in Speaking and Listening
- examine candidates' responses and see how well they have performed
- undertake activities and an extended practice task.

Why is preparation of this kind important?

- The example responses in this section allow you to take time to think about how well others speak and listen.
- Taking the opportunity to consider and discuss how activities can be approached and how others have performed will help you to improve the quality of your own performances.

Key Information

Unit 2 is the Speaking and Listening assessment.

- It has three parts: Presentation, Discussing and Listening, and Role-Play.
- The three activities are worth **20%** of your overall English GCSE mark.

What will the assessments involve?

The essential requirements are that you

- make an individual presentation
- perform in a group, discussing and listening
- play a role.

You are likely to complete more than one assessment in each of the three areas, with your best mark in each case being used.

It is crucial that you avoid reading from notes in any of the activities. You are allowed to use notes if they are appropriate (for example, in the presentation), but you are expected to refer to them as you talk, not simply read them.

The Assessment

The assessment objective for Speaking and Listening (AO1) states that you must be able to do the following:

- Speak to communicate clearly and purposefully; structure and sustain talk, adapting it to different situations and audiences; use standard English and a variety of techniques as appropriate.
- Listen and respond to speakers' ideas and perspectives, and how they construct and express meanings.
- Interact with others, shaping meanings through suggestions, comments and questions and drawing ideas together.
- Create and sustain different roles.

Targeting Grade A

Some of the key features of Grade C and Grade A responses are as follows:

Grade C candidates	See
<ul><li>adapt their talk to the situation</li><li>use standard English confidently</li><li>clearly present information, ideas and feelings</li><li>interest the listener through their use of language</li><li>listen carefully and develop their own and others' ideas</li><li>make significant contributions to discussions</li><li>develop and sustain roles through appropriate language and effective gesture and movement</li><li>interest the audience by showing understanding of characters, ideas and situations.</li></ul>	*example on page 158–159*

Grade A/A★ candidates	See
<ul><li>select suitable styles of English for a range of situations</li><li>show assured use of standard English when it is required</li><li>demonstrate a sophisticated vocabulary and vary sentence structures confidently</li><li>express information, ideas and feelings in an engaging way</li><li>initiate conversations and listen sensitively</li><li>make contributions which sustain and develop discussion</li><li>can fulfil the demands of challenging roles and can perform formally and imaginatively</li><li>listen sensitively, showing empathy for others' views.</li></ul>	*example on pages 157, 158–159 and 160*

Exploring Sample Responses

Individual presentation

ACTIVITY

Read the following extract from a student's presentation, in which she talks to her class about looking after a grandmother with Alzheimer's Disease.

Consider these key elements an examiner would look for:

- speaking appropriately in the situation
- using Standard English
- using a broad vocabulary and varied sentences
- being interesting.

Example

introductory complex sentence to begin/introduction to subject

precise vocabulary →

broken sentences, making it seem disturbing and emphasising 'Until'

personalised

> I imagine most of you will have some idea of what Alzheimer's Disease is: it progressively takes away the memory, so that sufferers lose touch with reality more and more, until they eventually can't even recognise their wife, their husband, or their children... They jumble the past and present. Until there is no past or present for them. They can't even recognise night or day. And my grandmother has Alzheimer's. We noticed it starting when her memory suddenly got worse. She struggled to cook our special meal on Friday night, which had always been her treat for us at the end of the week. Then she wasn't sure what day it was. She didn't know what she had done earlier in the day. People's names were forgotten even more easily than they had been before. She needed help.
>
> We actually thought that we needed help too, but as time goes on, you discover that the early stages were nothing. It is a degenerative disease which can only get worse. She takes tablets and somehow manages to still live alone, but now it is as if she is in a different kind of world altogether. Conversations are always the same:
>
> 'What day is it?'
> 'Wednesday.'
> 'Do I have meals on wheels tomorrow?'
> 'Yes, they'll be here.'
> 'Do I have to pay for them?'
> 'No, they are all paid for'
> 'What day is it?'
> 'Wednesday.'
> 'Do I have meals on wheels tomorrow...'

possible pause before this word, for effect

← sense of climax for the paragraph

← examples, to shock/ emphasise the seriousness

short sentences hammering like nails

sophisticated vocabulary

reality of conversation makes situation clear and tragic

Examiner feedback

This is a candidate who engages the audience and offers a variety of information, presented in interesting ways. Sentences are varied, there is some excellent vocabulary and the grandmother's situation is brought to life with the examples and conversation. The candidate can use standard English with great confidence.

Suggested grade: A★

ACTIVITY

With a partner, decide how the audience is likely to respond to each section and which language techniques will provoke that reaction.

Discussing and listening

ACTIVITY

The example below is a transcript from part of a discussion between two boys about the national anthem.

Consider these key elements an examiner would look for:

- speaking appropriately in the situation
- using vocabulary and sentences effectively
- initiating ideas and sustaining them
- listening carefully.

Example

Luke:	I love it. We sing it before international matches and things. *(He hums the tune)*
Sam:	I know lots of people do love it, but have you ever stopped to think about the words? It's not about the nation at all really, is it? We're all expected to stand up and sing about the Queen. I might prefer to sing about the Prime Minister or, better still, the people here. After all, we are supposed to be equal, aren't we? Why sing about the Queen, then?
Luke:	Because the tune represents the country. You know that. It makes everybody proud of where they come from. When you hear the tune, it stands for England, doesn't it?

simple opening

rhetorical questions to challenge and offer more ideas

moving the discussion on, and using logic

listening and responding; slight development of idea

Sam:	Ah, yes, England. But there is Wales and Scotland and Ireland too… *(He looks questioning, tongue-in-cheek)*	more challenge; ellipsis to leave the idea hanging; facial expression expects response
Luke:	You know what I mean. It includes them as well.	only brief retort
Sam:	Well, we did something on this in history, and it hasn't always been like that. There's one verse that goes:	moving the discussion on using fresh idea/evidence
	May he sedition hush and like a torrent rush,	
	Rebellious Scots to crush	
	Not much fun if you're Scottish, eh?	sarcasm

Examiner feedback

Sam is clearly offering more to the conversation and challenges Luke throughout. Even when he uses sarcasm, he is giving reasons for consideration. He includes questions, directs the debate, offers some evidence and fresh ideas. He is demonstrating high-level skills. Luke is listening carefully but only develops one idea in this extract. He uses a rhetorical question and language appropriately and contributes some ideas to the discussion.

Suggested grades: Sam A, Luke C

ACTIVITY

With a friend, discuss the national anthem, deciding whether we should retain it or choose another hymn or song to replace it – and if so, what you would choose.

Adopting a role

This example is an extract from two students delivering a modern-day version of part of *Romeo and Juliet*.

Consider these key elements an examiner would look for:

- speaking appropriately in the situation
- being interesting and being able to be creative and convincing in a complex role.

Juliet:	Don't go. I want you to say with me. Stay with me! ◄── *emotional opening*
Romeo:	I don't want to leave. I'm happier now than I've ever ◄── *explanation of* been in my life. But it's morning, and that means I *situation* have to go. If I'm found here today, I'll be executed – that's what the Prince said – and then there'll be no one for you to love. *(He stands)* I'll be dead and you'll ◄── *logic of why he must go* be a widow. What would you do then?
Juliet:	*(She rises to join him)* I'd kill myself. I'd come to join ◄── *movement to link them* you. You would lie about… *(She gestures)* here… and *interests – offers more* I would lie *(She gestures)* …here. *than just the spoken idea*
Romeo:	*(Laughing)* And much good that would do us. I'd like to live a very long time. With you. And we will live ◄── *irony* for a long time, I promise. But can you hear the lark? It's morning, and I must go. *(He takes her hand)* ── *direct reference to play* Believe me, only death could ever separate us; and if ── *further irony* I am in Mantua and you are still here, we are still together. We are in love and always will be…
Juliet:	I know. It's just… *(She turns away)* I just know ── *movement shows upset* something is going to go wrong. I dreamt about you and you were pale, as if in a tomb. Oh, I don't want ── *further reference to play* you to go. I may never see you again… ◄── *continued irony for effect*

variety of mood ── *touching* ──

Examiner feedback

The candidates approach a difficult scene seriously; both use irony and make their situation credible. The characters seem complex, emotional and realistic. Movements and gestures add to the effect and the candidates work well together to move the scene along. Although this is only the beginning of the activity, there is clear evidence that the candidates are likely to reach a high grade.

Suggested grade for both students: A

Working with a partner or partners, take characters from a literary text you have studied, and either produce a modern version of part of a scene or produce an extra scene.

After you have rehearsed, perform for the group and ask for feedback on how you have done.

EXAM PRACTICE TASK

Prepare and deliver a presentation from one of the options below:

- argue in favour of Britain being closer to Europe and try to persuade your class to think of themselves as European rather than British
- argue that Britain should not be a part of the European Union and is better off as a totally independent country
- persuade your class to be more interested in current affairs
- argue that the world would be a better place if only young people could be put in charge
- argue that we are very lucky to be living in this country at this time in history.

Whichever topic you choose, remember to

- plan carefully
- aim to interest your audience
- use the techniques and approaches you have practised in this chapter.

If you only do five things...

1 Observe and take note of people using standard English so you can use it confidently when you need to. Try to speak appropriately in any given situation: formally, perhaps,
for a presentation; much less formally, perhaps, if you are playing a character from a literary text.
2 When you are undertaking assessment tasks, avoid the temptation to use only simple words and short sentences – remember that you will be rewarded for variety.
3 If you are given the opportunity to plan, grasp it with both hands, because it will prove to be time well spent when you have to perform.
4 Try to be confident when giving a presentation – if people respond positively to you, you will perform better and gain more marks.
5 Take Speaking and Listening seriously. The 20% of marks awarded to it can be the difference between success and failure in your GCSE.

Unit 3A **Understanding Creative Texts** (Literary Reading)

What's it all about?

Reading a range of imaginative and creative texts enables you to discuss and explore some powerful ideas and writing techniques. This can be enjoyable, as well as feeding into your own writing and speaking work.

How will I be assessed?

You will get **20% of your English marks** for your ability to respond to a range of texts. You must study one or more Shakespeare plays, one or more texts from the English Literary Heritage and one or more texts from Exploring Cultures.

You will

- complete a Controlled Assessment task on **Characterisation and voice** or **Themes and ideas**, in which you write separately about one text from each of the three areas above (making sure you cover drama, poetry and prose) in **3 to 4 hours**.

The recommended total word limit is 1600 words.

What is being tested?

You are being examined on your ability to

- read and understand texts, selecting material appropriately to support what you want to say
- develop and sustain interpretations of writers' ideas and perspectives
- explain and evaluate how writers use particular linguistic or grammatical effects (for example, imagery) to influence or engage the reader
- explain and evaluate how writers use structural or presentational features (such as rhyme patterns in poetry) for effect
- write about these effects and features in relation to 'characterisation and voice' and 'themes and ideas'.

Shakespeare: Characterisation and Themes

Introduction

This section of Chapter 4 shows you how to

- understand what a Controlled Assessment task on 'Characterisation and voice' and 'Themes and ideas' is about, in relation to *Romeo and Juliet*
- develop responses to tasks in these areas.

Why is it important to learn about characterisation and themes?

- Characters and themes are key ingredients of any text, so learning about them will enrich your study and help you do well.
- They will also be the focus of the responses you write.

A **Grade C** candidate will

- show clear evidence that he or she understands the main ways in which a character or theme has been presented
- explain writers' presentation of character and theme clearly
- display understanding of various features of language and structure used by writers to create characters and explore themes
- support points with relevant and appropriate quotations.

C

A **Grade A/A*** candidate will

- sustain his or her interpretation of how characters and themes are presented (in other words, develop and write about these ideas at length)
- imaginatively select quotation and detail from the text to support these ideas
- analyse in a sophisticated way how characters or themes are presented through language and structure, going beyond the obvious to explore different layers of meaning
- make their own original interpretations.

A

A*

Prior learning

Before you begin this unit, think about

- what you already know about analysing character and theme
- any recent text you have read in which a particular character made an impression on you, or in which a theme or idea really interested you.

> What do you understand these terms to mean?

> What adjectives would you use to describe this character, for example 'kind', 'cruel', 'powerful'? What kept you interested in him/her?

Learning objective

- *To look at key themes and characters in Shakespeare's plays.*

Why is it important to read Shakespeare?

Many of Shakespeare's stories and characters will already be familiar to you, even if you have not read or seen the plays. Words and phrases from his plays form part of our everyday speech (for example, 'All the world's a stage'). But what was Shakespeare really interested in writing about?

Here are three pupils discussing Shakespeare's play *Macbeth*.

Jude:	Well, it's clear that the protagonist is Macbeth. He's the one who's ambitious and wants to be King.
Kaleem:	Yeah… he kind of makes things happen. OK, his wife pushes him but he *does the killing.* That's why he hesitates at the start. It's like his conscience talking.
Jude:	That bit when he says, after he kills the King, 'I am afraid to think what I have done'.
Liam:	And he's there all the way through, but his wife isn't. Shakespeare kills her off before the end and she doesn't say much in the second half of the play.
Jude:	'Cept when she's sleepwalking and feeling guilty herself. When she washes imaginary blood from her hands.

ACTIVITY

With a partner, decide:

- Is this a discussion about character or about themes?
- How can you tell? Think carefully.

The reason this isn't clear-cut is, of course, that the two areas overlap. If a character promises to help his best friend and then kills him, you could say:

- This tells us about his **character** – he's nasty, vindictive and cruel!

But you could also say:

- The writer is possibly interested in the **idea** or **theme** of betrayal.

Focus for development: Predicting themes and character

The opening Prologue of *Romeo and Juliet* tells us a lot about what is to come. A student has begun to make some notes about character and theme around the Prologue.

'households' means 'families' so people are mentioned straightaway – that's character.

Like 'hatred' going back years. Is 'hate' a theme? What sort?

Two **households**, both alike in dignity,
In fair Verona, where we lay our scene,
From **ancient grudge** break to new mutiny,
Where civil blood makes civil hands **unclean**.
From forth the fatal loins of these two foes
A pair of star-cross'd lovers take their life;
Whole misadventur'd piteous overthrows
Doth their death bury their parents' strife.
The fearful passage of their death-mark'd love,
And the continuance of their parents' rage,
Which, but their children's end, nought could remove,
Is now the two hours' traffic of our stage;
The which if you with patient ears attend,
What here shall miss, our toil shall strive to mend.

Don't get this – but sounds like this hate is making life dirty – almost sinful?

Examiner's tip

Openings are very important for both characters and themes. A character's first appearance can tell us a great deal about them. Be aware that the opening of a play can suggest themes, sometimes through quite subtle hints.

ACTIVITY

Complete these notes on the Prologue, adding any references you can find to people (even if not mentioned by name) and any themes or ideas.

- Are there references to relationships?
- Are there further references to hate, or to new ideas or themes?
- What does it tell us about what will happen in the play?

Why do you think Shakespeare tells his audience so much about the story before it begins?

ASSESSMENT FOCUS

Using your notes, write two paragraphs summarising how the Prologue introduces both the characters and themes to come.

- If you don't know the play, use the Prologue to predict.
- If you do, say how the prologue 'foregrounds' or looks ahead to what is to come.

Remember

- **Writers give clues and foreground ideas.**
- **Themes and characters are always linked.**

Writing about the character of Romeo

What does writing about character mean?

Examiners will be looking for your ideas on *how* the character has been created (characterisation) and your ability to imaginatively select textual detail to support these ideas.

To explore characterisation, you need to deduce information about character from the text, using pointers such as

- what the character **does**
- what the character **says**
- what other characters **say about** the character and how they **behave towards** them.

ACTIVITY

First, consider the facts. Here is the start of a list of things Romeo does in the play.

> *Romeo – what he does*
> - *Wanders around on his own apparently dreaming about Rosaline*
> - *Goes to the Capulet ball, disguised*
> - *Approaches Juliet, speaks to her and kisses her*
> - *Hides in her garden and then speaks to her when she appears*
> - *Promises to marry her and leaves.*

Quickly jot down anything you think this tells us about how Romeo is presented – for example, he is interested in girls because he seems to move on from one to the next quickly.

Here are two quotations related to Romeo's love interests.

1 Romeo on Juliet

Did my heart love till now? Forswear it, sight;
For I ne'er saw true beauty till this night.
(Act 1 Scene 5, lines 51–52)

2 Friar Lawrence to Romeo

Is Rosaline, that thou didst love so dear,
So soon forsaken? Young men's love, then, lies
Not truly in their hearts, but in their eyes.
(Act 2 Scene 3 , lines 66–68)

Discuss with a partner:

- What is Shakespeare telling us about Romeo through these lines?

ACTIVITY

So is Romeo a brave romantic or immature hothead?

- Complete your list of things that Romeo does in the story.
- From this list, decide where would you place Romeo on a spectrum like the one below.

Brave romantic ←————————————→ **Immature hothead**

Discuss your view with a partner.

Focus for development:
Interpreting the evidence

A key to getting a higher mark is to put your own interpretation on the 'evidence'. Read these responses, which both provide interesting perspectives on Romeo:

Grade B response

> Shakespeare shows us that Friar Lawrence, as an adult, recognises Romeo is essentially like any other young adolescent, falling in and out of love. Juliet isn't anything special, she is just another infatuation, who will be, like Rosaline, 'so soon forsaken'.

Grade A response

> Friar Lawrence completely misjudges Romeo. He thinks Juliet is just another girl, whom Romeo is attracted to, when in fact Romeo had never seen 'true beauty' till he saw Juliet. The Friar represents the adult world which in the end drives the two lovers to their deaths.

The second response is **Grade A** standard because it

- focuses clearly on character
- makes a personal interpretation and develops this further than the Grade B response
- supports it with apt quotation
- puts these ideas together very fluently (embedding the quotation neatly in the text).

Romeo in films
How do Leonardo di Caprio and Leonard Whiting portray Romeo in Baz Lurhmann's version (1996) and Franco Zeffirelli's version (1968)?

Examiner's tip ★

Try beginning your paragraphs with quotations – they don't have to come after the point you make. Try reorganising the examples above and see the effect.

ACTIVITY

Write your own point about Romeo which argues against Friar Laurence's notion that Romeo is just infatuated with love. Make sure you embed any words or phrases from the quotations. You could begin:

> Shakespeare presents Romeo through the eyes of Friar Laurence as a young man who ...

Remember

- **When making a point about characterisation, give it your own interpretation and use evidence from the text to support your views.**

Planning a character response

Checklist for success

In planning a response to the typical Controlled Assessment task below, you need to consider:

- how Romeo is presented through the things he says and does
- how he is presented through what others say and how they behave towards him
- your own personal interpretation – possibly linking Romeo to key themes in the play.

> **Explore the way a central character is presented in a text you have studied.**

Here is one student's plan for his response to this task.

Stage 1: 50–75 words (paragraph 1) Introduce subject in interesting way: quotation from Romeo? Or quotation about him? Will not reveal what I think at this moment, just explore different ways we could interpret how Shakespeare has characterised him.
Stage 2: 150–175 words (paragraphs 2 and 3) Paragraph 2: how Shakespeare presents Romeo at the start of the play (Act 1 Scene 1) Paragraph 3: how Romeo is presented through what he says about himself (same scene)
Stage 3: 175–200 words (paragraphs 4,5 and 6) Paragraph 4: other elements of Romeo's behaviour and language: with Mercutio (Act 2 Scene 4), Tybalt (Act 3 Scene 1), speeches before and after he goes to apothecary (Act 5 Scene 1) Paragraph 5: the final scene – Paris, death (Act 5 Scene 3) Paragraph 6: draw conclusions about his actions: fighting, exile, suicide.
Stage 4: 50-75 words (Paragraph 7): my conclusion
Total 500 words

Modals verbs like 'could' are useful for suggesting an idea

Connectives like 'however' allow you to bring in another perspective

If you were looking to consider different ways of characterising Romeo, you would need to find evidence and use comparative words or phrases, as in this example.

> It could be said that Friar Lawrence, one of the more caring adults, believes that Romeo is essentially like any other young adolescent, falling in and out of love. Juliet isn't anything special, she is just another infatuation, who will be, like Rosaline, 'so soon forsaken'. However, perhaps we shouldn't take Friar Laurence's views at face value. Shakespeare shows us that he makes some bad errors of judgement in the play.

ACTIVITY

Develop Stage 3 of the plan, in which Romeo and Tybalt meet (Act 3, Scene 1). Use this paragraph to explore Romeo's characterisaton in this part of the play.

Introduce your idea with a modal verb, such as 'One *could*…' or 'It *would be* possible to…' and then use a connective to contrast, such as 'However' or 'on the other hand'.

Focus for development: Romeo versus Juliet

Here is what another student has written for the same assessment task on Romeo.

> *Shakespeare presents Romeo as an idiot. He's naïve, foolhardy and acts without thinking. The truth is he fancied Juliet, and knew he would have to marry her to get his way. If anyone's guilty for Juliet's death it's him. Shakespeare makes Juliet take all the risks, too – marrying against her parents' orders, facing her father's anger, taking the sleeping drug that could have killed her ...*

ACTIVITY

Discuss with a partner:

- Do you agree with this view of the two lovers? Why? Why not?
- How could this be seen as an unusual view, with Juliet set against Romeo?
- What is missing from the paragraph to support this view and what needs to be improved?

ASSESSMENT FOCUS

To develop this response showing Romeo in a different light, you would need to refer to one of the 'Juliet episodes' in more detail, analysing her behaviour, with supporting quotations from the text. For example:

> **Point**: Shakespeare shows Juliet is brave.
>
> **Evidence**: How Juliet stands up to her father and how he responds (quotations from beginning and middle of Act 3 Scene 5).
>
> **Explanation**: he's pretty nasty to her!
>
> **Further reflection**: there are signs that Juliet doesn't wish to oppose her father altogether: for example, when she thanks him for trying to find her a husband.
>
> **Tie this back to Romeo**: what he is doing at this point in the play.

- Write a paragraph based on the notes above. You could begin:
  > *Shakespeare demonstrates Juliet's bravery when ...*
- Watch how you express yourself – phrases like 'he fancied her' in the response above were not appropriate. Use a more formal style.

Remember

- **Make your point, provide direct evidence, explain, and add a further layer of reflection.**
- **Bring in original interpretation, for example by contrasting your chosen character with another to make a point about them.**

Themes in *Romeo and Juliet*: fate and destiny

Why are writers' themes and ideas important?

Themes are the ideas or issues that emerge as being important to the writer as you read a text.

Checklist for success

- You need to be able to trace the development of an idea or theme through a text.
- You need to make your own personal interpretations of the theme and support them with evidence and quotation.
- You need to show how writers' choices about language and structure help to develop a theme or idea.

Here, two theatre directors talk about versions of *Romeo and Juliet* that they have put on.

> **Director 1**: For me, the play is about love, but not in a simplistic way. It's more about types of love, such as superficial infatuation, duty, tribal love, optimistic love, caring, and so on. This is why the roses are part of the design I wanted – fresh, withered, sharp thorns. Each character uses them in a different way.

> **Director 2**: This is not really a play about love at all. Love and desire are in it, but actually it is about two worlds that don't understand each other – young and old, families and individuals.

ACTIVITY

- Do you agree with either of the directors above? Or is the play about other things?

> It's about fate and destiny – the idea that you can't escape your future. The Prologue tells us what's going to happen, and the letter to Romeo going astray in Act 5 Scene 2 means this comes true.

> It's all about feud and conflict. Act 1 Scene 1 is a fight, the play ends with killing and death. You can't escape it!

- Discuss in a group what you think interested Shakespeare in particular in this play. Try to base what you say on events, characters and relationships.

Focus for development: Revealing theme through language

Shakespeare often uses **motifs** – repeated ideas or images – to support themes or character development. For example, Shakespeare's repeated imagery of omens can be linked to the larger theme of fate and destiny in the play.

1 The Friar to Romeo

> *These violent delights have violent ends,*
> *And in their triumph die; like fire and powder,*
> *Which, as they kiss, consume.*
> (Act 2 Scene 6, lines 9–11)

2 Juliet to Romeo, foreseeing his fate

> *O God, I have an ill-divining soul!*
> *Methinks I see thee, now thou art below,*
> *As one dead in the bottom of a tomb;*
> *Either my eyesight fails or thou look'st pale.*
> (Act 3 Scene 5, lines 53–56)

ACTIVITY

- Quickly note down the similes used in these extracts. Why are they particularly well-chosen? (What is moving about Juliet's words to Romeo at this stage in the play?)
- What ideas about Fate do you think Shakespeare wants to convey?

Grade C response

> Romeo obviously worries about the future when he is on the way to the Capulet party. He says, 'my mind misgives some consequence' and we know that he'll meet Juliet and that will lead, in the end, to his death. So this is a sort of omen.

There are many other omens and clues to future events in the play. Here is a further example from Romeo at the end of Act 1 Scene 4:

> *I fear, too early; for my mind misgives*
> *Some consequence, yet hanging in the stars,*
> *Shall bitterly begin his fearful date*
> *With this night's revels, and expire the term*
> *Of a despised life clos'd in my breast,*
> *By some vile forfeit of untimely death.*
> *But He that hath steerage of my course*
> *Direct my sail! On, lusty gentlemen.*

- Now read these responses to Romeo's words from two students.

Grade A response — interpretation — quotations to support this

> Shakespeare wants to convey the idea that characters are powerless in the face of fate, and he demonstrates this through the metaphor Romeo uses of our lives being like ships that are directed by God who has 'steerage' of our voyage, and can 'direct' our sails. So, he shows Romeo ignoring his own feelings as his mind 'misgives some consequence', even while we, as an audience, are aware that this is an omen of what is to come.

— develops the point fully

ASSESSMENT FOCUS

Re-read Juliet's lines in extract 2 above. Then write your own paragraph focusing on Shakespeare's use of omens.

Remember

- **Refer to what the imagery suggests.**
- **Develop points fully and with embedded quotations.**

Themes in *Romeo and Juliet*: feud and conflict

Learning objective

- To consider key themes in a Shakespeare play and how to write about them.

It might sound obvious to say that *Romeo and Juliet* is a play about conflict. So how can we find interesting or new things to write about this theme that will make an examiner take notice?

First of all, there are many **different types of conflict** in the play. Consider two of them in the next activity.

ACTIVITY

Make notes under these headings:

The Capulet and Montague feud

- What caused the feud and how long has it gone on for?
- What events in the play *particularly* show it in action?
- Who is in conflict with whom?
- Does anything change about the feud between the start and end of the play?

Parents and children

- Who is in conflict in the play? All parents and children?
- Which events show this conflict in action?
- Why are these people in conflict?

- Can you think of other types of less serious conflict, such as the banter between Mercutio and Romeo?
- Does any 'self-conflict' exist – where a character questions themselves about what to do?

Focus for development: Sustaining writing about a theme

Here is the start of one student's response to a task about the theme of conflict.

> *Conflict is a really important theme in the play. It affects everyone and everything, from the rioting in the street at the start of the play to the deaths of Mercutio, Tybalt, Paris, Romeo and Juliet. As the Prince says in Act 5 Scene 3, 'All are punish'd'.*

This is a good response because it

- states how conflict is central to the play
- gives a suitable quotation about the effect of the conflict
- provides evidence in terms of the riot and deaths.

Examiner's tip

The beginning of any response is vital. It is important to be clear about what you are discussing, but it is equally important to interest the examiner in what you have to say.

- Compare the response on page 172 with this introduction from **a Grade A/A★ response**:

> Conflict is like a poison or illness that infects everything in the play, shown when the Prince condemns the Capulets and Montagues by telling them, 'what a scourge is laid upon your hate' in Act 5 Scene 3. This links with other references such as Tybalt's promise to 'convert to bitt'rest gall' his temporary peacefulness at the feast on seeing Romeo (Act 1 Scene 5).

Discuss with a partner these improvements on the first response:

- the **analogy** that the writer makes between conflict and other unpleasant things
- the close reference to Shakespeare's **individual word choices**
- **the way** the quotations are embedded
- the **range** of reference from the play.

> **Glossary**
> **Analogy**: when a writer draws a comparison between one situation or description and another to shed light on the topic in question.

ASSESSMENT FOCUS

To sustain the disease/poison analogy through a response, you will need more examples from the play.

First, find appropriate quotations from these sections of the play:

- the Prince's references to peace and hate in Act 1 Scene 1 when he stops the street brawl
- Romeo's references to 'feasting with mine enemy' in Act 2 Scene 3, lines 48–54
- Mercutio's words about the two families when he is killed in Act 3 Scene 1, lines 86–88
- Juliet's speech on hearing about the death of Tybalt in Act 3 Scene 2, lines 73-85.

Then write two paragraphs in which you refer to the poison/disease analogy in your response. You could begin:

> The idea of conflict between the families as something poisonous or sickening is further emphasised when ...

Remember

- **Find interesting analogies or creative ways of describing themes and ideas.**
- **Choose specific quotations or focus on individual works to match your interpretation.**

Grade Booster

Extended Assessment Task

For any Shakespeare play you have studied, write a response of around 600 words about one of the key themes or ideas – for example, family, conflict, ambition or whatever is central to your text.

Make sure you

- consider how the idea or theme is presented at the start of the text, including subtle hints and suggestions
- look at how the theme or idea is developed by significant incidents, moments or situations, and how what we read about it may have changed by the end
- explore how the theme is presented through the use of language, setting, movement, key details or imagery.

Evaluation – What have you learned?

With a partner, use the grade checklist below to evaluate your work on the Extended Assessment Task.

- I can sustain sophisticated and original interpretations of texts I have read, engaging fully with writers' ideas and attitudes.
- I can imaginatively select detail and evidence, and make subtle links and connections between ideas.
- I can refer to a wide range and variety of linguistic devices and techniques used by writers.

- I can sustain my interpretation of the texts I have read.
- I can engage fully with writers' ideas and attitudes.
- I can use precisely selected supporting evidence and textual detail.
- I can analyse language and structure in convincing detail.

- I can develop ideas, and show engagement with many ideas and themes.
- I can select relevant evidence and quotations.
- I can analyse language and structure, sometimes in detail, sometimes broadly.

- I can show I clearly understand main ideas and themes.
- I can explain these main ideas and themes in clear and logical ways.
- I can understand how language features and structure work, and can support main ideas with relevant quotations.

- I can show some awareness of main themes and ideas.
- I can support ideas with quotations and evidence but they are not always well-chosen or appropriate.
- I can make my own points but they are not developed in as much detail as they should be.

You may need to go back and look at the relevant pages from this section again.

English Literary Heritage: Characterisation and Themes

Introduction

This section of Chapter 4 shows you how to

- understand what Controlled Assessment tasks on Characterisation and voice and Themes and ideas are asking you to do
- develop responses to tasks based on *Great Expectations* and a range of poems.

Why is learning about characterisation and themes important?

- You will only have to write on one of these two aspects of English Literary Heritage texts, but you need to be prepared for both, not least because there are often links between them.
- It is important to understand what they mean, how you can explore them, and how they relate to the English Literary Heritage texts you are studying.

A **Grade C** candidate will

- show clear evidence of understanding the main ways in which a character or theme has been presented
- explain writers' presentation of character and theme clearly
- display understanding of various features of language and structure used by writers to create characters and explore themes
- support points with relevant and appropriate quotations.

C

A **Grade A/A*** candidate will

- sustain an interpretation of how characters and themes are presented (in other words, develop these ideas at length)
- imaginatively select quotation and detail to support these ideas
- analyse in a sophisticated way how character or theme is presented through language and structure (going beyond the obvious)
- make original interpretations.

A

A*

Prior learning

Before you begin this unit, think about

- any 'typical' character types you remember from reading classic English stories and poems, for example the wicked stepmother or the innocent poor child
- any modern stage or film versions of classic stories from the literary heritage that you have seen.

> Why do you think such characters have remained memorable?

> What is it about these older stories that has made film makers and playwrights come back to them again and again?

Writing about the writer's craft

Learning objective

- To review how to write in a mature and precise way about literary texts.

⭐ Examiner's tip

Technical language, such as 'verse', 'stanza', 'alliteration', will not on its own improve your writing, but when it is linked closely to comment on content and effect, it becomes impressive.

Glossary

Symbol: something that represents or suggests an idea or emotion, such as poppies symbolising fallen soldiers in WW1

Stanza: a grouping of lines in a poem; sometimes called a verse

Alliteration: repeated consonant sounds at the start of words: 'the lion's long, lonely walk to its cage'

Checklist for success

Whether you are writing about theme or characterisation:

- You need to use appropriate technical terms: for example, 'chapter' when writing about novels, or 'scene' when referring to plays.
- You need to select a range of vocabulary which accurately explains what the writer is doing (for example, 'the writer *implies* that...').

ACTIVITY

Read this extract from William Blake's poem, 'London'. You will read the whole poem later.

> But most, thro' midnight streets I hear
> How the youthful Harlot's curse
> Blasts the new born Infant's tear,
> And blights with plagues the Marriage hearse

This is what one student said about these lines.

> The bit at the end of the poem has this idea which was really good that women pass on bad stuff to their kids.

Not great, is it? Now look at this second student's attempt. Identify where she has

- used technical terms **specific to poetry**
- used **vocabulary** that explains what the writer does
- been **precise** in her comment about society and children.

> In the final verse, in particular the opening couplet, the writer conveys the idea that the 'Harlot' is symbolic of how people pass on the ills of society to their children and contaminate them. The choice of this symbol is extremely powerful and with its reference to 'loose' women, would have made many readers in the late 18th century extremely uneasy.

Of course, the student does more than this, displaying several of the key elements that should go on to earn a higher grade. For example, she has included

- an **apt quotation** ('Harlot') to support the point made
- reference to a **language technique** and its **effect** (how the 'Harlot' is 'symbolic' of social problems)
- reference to the **social and historical setting** – and why it is relevant.

Focus for development: Commenting on writers' choices

The task you are given might ask:

> *How does the writer present the theme of ... (conflict, power, family, etc.)?*

The more precise and varied your comments are, the better. There are many alternatives to 'the writer presents' or 'says' that you can use.

The writer ...

introduces / conveys / suggests / proposes / implies / comments / reflects / recalls / anticipates / says / emphasises / stresses / questions / challenges / summarises / resolves / depicts / narrates / sets up

ACTIVITY

With a partner, discuss which of these you use regularly when you write about texts and decide on two you will try and use more.

ASSESSMENT FOCUS

Now, read this first verse of the poem 'London', by Blake.

London

I wander thro' each charter'd street,
Near where the charter'd Thames does flow,
And mark in every face I meet,
Marks of weakness, marks of woe.

> **Glossary**
> **Charter'd**: here, may mean 'controlled or owned by powerful people'

- Using at least two of the words from the panel above, write a paragraph about the ideas which Blake presents in this verse. You could comment on
  - his view of humanity
  - or the 'feel' of the opening.
- Include a suitable quotation, and use one or more technical terms about the form or structure of the poetry.

Remember

- Use technical terms appropriate to the form, whether it is a poem, prose or a play.
- Link these terms to their effect – don't just point them out.
- Express yourself using a range of words and phrases to describe how the writer presents his or her ideas.

Exploring theme in English Literary History poetry

Learning objective

- *To respond to the similar themes as dealt with by two different poets.*

Why is it important to explore themes?

When we talk about themes and ideas, these are the things that seem to interest writers and emerge from their work as you read it. These ideas are sometimes expressed in subtle ways, at other times more directly.

ACTIVITY

Read the following poem by William Blake.

London

I wander thro' each charter'd street,
Near where the charter'd Thames does flow,
And mark in every face I meet
Marks of weakness, marks of woe.

In every cry of every Man,
In every Infant's cry of fear,
In every voice: in every ban,
The mind-forg'd manacles I hear.

How the Chimney-sweeper's cry
Every black'ning church appalls;
And the hapless Soldier's sigh
Runs in blood down Palace walls.

But most thro' midnight streets I hear
How the youthful Harlot's curse
Blasts the new born Infant's tear,
And blights with plagues the Marriage hearse.

ACTIVITY

On your own, read the poem and make some basic notes about it: for example…

- What seems to be the 'subject' of the poem? It is called 'London' – does that mean the poet is especially interested in the city, or the people who live in it? Or perhaps something else?
- What particular words, phrases or lines stand out? Are there any that are especially powerful or difficult to understand?
- Do you see any evidence of the use of symbolism (something representing an idea or feeling?)

Here are three students discussing the poem's theme. Which view is closest to yours?

> **Jo:** This is a poem about cities – how they corrupt people. I mean you don't get 'harlots' in the countryside, do you?

> **Ryan:** Not any city – it's London – the capital. It's like he's having a go at the king 'cos he mentions the walls of the palace.

> **Joel:** It's nothing to do with cities, it's people in general. He says they're weak and their minds have 'manacles' in them – that's 'chains' isn't it?

Examiner's tip ⭐

A good essay might well mention all these things, if the theme was 'ruin'. With a symbolic poem like this, it can be difficult to settle on one definite view. Offering a range of detailed ideas can lead to higher grades.

Focus for development: Researching William Blake

ACTIVITY

Read this background information about William Blake.

> ### William Blake (1757–1827)
>
> English poet and artist, lived most of his life in London, and experienced turbulent riots against the government of the day. Whilst living for a short while in the Sussex countryside he commented on the clarity and pureness compared with the 'vapours' of the city. Blake was extremely critical of the Church of England, and ordered religion in general, and whilst he was greatly influenced by the Bible, he invented his own mythology and religious figures in his poetry and art. From a very early age, Blake claimed to have seen visions such as angels walking amongst every day working people. 'London' comes from his most famous collection of poems, *Songs of Innocence and Experience*. Many of the 'innocence' poems are associated with the countryside and unspoilt childhood, whilst the 'experience' poems are about growing-up, anger and the lives of working people.

Try finding out four more facts about Blake using these websites:

http://www.literaryconnections.co.uk/resources/blake.html
http://www.bbc.co.uk/poetryseason/poets/william_blake.shtml

Write two paragraphs in which you analyse Blake's attitude to London as presented in at least two of the verses. Make sure you include suitable quotations to support your point of view.

ASSESSMENT FOCUS

With your research in mind, re-read the poem. Does it add to your understanding?

Remember

- **Offer your own personal interpretation of the words.**

Comparing theme in two different poems

Learning objective

- To respond to similar themes as dealt with by two different poets.

About 80 years after Blake wrote his poem, Thomas Hardy wrote 'The Ruined Maid'. The key word to understand is 'ruined' which usually meant a woman whose reputation had been spoiled by sex outside marriage, or by living as a 'kept woman' – the mistress of a rich man.

ACTIVITY

The poem imagines the first speaker meeting 'Melia in town, and noticing the change in her.

The Ruined Maid

'O 'Melia, my dear, this does everything crown!
Who could have supposed I should meet you in Town?
And whence such fair garments, such prosperi-ty?'
'O didn't you know I'd been ruined?' said she.

– 'You left us in tatters, without shoes or socks,
Tired of digging potatoes, and spudding up docks;
And now you've gay bracelets and bright feathers three!' –
'Yes: that's how we dress when we're ruined,' said she.

– 'At home in the barton you said "thee" and "thou",
And "thik oon",' and "theäs oon", and "t'other"; but now
Your talking quite fits 'ee for high compa-ny!' –
'Some polish is gained with one's ruin,' said she.

– 'Your hands were like paws then, your face blue and bleak
But now I'm bewitched by your delicate cheek,
And your little gloves fit as on any la-dy!' –
'We never do work when we're ruined,' said she.

– 'You used to call home-life a hag-ridden dream,
And you'd sigh, and you'd sock; but at present you seem
To know not of megrims or melancho-ly!' –
'True. One's pretty lively when ruined,' said she.

– 'I wish I had feathers, a fine sweeping gown,
And a delicate face, and could strut about Town!'
'My dear – a raw country girl, such as you be,
Cannot quite expect that. You ain't ruined,' said she.

With a partner, practise a rehearsed reading. Try using distinct voices for each speaker. Would 'Melia's accent have changed or is she still a country girl at heart?

On your own, make some notes about the poem in response to these questions:

- What is the difference in circumstances between 'Melia and her friend?
- How is the difference portrayed in the way they look and speak?
- What appears to be 'Melia's and her friend's attitude to her situation?
- What effect does the last line of each verse have on the reader?

Glossary

spudding up docks: digging up weeds

barton: barn or farmyard

megrims: headaches

Focus for Development:
Comparing the poems

Even if you deal with each poem in turn, refer to the other poem where relevant. For example, you could be focusing on 'London' but find a related point about 'The Ruined Maid', like this:

> The poet is very much present in Blake's poem as he 'wanders' the streets of London and this gives the impression of a man who feels these experiences very closely. Hardy, **on the other hand**, is much more distant, like an unspeaking observer who has just recorded the conversation...

ASSESSMENT FOCUS

Plan a response to this task:

> *How is the theme of ruin and corruption explored in any text(s) you have studied?*
>
> *Write about 'London' and 'The Ruined Maid', exploring how the writers present the ruinous effects of places or society on people's lives.*

Follow this plan, fleshing it out by adding your own notes.

> **Introduction:** the main links or comparisons between the poems

> **First poem:** how poet presents ideas on ruin/corruption
> Consider choice of vocabulary, voice of poet, imagery, structure

> **Second poem:** how poet presents ideas on ruin/corruption
> Consider choice of vocabulary, voice of poet, imagery, structure

> **Conclusion:** draw together key points (similarity/difference)

Examiner's tip ★

Don't force points of comparison that aren't there, however. For example, Blake talks about blood on palace walls but there is no obvious link to this comment on violent city life in 'The Ruined Maid'.

ACTIVITY

Thomas Hardy does not include himself in this poem (as Blake does in his poem, 'London').

Write a short paragraph in which you say why Hardy might have written it. Does he have a 'message' to get across, and is it in any way similar to Blake's or different?

Remember

- **Themes can be similar but dealt with in subtly different ways by writers.**
- **Include some references to social or historical background but not too many.**
- **Focus on the writer's techniques and how these create effects and meanings.**

Characterisation and voice in Charles Dickens

Learning objective

- *To consider how Charles Dickens portrays character in* Great Expectations.

Checklist for success

You need to apply what you know about commenting on the writer's craft (see pages 176–177) to some longer prose extracts.

Dickens's characterisation

Read these two short extracts from two of Charles Dickens's most well-known stories.

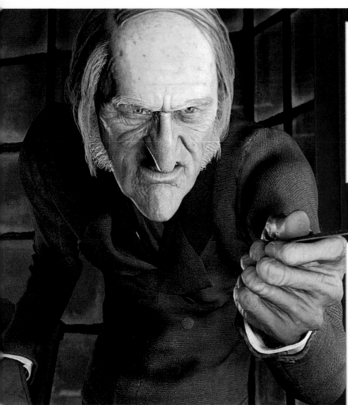

Scrooge from *A Christmas Carol*

Hard and sharp as flint, from which no steel had ever struck out generous fire; secret, and self-contained, and solitary as an oyster. The cold within him froze his old features, nipped his pointed nose, shrivelled his cheek, stiffened his gait; made his eyes red, his thin lips blue; and spoke out shrewdly in his grating voice.

Mrs Joe from *Great Expectations*

My sister […] with black hair and eyes, had such a prevailing redness of skin that I sometimes used to wonder whether it was possible she washed herself with a nutmeg-grater instead of soap. She was tall and bony, and almost always wore a coarse apron, fastened over her figure behind with two loops, and having a square impregnable bib in front, that was stuck full of pins and needles.

★ Examiner's tip

Authors sometimes associate one clear idea with a character, for example Scrooge's 'coldness' – in both heart and body.

ACTIVITY

With a partner, make brief notes about how Dickens presents both characters. Consider

- detailed visual information about face and body
- similes or metaphors describing appearance, movement or dress
- the style of language, in particular sentence construction and choice of vocabulary.

Focus for development: Dickens's use of speech

ACTIVITY

Read this further extract from *Great Expectations* in which the narrator, a young boy named Pip, is talking to Joe, his brother-in-law.

Then discuss with a partner:

- What does Dickens reveal about Joe's upbringing from what he says?
- What distinctive features of Joe's voice does Dickens bring out?

Examiner's tip ★

Irony occurs when a writer deliberately reveals things characters are unaware of. For example, when Joe says how his father's violence affected his 'learning', this is clearly an understatement as it might well have caused Joe some brain damage, as well as stopping him going to school!

'Why didn't you ever go to school, Joe, when you were as little as me?'

'Well, Pip,' said Joe, taking up the poker, and settling himself to his usual occupation when he was thoughtful, of slowly raking the fire between the lower bars: 'I'll tell you. My father, Pip, he were given to drink, and when he were overtook with drink, he hammered away at my mother, most onmerciful. It were a'most the only hammering he did, indeed, 'xcepting at myself. And he hammered at me with a wigour only to be equalled by the wigour with which he didn't hammer at his anwil. – You're a listening and understanding, Pip?'

'Yes, Joe.'

''Consequence, my mother and me we ran away from my father, several times; and then my mother she'd go out to work, and she'd say, "Joe," she'd say, "now, please God, you shall have some schooling, child," and she'd put me to school. But my father were that good in his hart that he couldn't abear to be without us. So, he'd come with a most tremenjous crowd and make such a row at the doors of the houses where we was, that they used to be obligated to have no more to do with us and to give us up to him. And then he took us home and hammered us. Which, you see, Pip,' said Joe, pausing in his meditative raking of the fire, and looking at me, 'were a drawback on my learning.'

'Certainly, poor Joe!'

ASSESSMENT FOCUS

Write a paragraph summing up your impressions of Joe, and his relationship with Pip, based on this extract.

Remember

- **Comment on how characters speak about themselves.**
- **Describe how others speak or respond to them.**
- **Focus on specific character details, such as appearance, decisions or movement.**

Character development: from boy to man

Learning objective

- *To analyse character development through two passages from the same novel.*

Why is learning about character development important?

You may be asked to write about how a character changes or develops over the course of a text. This will require particular analysis and comparison skills.

In *Great Expectations*, Pip is introduced as a young boy on the very first page. As the novel unfolds, the reader sees him change because of events – some of his making, some not.

In his first appearance below, he is visiting the churchyard where his parents and his five brothers and sisters are buried, when he gets a huge shock.

ACTIVITY

As you read, think about

- how Pip speaks (How does Dickens convey his fear?)
- how he views the convict, called Magwitch, and what that tells us about Pip's age and character at this point in the book
- how we know, even at this early point, that the narrator is an 'older Pip', looking back at events?

Make a note of your ideas.

Extract 1

'Hold your noise!' cried a terrible voice, as a man started up from among the graves at the side of the church porch. 'Keep still, you little devil, or I'll cut your throat!'

   A fearful man, all in coarse grey, with a great iron on his leg. A man with no hat, and with broken shoes, and with an old rag tied round his head. A man who had been soaked in water, and smothered in mud, and lamed by stones, and cut by flints, and stung by nettles, and torn by briars; who limped, and shivered, and glared and growled; and whose teeth chattered in his head as he seized me by the chin.

   'O! Don't cut my throat, sir,' I pleaded in terror. 'Pray don't do it, sir.'

   'Tell us your name!' said the man. 'Quick!'

   'Pip, sir.'

   'Once more,' said the man, staring at me. 'Give it mouth!'

   'Pip. Pip, sir.'

   'Show us where you live,' said the man. 'Pint out the place!'

   I pointed to where our village lay, on the flat in-shore among the alder-trees and pollards, a mile or more from the church.

> The man, after looking at me for a moment, turned me upside down, and emptied my pockets. There was nothing in them but a piece of bread. When the church came to itself – for he was so sudden and strong that he made it go head over heels before me, and I saw the steeple under my feet – when the church came to itself, I say, I was seated on a high tombstone, trembling, while he ate the bread ravenously.
>
> 'You young dog,' said the man, licking his lips, 'what fat cheeks you ha' got.'
>
> I believe they were fat, though I was at that time undersized for my years, and not strong.
>
> 'Darn Me if I couldn't eat em,' said the man, with a threatening shake of his head, 'and if I han't half a mind to't!'
>
> I earnestly expressed my hope that he wouldn't, and held tighter to the tombstone on which he had put me; partly, to keep myself upon it; partly, to keep myself from crying.

Here is one student writing about how a character 'grows up' in a novel they have studied. He uses Pip as his example.

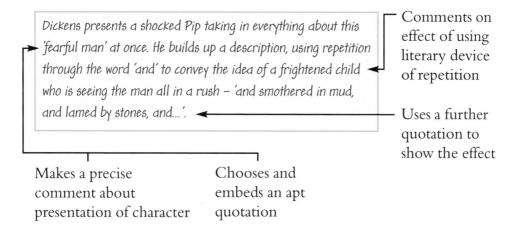

Dickens presents a shocked Pip taking in everything about this 'fearful man' at once. He builds up a description, using repetition through the word 'and' to convey the idea of a frightened child who is seeing the man all in a rush – 'and smothered in mud, and lamed by stones, and…'.

Comments on effect of using literary device of repetition

Uses a further quotation to show the effect

Makes a precise comment about presentation of character

Chooses and embeds an apt quotation

As the annotations show, this response includes many of the features identified on pages 176–177 for commenting effectively on writer's craft.

ACTIVITY

Using your notes on the extract, write two further paragraphs to establish clearly what picture of Pip is presented in this opening.

Focus for development: Tracing character development

The extract on the next page comes from much later in the novel. Pip is now a 'gentleman', having had his education paid for by a mysterious benefactor. Here, Magwitch turns up unexpectedly and asks to speak to Pip at his lodgings.

Extract 2

Moving the lamp as the man moved, I made out that he was substantially dressed, but roughly; like a voyager by sea. That he had long iron-grey hair. That his age was about sixty. That he was a muscular man, strong on his legs, and that he was browned and hardened by exposure to weather. As he ascended the last stair or two, and the light of my lamp included us both, I saw, with a stupid kind of amazement, that he was holding out both his hands to me.

'Pray what is your business?' I asked him.

'My business?' he repeated, pausing. 'Ah! Yes. I will explain my business, by your leave.'

'Do you wish to come in?'

'Yes,' he replied; 'I wish to come in, Master.'

I had asked him the question inhospitably enough, for I resented the sort of bright and gratified recognition that still shone in his face. I resented it, because it seemed to imply that he expected me to respond to it. But, I took him into the room I had just left, and, having set the lamp on the table, asked him as civilly as I could, to explain himself.

He looked about him with the strangest air – an air of wondering pleasure, as if he had some part in the things he admired – and he pulled off a rough outer coat, and his hat. Then, I saw that his head was furrowed and bald, and that the long iron-grey hair grew only on its sides. But, I saw nothing that in the least explained him. On the contrary, I saw him next moment, once more holding out both his hands to me.

'What do you mean?' said I, half suspecting him to be mad.

He stopped in his looking at me, and slowly rubbed his right hand over his head. 'It's disapinting to a man,' he said, in a coarse broken voice, 'arter having looked for'ard so distant, and come so fur; but you're not to blame for that – neither on us is to blame for that. I'll speak in half a minute. Give me half a minute, please.'

He sat down on a chair that stood before the fire, and covered his forehead with his large brown veinous hands. I looked at him attentively then, and recoiled a little from him; but I did not know him.

ACTIVITY

How does Dickens present the changed character of both men in this extract?
Start by completing a grid like this.

Character feature	Magwitch	Pip
Movement/appearance	'substantially dressed'	
Speech		Spoke 'inhospitably enough'
Feelings (where stated)		Pip 'resented' how the man seemed to know him

186

Below is a plan that a student wrote in response to this task:

> *Write about how Pip has changed and developed over the course of* **Great Expectations**. *Focus on two or three key chapters to explain how Dickens presents this change, particularly in his relationship with Magwitch.*

Read the plan, then write part or all of your response to the task.

> **Introduction**: present very briefly the key facts about the story and what happens to Pip over the course of the novel. (1 paragraph)

A student writes…

I have lots of notes, but how can I link the two extracts?

Answer…

As you are writing about *character development* over the course of a story, it will help to use sequence words or phrases such as, 'Firstly / Initially / As the novel opens' and 'Later / Consequently / As it turns out'. You can also connectives to contrast extracts, such as 'However / On the other hand / Yet'.

> **Development:**
>
> **1.** Write about the **opening chapter**:
>   - how Pip is presented in relation to Magwitch
>   - Pip's family life with Joe and Mrs Joe
>   - his kindly character as a boy
>   - how he deals with and recalls the situation in the graveyard. (2–3 paragraphs)
>
> **2.** Write about **Chapter 39**, when Pip is 23 and meets Magwitch again, commenting on:
>   - what has changed in Pip's and Magwitch's life by this point
>   - how Pip reacts to Magwitch, especially when he hears the news he brings
>   - the change in the way Pip sees himself as a result. (2–3 paragraphs)
>
> **3.** Write about **Chapter 56** which shows Pip as an improved and more understanding person when Magwitch is ill. (1–2 paragraphs)

> **Conclusion**: give a **general comment** on how Pip develops in the novel: how he has changed and what he and Magwitch have learned. End with an **appropriate quotation** which sums up how one or other of them feels. (1 paragraph)

Remember

- **Trace the character's development through comparison of key moments, speech and description.**
- **Select and then analyse relevant quotations to support your points.**

Grade Booster

Extended Assessment Task

Write a response of around 600 words to this task.

> *How is the theme of ruin or corruption presented in any text(s) you have studied?*

Make sure you

- consider how the idea or theme presents itself at the start of the text
- look at how the theme or idea is developed by key incidents, and how it may have changed by the end
- explore how the theme is presented through the use of language, setting, movement, key detail, imagery and structure.

You may wish to refer back to your work on the Thomas Hardy and William Blake poems on pages 178–181.

Evaluation What have you learned?

With a partner, use the grade checklist below to evaluate your work on the Extended Assessment Task.

- I can sustain sophisticated and original interpretations of texts, engaging fully with writers' ideas and attitudes.
- I can imaginatively select detail and evidence, and make subtle connections between ideas.
- I can refer to a wide range and variety of linguistic devices and techniques used by writers.

- I can sustain my interpretation of the texts.
- I can engage fully with writers' ideas and attitudes.
- I can use precisely selected supporting evidence and textual detail.
- I can analyse language and structure in convincing detail.

- I can develop ideas, and show engagement with many ideas and themes.
- I can select effective evidence and quotations.
- I can analyse language and structure, sometimes in detail, sometimes broadly.

- I can show I clearly understand main ideas and themes.
- I can explain these main ideas and themes in clear and logical ways.
- I can understand how language features and structure work, and can support ideas with relevant quotations.

- I can show some awareness of main themes and ideas.
- I can support these ideas with quotations and evidence but these not always well-chosen or appropriate.
- I can make my own points but they are not developed in as much detail as they should be.

You may need to go back and look at the relevant pages from this section again.

Exploring Cultures: Characterisation and Theme

Introduction

This section of Chapter 4 shows you how to

- understand what is involved in a Controlled Assessment task on Characterisation and voice and Theme and ideas in relation to *Of Mice and Men* and a range of poems
- develop responses to tasks in these areas.

Why is learning about characterisation and themes important?

These are key elements of any text you read, and can both enrich your study and help your understanding of how texts work.

It is important to understand what they mean, how you can explore them, and how they relate to the Exploring Cultures texts you are studying.

A **Grade C** candidate will

- show clear evidence that he or she understands the main ways in which a character or theme has been presented
- explain writers' presentation of character and theme clearly
- display understanding of various features of language and structure used by writers to create characters and explore themes
- support points with relevant and appropriate quotations.

A **Grade A/A*** candidate will

- sustain his or her interpretation of how characters and themes are presented (in other words, develop and write about these ideas at length)
- imaginatively select quotation and detail to support these ideas
- analyse in a sophisticated way how character or theme is presented through language and structure (going beyond the obvious to explore layers of meaning)
- make their own original interpretations.

Prior learning

Before you begin this unit, think about

- any memorable stories set in different (non-UK) settings you have read
- whether there are particular themes or issues that arise in texts set in, or written by people from, different cultures.

> How important was the different setting – and the effect it had on the characters – to the story?

> Where writers 'belong' to two cultures, for example British and a country or state overseas, what personal ideas might they choose to write about?

Exploring characterisation in *Of Mice and Men*

Learning objective

- *To explore how an author presents a character in a different cultural setting.*

Checklist for success

You need to understand the different techniques a writer uses to present and develop a character in a text. These will relate to

- the writer's **physical description** of characters
- how characters **speak** and **what they say**
- what the characters **do** – or **how they respond** to particular acts or events.

ACTIVITY

Discuss with a friend: how might the historical or cultural background in which a character lives affect how they behave?

We are going to look at the presentation of character in the novel *Of Mice and Men* by John Steinbeck. One student has started by making some basic background notes …

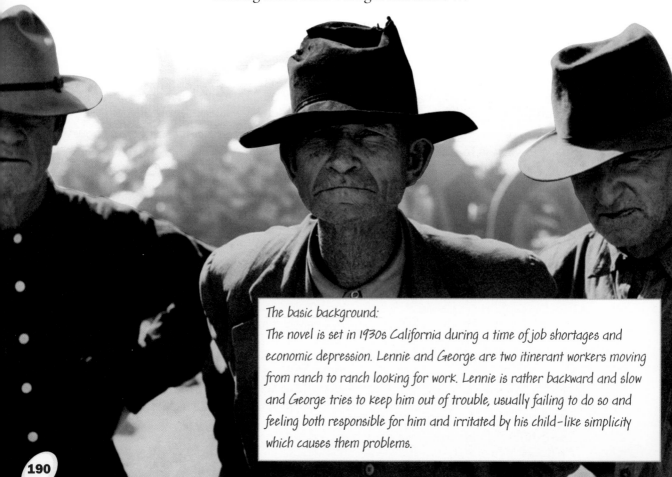

The basic background:
The novel is set in 1930s California during a time of job shortages and economic depression. Lennie and George are two itinerant workers moving from ranch to ranch looking for work. Lennie is rather backward and slow and George tries to keep him out of trouble, usually failing to do so and feeling both responsible for him and irritated by his child-like simplicity which causes them problems.

ACTIVITY

From reading this information, what aspects of a culture and time different from our own might influence the events, the themes and the characters of the novel?

Discuss with a partner:

- When and where is the novel set?
- What sort of society or lifestyle is being presented?
- Why does the writer choose to focus on Lennie and George rather than, for example, rich bankers in cities at this time?

You can find out more about the Great Depression of the 1930s in the USA by visiting these sites:

www.bbc.co.uk/schools/gcsebitesize/history/mwh/usa

www.learningat.ke7.org.uk/english/ks4/year10/ mmbackground

Focus for development: Characterising Lennie

Through his actions

If one of the key ways to understand a writer's presentation of character is through what he or she does, the first step is to be very clear about the important events.

Here, the same student has begun a list detailing the actual things Lennie does in the novel.

Lennie – what he does

- (before the novel begins) Touches/grabs girl's dress in Weed causing her to think she is going to be assaulted. This causes Lennie and George to leave town and hide from the townspeople.
- Accidentally kills mouse he has been 'petting'; tries to keep it when George tells him to get rid of it.
- Works hard to lift grain on the new ranch once they get their jobs.

ACTIVITY

The writer has chosen these events for a reason. With a partner, discuss what you think these events alone tell us about Lennie.

Here are the notes one student wrote to summarise the discussion.

> Lennie causes trouble in Weed and this means he and George have to leave. On the way to their new job, when they stop by the pool to drink, George finds out Lennie has kept hold of a dead mouse he was petting and has accidentally killed. He reluctantly gets rid of it, but only after George takes it from him. This shows that Lennie is sort of accident-prone and that he relies on George to get him out of trouble. As George says, 'You get in trouble.'

This is a **Grade C** response because it

- says clearly what Lennie did
- backs it up with a (very short) quotation
- explains what we find out about Lennie as a result.

However, it doesn't analyse how the writer *presents* Lennie to the reader through his actions. The student could also have commented on the more positive aspect of Lennie – his ability to work hard.

ACTIVITY

Make brief notes saying why this extract from a **Grade A★** response (dealing just with the incident in Weed) is better.

> By describing the incident in Weed, in which Lennie 'jus wanted to feel that little girls' dress', the writer conveys a picture of Lennie's accident-prone nature and his dependence on George, and sets up a key idea about him which will recur throughout – Lennie's clumsy strength and dumbness. This will have a big effect on the events to come.

Notice in particular how the student uses words and phrases that show the writer's craft – what Steinbeck is doing. Look back at pages 176–7 if you are not sure about this.

Through physical description

Now read the following longer extract from the novel. George is watching Lennie...

> His huge companion dropped his blankets and flung himself down and drank from the surface of the green pool; drank with long gulps, snorting into the water like a horse. The small man stepped nervously beside him.
>
> 'Lennie!' he said sharply. 'Lennie, for God's sake don't drink so much.' Lennie continued to snort into the pool.

The small man leaned over and shook him by the shoulder. 'Lennie. You gonna be sick like you was last night.'

Lennie dipped his whole head under, hat and all, and then he sat up on the bank and his hat dripped down on his blue coat and ran down his back. 'Tha's good,' he said. 'You drink some, George. You take a good big drink.' He smiled happily.

George unslung his bindle and dropped it gently on the bank. 'I ain't sure it's good water,' he said. 'Looks kinda scummy.'

Lennie dabbled his big paw in the water and wiggled his fingers so the water arose in little splashes; rings widened across the pool to the other side and came back again. Lennie watched them go. 'Look, George. Look what I done.'

ACTIVITY

Focusing on Lennie, note down how he is presented in this extract. In particular, consider

- how he is **physically** described (his movements, and how he is contrasted with George)
- how he **speaks and responds** to George
- the way **imagery** is used – similes and metaphors.

Make sure you begin by focusing on Lennie, not George. Which one of these responses gets this right?

Response A
Here, Steinbeck presents George as a character who bosses Lennie around, at the same time watching out for his well-being.

Response B
Here, Steinbeck presents Lennie rather like a child with a father who both bosses him around, but also looks after him.

Examiner's tip ★

If the task you have been set asks you to focus on Lennie, then make sure this is what you do. Don't be diverted into commenting more on George. There is nothing wrong with mentioning their relationship but, if you do, it needs to reveal what it tells us about Lennie.

Examiner's tip ★

Sometimes it is not the actual words spoken by a character but patterns of speech. For example, notice how Lennie repeats simple words – how does that add to the way Steinbeck characterises him?

ASSESSMENT FOCUS

Using your notes and understanding of Lennie so far, write two paragraphs about how he is characterised by his actions, physical appearance and speech in the extract above.

Remember

- What characters do – their effect on the action of the story – tells us a great deal.
- Focus on the character required by the task. Don't get diverted by another character.

Producing sophisticated responses on characterisation

Learning objective

- To learn how to use sophisticated techniques to put original ideas across.

Why is it important to say something original?

- One challenge you will face in trying to reach the higher grades is finding something original to say about characterisation.
- This does not mean making wild claims you cannot support. Often the best way to show originality is to analyse small details and relate them to a larger point. Small touches of originality count a great deal.

ACTIVITY

Read these two ideas about Lennie. With a partner, choose one of them and argue the case for it or against it, backing up what you say as persuasively as you can with evidence from the text.

> Lennie's death isn't tragic; despite his child-like nature he has to take responsibility for his actions and the truth is that he does kill someone.

> Lennie has held George back too long. Now he is dead, George is free to follow his dreams.

Focus for development: Presenting a personal interpretation or challenging perspective

It is probably best if you wish to pursue such a point of view that you use some clever techniques to get the reader 'on-side'.

Technique	Example	Effect
Temper your language	*It **could be said that** Lennie's death isn't intended by the writer to be completely tragic…*	By using gentler modal forms like 'could' and a more objective style (not 'I believe' but 'it could') you come across as reasoned and well-informed.
Anticipate arguments	*Of course, Steinbeck might be saying that, **whilst it is clear that Lennie cannot help his child-like simplicity**, ultimately he must take responsibility for his violent actions.*	By predicting what others might say in defence of Lennie (that he is child-like), you 'take the sting' out of that argument.
Choose apt and selective quotations	*Slim, **respected in the book as a decent man**, says '**You hadda, George. I swear you hadda**' after Lennie is killed.*	By drawing attention to this quotation rather than others (for example, George's own anger with Lennie at various stages), this stresses Lennie's faults and that George had no choice but to shoot him.
Sustain your idea	***By the end of the text**, with Lennie back at the pool facing death for a real murder, **Steinbeck reminds us that this is where it all began**: where we met Lennie, learned about Weed, saw the dead mouse.*	Develop your idea so it shows you have taken into account the overall arc of the narrative – where it starts, goes and ends (in relation to the character in question).

ASSESSMENT FOCUS

You have now explored a number of key areas in relation to characterisation:

- how they shape and are shaped by events
- what they look like, how they behave and how others respond to them
- particular ways they are described which the author has chosen (for example, Lennie as a big child, animalistic, etc.)
- how your own interpretation and analysis might refresh the way we view a character

Taking these ideas on board, choose one of the following three characters from *Of Mice and Men* to write about, and follow the planning stages below.

- Slim
- Curley
- George

Stage 1

Make **detailed notes** on your chosen character using a grid like this.

Information	Quotation (if appropriate)	What this tells us
What they actually do in the plot		
How they appear, look, move, speak		
How others respond to them (what they say and do)		
Key moments or scenes★ (see below)		

★ A further step to higher level response is to consider carefully two or three key moments for your character. For example, for Lennie it might be

- breaking Curley's hand
- killing Curley's wife.

By focusing on these, you can comment in detail on how and why the writer chooses these particular moments of drama, humour or information to alter our view of the character.

Stage 2

Carefully **select** from your notes what you want to use.

To answer the task you will probably need to tailor your notes to show how Steinbeck presents the character in a particular way – in which case, selecting ideas and evidence to emphasise or develop certain points more than others becomes very important.

You are now ready to write a draft or more detailed plan of your response.

You may wish to use the plan below as a guide for your own plan.

Explore how the writer presents a key character in any text you have studied.

START: Impress with an imaginative opening (para 1)
You could use a quotation: 'he walked heavily, dragging his feet a little, the way a bear drags his paws.' This is how the writer first presents Lennie, and it gives an insight into how he will be viewed from now on.

DEVELOP: Pick up on the first point – the 'physical description' and look to explore further (para 2)
Why is Lennie's bear-like appearance so important? The simile conveys the idea of slowness, yet also animal aggression, which we will learn is a key part of Lennie's make-up. This is explored further in the opening chapter.

FOCUS: 1 – opening chapter (para 3) Further 'animal' similes or metaphors	**FOCUS: 2 – his relationship with George** (para 4)	**FOCUS: 3 – past and future events** (para 5) What we know about what happened in Weed, plus killing of mouse

DEVELOP AGAIN: a new point (para 6)
How Lennie is presented in three key scenes: first, when Slim talks about him with George; second, when he kills Curley's wife; third, when he meets George by the pool at the end of the novel

FOCUS: 1 - their attitude to Lennie as harmless (para 7)	**FOCUS: 2 - his panicky, child-like strength** (para 8)	**FOCUS: 3 - his innocent sense of what he's done and what it means** (para 9)

CONCLUSION: end by summarising, in flowing phrase, with a question or a good quotation, for example...
Lennie is no murderer, just a victim of the times and his own fate, a gentle simple man with a dream to live off 'the fatta the lan'. (para 10)

Remember

- **Comment on how Steinbeck presents your chosen character but always include your personal interpretation of the characterisation.**
- **Your plan will alter according to the perspective you take and as you prepare for the task. The plan you take into the Controlled Assessment is unlikely to be as detailed as the plan above.**

Themes in Exploring Cultures poetry

Learning objectives

- To explore how less obvious aspects of poetry, like its grammatical features, can convey meaning.

- To respond to a whole poem, drawing on these aspects and more conventional ones such as imagery and vocabulary.

Why is it important to explore themes?

Themes are the issues and ideas that seem to interest poets and emerge from their work as you read it. These ideas are sometimes expressed in subtle ways, at other times more directly.

Checklist for success

- You need to be able to trace the **development** of an idea or theme through a text.
- You need to make your own **personal interpretations** of the theme and support these with **evidence and quotation**.
- You need to show how writers' decisions about **language, structure** and **form** help to develop a theme or idea.

Making connections

One of the things that can make a difference to both your enjoyment of reading and your grade, is a very close focus on words or phrases from the texts you read. The best readers see all sorts of connections and ideas in even the simplest of words.

However a range of language features, beyond imagery and vocabulary, can convey meaning, for example grammatical points such as

- the verb tense used
- the order of words
- the narrative voice (first, second or third person).

ACTIVITY

Imagine you found this scrap of poetry. What might you conclude about the poem and its subject from reading just this?

> ... *my first god*

Discuss with a partner:

- Is this poem likely to be a personal one? Why or why not?
- What sort of 'god' is being referred to? A religious one?
- What does the word 'first' imply about the god(s) the speaker has had?
- Who or what might the god be?

We will return to this line, and the rest of the poem later.

Focus for development:
'Praise Song for my Mother'

Examiner's tip ★

Using an investigative approach, like the annotations shown around this poem, is a good way of really getting inside the text and to grips with the language techniques being used.

ACTIVITY

- Read the following poem by Grace Nichols to yourself and look at the annotations that one student has begun.

Make your own notes about the structure, choice of vocabulary, grammatical features such as verb tense, and any powerful words, patterns of phrasing or punctuation.

What impression of the poet's voice and reflections of her Guyanan childhood come through in the poem?

Song links to childhood?

Praise Song for my Mother

You were
Birth? Or washing child? → water to me
deep and bold and fathoming

You were
moon's eye to me
pull and grained and mantling

You were
sunrise to me
rise and warm and streaming

You were
the fishes red gill to me
the flame tree's spread to me
the crab's leg/the fried plantain smell
          replenishing replenishing
Go to your wide futures, you said

Grace Nichols

ASSESSMENT FOCUS

Is this just a poem about the poet's mother? Or is there more to it?

- Read the poem again and decide
  - what you think is the central idea that Grace Nichols wanted to get across
  - what evidence you can find for this.
- Then write a paragraph to summarise your ideas, incorporating your evidence skilfully.

Remember

- **Focus closely on individual words and phrases when you annotate and then write about poetry.**
- **Read for meaning in grammatical features and the order of words, as well as in the words themselves.**

Comparing themes in Exploring Cultures poems

Learning objective

- *Respond in an informed and intelligent way to a poem on a similar theme, but with subtle differences of style, approach and content.*

Read this poem by James Berry.

Thoughts on my Father

You are boned clean now.
You are lost like dice and teeth.
Don't bother knock
I won't represent you.

A sound brain you were,
your body a mastery,
but no turning into any stepping stone
or handing anybody a key.

Simply, it hurts that needing
we offended you
and I judge you by lack.

Playing some well-shaped shadow
the sun alone moved,
you wouldn't be mixed with cash
or the world's cunning.

So perfectly exclusive,
you tantalised me.
You split our home in passions.
Every year we were more blunted.

I knew nowhere.
My eyes looked out from you
my first god.

Omnipotence breathed
come boy come
to hungrybelly revelations

Lift your hat to doom
boy, in the manner that roadside
weeds are indestructible.

Stubborn tides you echo.

I moved your sterile tones
from your voice.
I lifted your mole from my back.
You scar me man,
but I must go over you again and again.
I must plunge my raging eyes
in all your steady enduring.

I must assemble material
of my own
for a new history.

ACTIVITY

Begin by 'interrogating' the poem in the same way as you did 'Praise Song for My Mother' on page 199. Make notes on

- key words and phrases that stand out
- features and effects of language and structure
- any links between ideas that you notice
- words and phrases that give a sense of the poet's voice or of Caribbean culture.

You could write your notes as annotations. For example…

My eyes looked out from you — how is that possible? Is it like when a child is told stories by a parent when they are little so that's all they know?

Focus for development: Comparing Themes

Before you go on to explore in detail all aspects of two poems, a good place to start is to focus on some obvious thematic similarities. For example, with 'Praise Song for my Mother' and 'Thoughts on my Father', the titles come to mind.

This might be a **Grade C** response about the titles.

> The first poem is called 'Praise Song for my Mother' and the second is called 'Thoughts on my Father'. From this we can immediately see that both poems are about the relationships between a child and a parent and how they feel about them.

A **Grade A** response would go further.

> The writers' choice of titles immediately suggest that their theme is an exploration of what their mother and father, respectively, mean to them. Here, whilst the broad subject may be similar (the poems are, after all, about parents), how they perceive them might be subtly different. On the one hand, Nichols poem is a 'praise song' – the noun 'praise' clearly positive and uplifting. Berry's choice of noun, however, 'thoughts' is more neutral, and he makes us wait to hear what he thinks – good or bad.

This student implies that while the 'broad subject' is the same, there are subtle differences. The response also uses

- essay language that is **clear and analytical** ('on the one hand', 'however')
- **apt quotations**
- analysis of the **writers' choice of language and its effect**
- an **interpretation** of why this has been chosen.

ASSESSMENT FOCUS

In fact, there is much more you can get from these poem titles. Try adding to the Grade A response above by commenting on

- the writers' use of 'my' (the possessive pronoun) in both titles and what it might convey
- Nichols's decision to call the poem a 'song' and what that might suggest
- Nichols's use of the preposition 'for'; Berry's use of the preposition 'on'.

Consider how these could further develop or support any of the points in the Grade A response.

Remember

- Refer to specific language features and techniques but always make sure you interpret what they suggest.
- Close analysis can reveal a great deal about a poem.

Comparing poems: how to write an extended response

Checklist for success

- You need to have a clear plan which addresses all the points you want to make.
- You need to ensure you have focused on theme at both a general and specific level.
- You need to address most, if not all, of the language choices the writers have made and their impact on the reader.

ACTIVITY

You have been set this task:

> *Compare the ways two poets use language and structure to explore the theme of family relationships.*

Read this advice on writing a comparison of the two poems, 'Praise Song for my Mother' and 'Thoughts on my Father'.

With a partner, discuss how you could apply it to your own notes about the poems.

Introduction

Your first paragraph or two could deal with the **general content** or **theme(s)**, without getting into the subtle differences and perspectives of the two writers.

A **Grade A** answer will start in a way which immediately engages the reader, for example by

- going straight into a discussion of the two titles, as in the example on page 201
- using a powerful quotation from one of the poems (*'A "new history" – so says James Berry as he tries to…'*)
- using an eye-catching question or phrase (*'What are the gifts we get from our parents? This is just one of the questions these poems try to answer…'*).

Development: the core of your essay

You will probably deal with each poem in turn. You need to comment on the structure of the poems and how this supports the theme of child/parent relationships.

Development A: 'Praise Song for my Mother'

You might comment on the use of

- repetition and tense ('You were')
- sound and rhythm and how that adds to the idea of relationship
- metaphor ('moon's eye to me')
- powerful images which suggest Caribbean culture

Use connective words to guide the reader through your ideas.

A student writes…

How do I link different cultures to the theme?

Answer…

First, be clear but careful about cultural references – be aware of stereotypes. Root your comments in what it says in the poem(s), as here.

> **Firstly,** the reference to water and tides in the poem **suggests** a childhood lived outdoors, so it is natural that the poet uses this **metaphor** to say something about her relationship with her mother. Grace Nichols **associates her with the 'moon's eye', guiding and controlling her** in a good way.

From this point, you could do one of two things:

- You could continue making points about 'Praise Song', for example by developing comments on imagery such as 'moon's eye', or 'deep water'.
- You could link the comment about tides to what Berry has to say about them ('stubborn tides you echo'), showing quite a different view of his father's influence. If you feel confident enough, you can take the opportunity to link or contrast ideas like this, rather than discussing one poem before the other.

Conclusion: both poems

Don't go over the same points again, but find a way of drawing together your overall thoughts about the way the poets have approached the same theme. Use simple connectives to help summarise the key ideas you have explored.

- *While* 'Praise Song' *is a hymn in gratitude to Nichols' mother, Berry,* **as we have seen,** *takes an* **altogether different view**.

Development B: 'Thoughts on my Father'

You might wish to start with some linking ideas or make an immediate contrast with what you have just said, as in these two examples.

- *Berry's poem* **addresses similar subject matter,** *commenting on …*
- *Berry, in contrast, has* **quite different things to say about his father**.

Then, you could comment on the following (referring back to Nichols's poem if you wish):

- Berry's use of structure (how the poem starts and ends, and what this tells the reader)
- any use of repeated words, phrases or ideas
- sound and rhythm – is it more disjointed than 'Praise Song'? Why might this be?
- imagery – is it positive and/or negative about his father and their relationship?
- use of grammar and tense ('You scar me man' is expressed in the present tense even though his father is dead).

ASSESSMENT FOCUS

Following the structure outlined, plan out your comparison of language and structure to explore the theme of family relationships. Add as much detail and evidence from the poems as you can.

Remember

- **Address as much of the two poems' language and structure as you can, linking it to their effect and the subject of the task.**
- **Make links between the poems where you can as you go along, but don't force this.**

Grade Booster

Extended Assessment Task

Write a response of around 600 words to this task.

> *How is the theme of love presented in any text(s) you have studied?*

Make sure you

- consider the idea or theme as it presents itself at the start of the text
- look at how the theme or idea is developed by significant incidents and how it may have changed by the end
- explore how the theme is presented through use of language, setting, movement, key detail, imagery and structure.

You may wish to refer back to your work on *Romeo and Juliet* on pages 164–173 or the Exploring Cultures poems on pages 198–203.

Evaluation – What have you learned?

With a partner, use the grade checklist below to evaluate your work on the Extended Assessment Task.

- I can sustain sophisticated and original interpretations of texts I have read, engaging fully with writers' ideas and attitudes.
- I can imaginatively select detail and evidence, and make subtle links and connections between ideas.
- I can refer to a wide range and variety of linguistic devices and techniques used by writers.

- I can sustain my interpretation of the texts I have read.
- I can engage fully with writers' ideas and attitudes.
- I can use precisely selected supporting evidence and textual detail.
- I can analyse language and structure in convincing detail.

- I can develop ideas, and show engagement with many ideas and themes.
- I can select effective evidence and quotations.
- I can analyse language and structure, sometimes in detail, sometimes broadly.

- I can show I clearly understand main ideas and themes.
- I can explain these main ideas and themes in clear and logical ways.
- I can understand how language features and structure work, and can support main ideas with relevant quotations.

- I can show some awareness of main themes and ideas.
- I can support these ideas with quotations and evidence, though they are not always well chosen or appropriate.
- I can make my own points, but they are not developed in as much detail as they should be.

Controlled Assessment Preparation

Introduction

In this section you will

- find out what is required of you in the Understanding Creative Texts Controlled Assessment task
- read, analyse and respond to three sample answers by different candidates
- plan and write your own answer to a sample question
- evaluate and assess your answer and the progress you have made.

Why is exam preparation like this important?

- If you know exactly what you need to do, you will feel more confident when you produce your own assessed response.
- Looking at sample answers by other students will help you see what you need to do to improve your own work.
- Planning and writing a full sample response after you have completed the chapter will give you a clear sense of what you have learned so far.

Key information

Unit 3 Section A is 'Understanding Creative Texts'.

- The controlled part of the task will last **3–4 hours**, and is worth **40 marks**.
- It is worth **20%** of your overall English GCSE mark.

What will the task involve?

- You have to complete **one** task, which will be made up of three smaller responses – one response for each text (or set of texts) you have studied.
- Your responses will be based on **one or more** of the **Shakespeare plays** you have studied, **one or more** of the **English Literary Heritage** texts and one text or a collection of texts from **Exploring Cultures**.

What does the task consist of?

It is likely that your teacher will have focused you on a task related to either

- Themes and ideas

   or

- Characterisation and voice

You will have to respond by writing three pieces with a recommended total of **1600 words**. This will be done in 'controlled conditions' over a period of up to four hours.

Here are some example questions based on the general task areas set by the exam board.

Character	• Explore the way a central character is developed in the text(s) you have studied. • How does a main character in a text you have read change as a result of events and/or relationships?
Theme	• Explore the way family relationships are presented in a text you have studied. • Explore the theme of power in a text or texts you have read.

The Assessment

The assessment objective for this unit (AO2) states that you must:

- Read and understand texts, selecting material appropriate to purpose.
- Develop and sustain interpretations of writers' ideas and perspectives.
- Explain and evaluate how writers use linguistic, grammatical, structural and presentational features to achieve effects and engage and influence the reader.
- Understand texts in their social, cultural and historical contexts.

Targeting Grade A

Some of the key features of Grade C and Grade A responses are as follows:

Grade C candidates	See example on pages 207-8
• show clear evidence of understanding key meanings in the text, with some ability to look for more significant or deeper interpretations • write clearly about writers' ideas supported by relevant and appropriate evidence/quotation • display understanding of language features used and support points with relevant quotations.	©

Grade A/A★ candidates	See example on see pages 211-212
• sustain ideas and interpretations so they are fully developed and explored • demonstrate real engagement with the writers' ideas, selecting not just relevant quotations but very carefully selected evidence, viewed in an original and often sophisticated way • analyse writers' use of language in focused detail, understanding the sometimes complex ways language operates.	A A★

Exploring Sample Responses

ACTIVITY

Read the following extract from the first part of a student's response to this task.

> **How is a central character presented in a text you have studied?**
>
> **Consider how Shakespeare presents the character of Romeo in Act 1 Scene 1 and Act 1 Scene 5, and what this reveals about his development over the course of the play.**

As you read the response, think about whether it is closer to a Grade C, B or A, and why.

Consider the key elements a marker would look for:

- Whether the author's and the student's ideas are clearly conveyed.
- How well the student comments on the language used.
- How well the student supports the points he or she makes.
- Whether there is any original or 'sophisticated' interpretation of ideas.

Example 1: Characterisation in Shakespeare's plays

It is clear to everyone that Romeo changes as the play goes on. For a start when Romeo first appears he is extremely moody and depressed because a girl called Rosaline is not interested in him. It says, 'Romeo shuts up his windows, locks fair daylight out' (Act 1 Scene 1). This means he does not want to be seen by anyone and is moping around. A bit like when your mum tells you off and you lock your door and won't speak to anyone, except this is about love and his feelings for a girl.

The scene is important because it shows first of all that Romeo's parents are worried about him and this is why they ask Benvolio to talk to him to find out what the matter is. When Benvolio does get to speak to him, Romeo talks in very lovesick language such as saying, 'Love is a smoke made with the fume of sighs:

Being purged, a fire sparkling in lover's eyes' (Act 1 Scene 1, lines 184–185).

This is a metaphor and is very over the top, making love sound fiery and bold. There isn't any proper description of Rosaline and later on in the scene Romeo admits that she isn't interested in love. This may be why he is attracted to her!

However everything changes when he meets Juliet at the ball in Act 1 Scene 5. This time he is seeing a girl in real life, not imagining her, and Shakespeare shows us how when he sees her he is just stunned by her looks and how she acts. He uses a metaphor which shows how

beautiful she is: 'She doth teach the torches to burn bright', he says (Act I Scene 5). You could say this links back with the 'smoke' idea in Act I Scene I but saying things in a different way.

Romeo is at the ball because his friend Mercutio told him to go, although Romeo did have some bad omens about it. But as it turned out he met Juliet, and they kiss and it is only afterwards that they find out who they are and that their families have an 'ancient grudge' for each other.

Romeo is now changing. He forgets all about Rosaline. He says 'did my heart love till now?' (Act I Scene 5) which sounds like he realises his love for Rosaline was just on the surface, not a deep love. It is like he has grown up in a minute from a boy to a man. But we must not forget that he still showed his foolish and unthinking side by going to the ball, as it was very dangerous and he wasn't supposed to be there. You could say he is ruled by his emotions.

These two sides of Romeo continue in the rest of the play as he faces danger just to see Juliet in Act 2 Scene 2, but also shows he has grown up by agreeing to marry her. His love for her which we see in Act 2 Scene 2 also means that he does not want to fight with Tybalt but then again his emotional side takes over and he kills Tybalt after his best friend Mercutio is stabbed to death.

All in all, I think that Romeo changes from the start of the play when he is miserable and depressed. He is made happy by Juliet's love but it doesn't completely stop him from being rather wild and unthinking in what he does later.

Examiner feedback

This is generally a clear response to the task. There is a focus on the question of character and development, although a little more reference to **how** Shakespeare presents Romeo would help. There is a good reference to the use of metaphor in terms of the 'torch' although some opportunities are missed to comment on the harmony of the sonnet Romeo and Juliet speak when they exchange vows. In addition, while a link is made between the 'smoke' of love and Juliet being like a 'torch', what this linked imagery represents is not stated. Style, too, could be a little more fluent: quotations could be woven into the sentences better. The candidate has also begun to comment on Romeo's headstrong nature and his increased happiness, but a greater range of reference to language techniques is required, as well as a more considered style.

Suggested grade: C

ACTIVITY

- Rewrite the first two paragraphs. Integrate the quotation, shortening it if necessary to fit your sentence.
- Try to make the personal references sound a little more professional, for example by saying 'this is rather like a teenager who…' and taking out the reference to 'your mum'.

Read the following extract from a response to this task.

> *Explore the theme of power in a text or texts you have read. You might wish to consider how someone in power achieves it and/or abuses it, or how someone powerful is brought down.*

The following is the first part of a response which draws on two Literary Heritage poems, 'Ozymandias' by Percy Bysshe Shelley and 'My Last Duchess' by Robert Browning.

Look at the annotations. How would these comments relate to your own work?

Example 2: Theme in English Literary Heritage poetry

The essay focus is introduced immediately →

Power can be treated respectfully, honestly or corruptly and as these poems show **if in the wrong hands can bring eternal damnation**.

← This sets up the discussion of the poem, but isn't actually borne out by what the student says

Ozymandias' is the name of an ancient king and on the surface the poem does not seem to have anything to do with power at all. It begins with the poet saying how he **'met a traveller from an**

Good quotation, raising an interesting question. Not sure it relates to the theme →

antique land', and this immediately draws us into the poem – but weirdly seems distant too. Why isn't the poet himself telling us the story? Is it to make what he recounts seem more trustworthy, because it's come from someone else?

Anyway the point is that when we hear the traveller's story, basically all it is is that he came across a fallen statue in the desert, with a **'shatter'd visage'**. It is clear that this was a statue of someone high and mighty because it states, **'vast' legs and that the face had a 'cold command'** which means they commanded lots of people, like a top ruler.

Good quotation to support point

Detailed explanation follows

It says that the sculptor was very skilled because he had managed to get the right look of this powerful ruler

Second quotation further supports point made →

with a **'sneer'** (looking down on people). It also says that he 'mock'd them' which I think means he treated his people really badly. It also says that his 'heart fed' on them which **sounds very unpleasant!**

Explanation could be better – *why* is 'heart fed' unpleasant? →

The really interesting bit is when Ozymandias seems to speak, like the time when there was a great city all around and he was arrogantly saying to the

The
explanation
put in
'modern'
words is a
little clumsy

Good
summing
up at this
point

> 'mighty' **you couldn't build a city like this, could you?**
> However, the catch is that it is left in the desert in the middle of
> sands now and no one cares for Ozymandias. The half-line
> 'Nothing beside remains' really stresses this.
>   **The message of the poem** seems to be that however mighty
> and powerful you are, eventually you will die and turn to dust.
>   A key thing to think about too, **is why Shelley wrote about**
> **a 'faraway' land. In his time, people were fascinated by**
> **travel to exotic places** so **whether Shelley is saying that we**
> **can learn something from other countries, I don't know.**
> But it is clear that he is saying having wealth and power isn't
> really worth it and isn't lasting.
>   I will now look at a different sort of power – that of one single
> person over another – in 'My Last Duchess'...

Good to
mention the
historical
context but does
it add to our
understanding of
'power'?

Nothing wrong
with thinking
things through
in the essay –
shows personal
engagement

Examiner feedback

The candidate has shown a well-argued response which sets out clearly what is going to be covered. Quotations from the poem are generally handled well and skilfully interwoven into the text, although sometimes the explanations that follow could interpret ideas a little more, as in the 'heart fed' example. The theme of power is explored and developed in real detail but the candidate gets a bit diverted at the end when mentioning the nineteenth century interest in exotic travel; unless something like this can be closely related to the theme, it would probably be better not to mention it. Finally, the response would be improved by further reference to the structure of the poetry: in particular, the fact that this is a form of sonnet, and the effect of the final 2-4 lines which make a final statement about the scene.

Suggested grade: B (based on this first part)

ACTIVITY

In what ways is this response a genuine improvement on Example 1 on pages 207–208?

Return to the feedback on the Grade C response on Characterisation and compare

- the fluency and expression of the two responses
- the development of ideas
- the use of quotations
- the reference to language and the particular devices the writer uses.

Read the following extract from a response to this task.

> *Explore the way the idea of personal identity is presented in a text(s) you have studied.*

This is the first part of a response to this task, relating it to the poems, 'Checking out me History' by John Agard and 'Thoughts on my Father' by James Berry (see page 200).

Example 3: Theme in Exploring Cultures poetry

Starting with a quotation draws reader in →

I carving out me identity

So ends, 'Checking out me History' by John Agard, which even in its title reminds us that those who speak English may have different roots and backgrounds, as the dialect word 'me' rather than 'my' shows.

Long quote isn't embedded but this doesn't matter as he explores each aspect in detail

Use of question to structure the response →

What, then, does John Agard have to say about his own identity? First, he makes an immediate connection between 'identity' and 'history' in the lines:

Bandage up me eye with me own history ←
Blind me to me own identity.

Good analysis of imagery →

The use of **medical imagery** such as this suggests that the people who have told him his 'history' have hurt him deep down. But how can 'history' hurt you? **We find out in the next stanzas** which follow a sort of pattern as they present famous figures from 'British' history (which is all white and English-based) and then present alternative Caribbean or African figures who the poet believes he should have been taught about.

Explains simply what poet does

So we have '1066 and all dat' but nothing about the 'slave with vision' – Toussaint l'Ouverture who beat Napoleon. Later we have his reference to Mary Seacole, a West-Indian nurse in the Crimean War who, **ironically**, helped the British. Agard uses the **powerful metaphors**, 'a healing star' and a 'powerful sunrise', to

> **Excellent juxtaposition of ways various people are described**

> **Covers structure but also its effect**

describe her which is a clever comparison with Florence Nightingale who was known as the 'Lady of the Lamp' when she helped the wounded and dying.

*The poem's structure also helps with what Agard has to say about personal identity. He keeps repeating the **refrain** 'Dem tell me' ('They tell me') which must refer to teachers, and by using the pronoun 'dem/they' it makes it seem even more as if these people oppose him. All the examples he gives of the well-known historical figures need no explanations to why they are famous because they are so celebrated in British history, but he has to give us lots of detail about Toussaint, Nanny and Mary Seacole because they are part of his history.*

*The poem ends very powerfully as he is now '**carving**' out his identity, like suggesting it will last forever – like in the bark of a tree.*

In contrast, 'Thoughts on my Father' deals with a very different aspect of personal history and identity ...

> **Personal engagement**

> **Language term used helpfully**

> **Interesting and relevant personal interpretation**

Examiner feedback

This is excellent: there is a real understanding of how the theme is explored and the range of quotations and references is varied and apt. The candidate also comments on aspects of structure, dialect and culture, thus addressing all elements of the assessment objectives.

On several occasions the style is a little loose, when the student appears to be 'thinking aloud on the page'. More focus here would help, with some more succinct sentences – don't over-use 'like'. The final comment on the poem is a bit blunt, too!

Overall, this part of the essay is successful from the start: it draws us in with a powerful and apt quotation and then uses that as a springboard into the answer. The short relevant reference to the historical background ('Lady with the Lamp') shows the candidate has done some research too.

Suggested grade: A (based on this first part)

EXTENDED PRACTICE TASK

Write about contrasts in a character or between characters who have made a particular impression on you in the text or texts you have read. You can choose to write about character(s) from

- a Shakespeare play (for example, Mercutio in *Romeo and Juliet*)
- an English Literary Heritage text(s) (for example, Magwitch in *Great Expectations* or two characters from different poems)
- an Exploring Cultures text(s) (for example, Crooks in *Of Mice and Men*, or two characters from different poems).

What made an impact on you, and how did the writers present the character(s)?

If you only do five things...

1. Prepare carefully in advance of the assessment on your chosen texts – this will be important.
2. Know the texts very well so you don't waste time looking for references on the day.
3. Stick to the focus of the task – if you are writing about theme, keep on coming back to the key word, for example 'power' or 'conflict'.
4. Make sure you keep referring to the *effect* of the choices writers make; don't just say what they did.
5. Strike a balance between comments on language choices (vocabulary, imagery), grammatical choices (tenses, sentence types) and structure (how and when information is revealed, ordered and patterned) and use appropriate technical terms (for example, stanza, chapter, scene).

⑤ Unit 3B **Creative Writing**

What's it all about?

Writing creatively really enables you to 'show off' your most imaginative ideas, original thinking and best writing techniques.

How will I be assessed?

- You will get **20% of your English marks** for your ability to write creative texts. You will have to complete two written pieces in a Controlled Assessment lasting up to **4 hours**.
- You will be marked on your writing of **two** written responses taken from a **choice of three areas**. These are
  - *Moving Images:* watching moving image texts and developing writing from them
  - *Prompts and Re-creations:* using a text or prompt to develop writing
  - *Me. Myself. I.:* writing from personal experience

- The two pieces of writing will total up to **1400 words**. They needn't be the same length: the way you split the total will depend on the tasks.

What is being tested?

You are being examined on your ability to

- write for specific creative purposes
- communicate clearly, effectively and imaginatively
- organise information in a structured and inventive way
- use a range of paragraphs
- use a variety of sentence structures and styles
- use a range of linguistic features for impact and effect
- write with accuracy in punctuation, spelling and grammar.

Moving Images

Introduction

This section of Chapter 5 shows you how to

- explore the area of creative writing linked to 'Moving images'
- understand what a Controlled Assessment task in this area is asking you to do
- produce responses to a range of moving image texts from which written texts will be developed
- practise and develop extended responses.

Why is learning about this area important?

- This is one of the three elements of your creative writing unit, from which you will choose two tasks to respond to.
- The skills you develop here will feed into your other reading, writing, speaking and listening tasks and responses.

A Grade C candidate will

- use the main conventions of creative texts consistently
- write clear and well-structured creative pieces, making the meaning clear to the reader
- try consciously to achieve certain effects in his or her writing to interest the reader, for example through vocabulary choices
- use clear paragraphing and sentences, which are sometimes varied.

A Grade A/A★ candidate will

- exploit the chosen form or conventions for effect and impact
- engage and delight the reader with language choices, devices and effects
- use varied and sophisticated vocabulary, sentences and paragraphs
- write with ambition and imagination.

Prior learning

Before you begin this section, think about

- a book you have read which would make a good film
- a memorable scene from a film you have seen and how you would describe it in words.

> Why would it make a good film? Is it the story, setting, themes, characters?

> What would you have to do to turn it into a successful piece of writing?

Moving images: generating ideas

What is involved in generating ideas from moving image texts?

You will be shown moving image texts (film sequences, video or DVD clips) from which you will be expected to compose your own extended creative text.

You will respond by using what you have seen as a 'springboard' for your own creative writing. This means you won't just describe what you see on the screen but will take elements of it and develop your own ideas from these.

Checklist for success

- You need to consider original and inventive approaches to the material.
- You need to use rich, varied language that engages the reader.
- You need to sustain your ideas, style and tone throughout your writing.

Focus for development: Building ideas, creating new directions

A student has chosen a memorable scene from a film to inspire his own piece of creative writing. He will take some of the powerful ideas from the original and add his own ideas to them.

His choice is the opening sequence to *Great Expectations* (David Lean, 1946).

The student has made notes about particular ideas that stood out from the sequence, and how these might be developed in his own story. Here are his notes as a spider diagram.

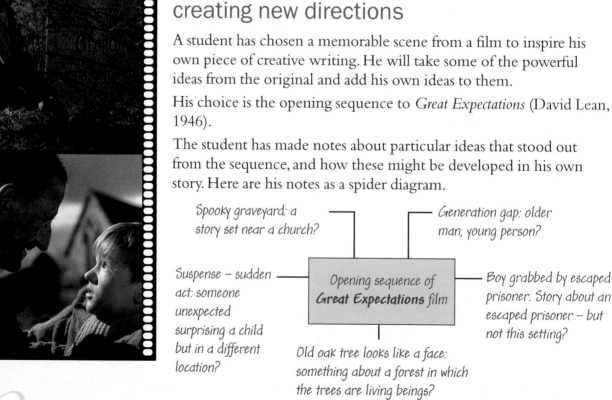

Spooky graveyard: a story set near a church?

Generation gap: older man, young person?

Suspense – sudden act: someone unexpected surprising a child but in a different location?

Opening sequence of *Great Expectations* film

Boy grabbed by escaped prisoner. Story about an escaped prisoner – but not this setting?

Old oak tree looks like a face: something about a forest in which the trees are living beings?

Choose one of the ideas on the previous page. Note down how you could develop it into a powerful and memorable scene or section from a story.

For example, the student decided that the idea of 'someone unexpected surprising a child in a different location' would work. Here is her set of notes on the plot.

> Girl on bus on way home from school.
> Is approached by a down-and-out woman who demands money.
> When she looks closely, amazed to see the woman looks identical to her mother!

Now, note down details for your own story.

- **Focus on character**: How do the characters in your section from the story dress, behave, speak?
- **Focus on setting:** Where does the scene take place? (A bus, a graveyard or…?) What objects are there in the scene? (An old tree? A rotten chair? A flashing computer screen?) Is there any reason to mention the weather or time of year?
- **Focus on dialogue:** Is anything said, or is this a scene of action or description? If there is speech, who speaks and why? How do they speak and what is their voice like? What happens as a result of the conversation?
- **Focus on atmosphere:** This is linked to setting. What is the overall tone of the piece? (Frightening? Thoughtful? Sad? Comic?) Or is it full of contrasts (Rich/poor? Young/old? Happy/sad? Dark/light?)

ASSESSMENT FOCUS

Based on your notes, write the first two paragraphs of your scene or story. Try to

- establish the setting and atmosphere
- introduce your main character and their situation.

Remember

- **Plan new ideas that springboard away from the original.**
- **This is a part response, so there is no need to waste time telling a lot of the story.**
- **Focus on *showing* what happens rather than *telling* your reader lots of information.**

Using images to write with impact

Learning objective

- To learn how to make your writing highly visual and easy for the reader to picture.

Checklist for success

You need to make sure the reader can 'see' a picture when they read your work, so focus on objects, people and locations and use vivid detail.

Based on the *Great Expectations* images on page 216, here is part of a **Grade C** response about a graveyard in which a runaway child is hiding from the police and the gang she has been forced to work for.

> The police-officer chased me as I ran away towards the graveyard. Getting closer I could see the gravestones all around me. I knew if I didn't reach the church I was finished. It would be back to work or off to prison. I got closer and could now see the windows of the church looking down.

Next read this extract from a **Grade A/A★** response.

> The gravestones, like grey jagged fangs sprouting from the earth, reared up towards me as I ran. I knew if I didn't reach the welcoming sanctuary of the church, the man pursuing me would trap me like a rat-catcher, and I would be destined for the cold concrete floors or the iron bars of a cell.

ACTIVITY

- Identify at least two ways this is an improvement on the Grade C response.
- Add a final sentence to the Grade A/A★ response which describes the windows of the church. Make it more visually detailed than the first.

Focus for development: Using visual detail

An excellent element of the Grade A/A★ extract was the simile for the gravestones, and the personification of them in the verb 'reared up'.

> The gravestones, **like grey jagged fangs sprouting from the earth, reared up** towards me as I ran.

Looking at objects in detail will enrich your writing. More importantly, they must

- **add to the atmosphere or tone**
- **advance the story**
- or **reveal something about a character**.

In the *Great Expectations* film sequence, the director focuses on the old tree which creaks and sways, and looks like an old man's face, to suggest the boy's fear and loneliness.

If this idea was put into writing it would need to contain

- original and powerful imagery which was mysterious and drew a picture in your reader's mind of that particular tree
- verbs conveying the movement and sound of the tree and its effect on the boy.

ACTIVITY

Does the following response achieve this?

> The tree was very high and looked down on me. The way it moved around, swaying and hanging down like arms from the sky, made me feel uneasy and I could feel my heart beat faster and faster. The branches seemed to be coming towards me, and the bark had the look of an old man's face watching me. They reminded me of who I had come to meet.

Improve the response, focusing on the two points above. You may need to change the order of the sentences too – it is not just a question of replacing individual words.

The overall tone needs to be creepy and suggest the boy's anxiety.

ASSESSMENT FOCUS

Continue the description of the graveyard, adding other evocative details. You could focus, for example, on a particular gravestone, or an aspect of nature (a crow? a yew tree?). If you wish, develop the opening into a longer sequence. You could link it to the runaway child idea, or come up with your own idea.

Remember

- **Match your description to the style and tone of your story.**
- **Show details of colour, sound and texture, making sure your details add to the atmosphere, reveal the characters' feelings or hint at the story to come.**

219

Writing for film

Learning objective

- To learn how to write creatively in a style that might be adapted for film.

What does writing for film mean?

You may be asked to write a sequence or a short story which has 'filmic' qualities. This means writing that

- is set in evocative locations
- has powerful dialogue
- includes memorable characters.

ACTIVITY

A student has come up with a story idea that he thinks would make an exciting film. It is called 'Brothers' and is about two teenagers, one who wants to work hard and succeed at school, the other who thinks this is a waste of time.

Here is his opening – it's a draft with some changes he has already made and notes for further changes.

> **Brothers**
>
> *Make opening more exciting – could his brother grab him/be violent?*
>
> *his older brother*
>
> As Peter walked out of his house, ~~Danny~~ stopped him.
>
> *as he stepped off their neat front lawn.*
>
> 'Why don't you come with me? School's naff and I got some cash. We could catch a bus into town, buy some gear. ~~You could come, it'd be a laugh...~~'
>
> Peter didn't know what to do. Part of him wanted to go, but he
>
> *with their curly, mop-like brown hair*
>
> knew his brother had plans ~~– bad plans~~. They looked alike but that was where the similarity ended. ~~Danny was a wild kid, always in trouble, while Peter was the studious one.~~
>
> Suddenly, a wreck of a car screamed around the corner, screeching to a halt by them both...

Discuss with a partner:

- How do the notes improve the **visual aspect** of the writing?
- What has changed about the **dialogue**? How is it improved?
- What else could be done to give this opening **more impact**? (Do you agree with the idea of making the brother more 'violent'?)

Focus for development: Writing sharper dialogue and description

You have already seen that good dialogue is key to writing 'filmically'. Now try writing dialogue that has impact and power.

ACTIVITY

Look at this **Grade A** opening to a story. Identify at least three features that make it particularly suitable for film.

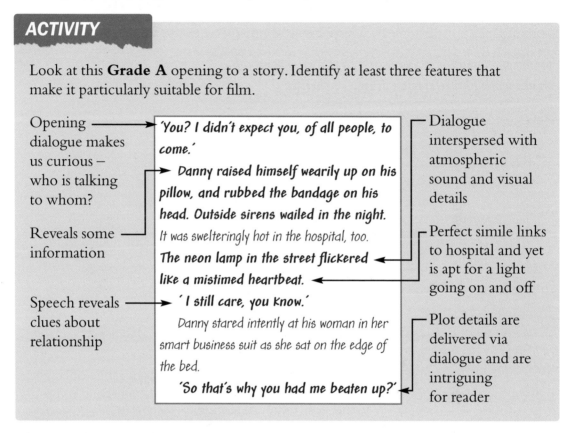

Opening dialogue makes us curious – who is talking to whom?

Reveals some information

Speech reveals clues about relationship

'You? I didn't expect you, of all people, to come.'

Danny raised himself wearily up on his pillow, and rubbed the bandage on his head. Outside sirens wailed in the night.

It was swelteringly hot in the hospital, too. The neon lamp in the street flickered like a mistimed heartbeat.

' I still care, you know.'

Danny stared intently at his woman in her smart business suit as she sat on the edge of the bed.

'So that's why you had me beaten up?'

Dialogue interspersed with atmospheric sound and visual details

Perfect simile links to hospital and yet is apt for a light going on and off

Plot details are delivered via dialogue and are intriguing for reader

ASSESSMENT FOCUS

Now take this **Grade B** opening to a similar scene, and improve it 'filmically'.

Jane made her way onto the dark nightclub floor. It had been closed for several hours and was quiet and still. By the bar stood a tall figure, her ex-manager Jason. He had phoned her to suggest they met as he had a proposition for her. What could he possibly want?
'Hi,' she said.
'I'm glad you're here,' he replied.
'It's late,' she said, 'what is it you want?'

For more on making your writing visual, see pages 218–9.

Remember

- **Hold back information – don't reveal everything about the character(s) straight away.**
- **Make sure the dialogue works for you – get rid of anything unnecessary.**
- **Add descriptive detail around the dialogue to convey atmosphere and tone.**

Grade Booster

Extended Assessment Task

Generate ideas, plan and write a response of about 700 words to this task.

> *Write the opening of a story set in the near future that*
> *would work as a television drama or thriller.*

Make sure you

- use convincing dialogue
- hold back key information to keep the reader guessing
- use a range of language devices and techniques, such as metaphor and simile
- don't waste time with unnecessary or dull details setting the scene.

Evaluation – What have you learned?

**With a partner, use the grade checklist below to evaluate your work
on the Extended Assessment Task.**

- I can write a sustained, vivid and original piece, based on film, which engages and delights the reader.
- I can make full and varied use of a wide and ambitious range of language devices, structures and effects, including the full repertoire of sentence and paragraphs.

- I can write a sustained, vivid and original piece which engages the reader and often delights through ambitious use of language devices, structures and effects.
- I can use a wide range of sentences and paragraphs for effect.

- I can write a well-developed creative piece with conscious use of a range of language devices and structures to create effects.
- I can use sentences and paragraphs fluently and creatively.

- I can write a clear and well-structured creative piece which uses some language devices and structures for purpose and effect.
- I can use clear and sometimes varied paragraphs and sentences.

- I can write a creative piece which mainly matches the task I have been set and is generally accurate and clear, but is sometimes undeveloped.
- I can show only a limited variety of vocabulary, and sentence or paragraph structures.

You may need to go back and look at the relevant pages of this section again.

Re-creations and Prompts

Introduction

This section of Chapter 5 shows you how to

- explore the area of creative writing linked to a prompt (usually a story's opening or closing sentence) or stimulus text, such as a poem
- understand what a Controlled Assessment task in this area is asking you to do
- develop creative writing responses to a range of ideas or other texts
- practise and develop extended responses .

Why is learning about this area important?

- This is one of the three areas of your creative writing unit from which you will choose two tasks to respond to.
- The skills you develop here will feed into your other reading, writing, speaking and listening tasks and responses.

A **Grade C** candidate will

- use the main conventions of creative texts consistently
- write clear and well-structured creative pieces, making the meaning clear to the reader
- try consciously to achieve certain effects in his or her writing to interest the reader, for example through vocabulary choices
- use clear paragraphing and sentences, which are sometimes varied.

C

A **Grade A/A★** candidate will

- exploit the chosen form or conventions for effect and impact
- engage and delight the reader with language choices, devices and effects
- use varied and sophisticated vocabulary, sentences and paragraphs
- write with ambition and imagination.

A **A★**

Prior learning

Before you begin this section, read

- the opening lines of a poem and jot down ideas about the potential new writing that could come out of it
- a range of beginnings of short stories, making notes about how the writer engages the reader straight away
- your previous creative writing – think about what you did well, and what needed more work.

> Who tells the story? Is it from the same viewpoint as the writer in the poem, or a different one?

> In what way does the first sentence grab your attention?

> How well did you use imagery, like simile and metaphor?

Structuring ideas

Learning objective

- To learn how to structure a story successfully from a simple prompt.

★ **Examiner's tip**

Remember, your word count is limited so simplicity is the key. You won't be expected to come up with a hugely complex narrative.

ACTIVITY

What does structuring ideas involve?

When you respond to a 'prompt' task, you will be given only a short extract or sentence to work from, so being able to structure your ideas from scratch is vital.

Checklist for success

- You need to develop a structure that follows one or two main characters.
- You need to focus writing around key moments and events that engage the reader.
- You need to plan for opportunities to 'show off' your creative and descriptive skills, such as use of imagery.

Read this short 'prompt' task.

> **Write a creative piece that leads up to these final sentences:**
> *He stood by the road looking over the marshland back to where his mother's cottage once stood. It would take some time to make sense of what had happened.*

With a partner:

- mind map **two or three story ideas** that could arise from these few simple lines
- choose the **best idea** from your discussion.

On your own, develop the initial idea.

- Jot down some of the key plot elements – the 'ingredients' for your story – for example, the main character or characters (no more than two, for a short story).
- What **happens** in the story? It must start

somewhere, then **develop** (due to a problem, piece of news or a change in character's circumstances).

- How will it end? For example, the development could focus on how
  - a character changes as the result of something profound or powerful that happens
  - a relationship between people develops or breaks down
  - a character learns something new about him or herself or the people/places around them
  - a secret is revealed
  - somebody or something turns out not to be what/they it appears.
- You will also need to decide on a **suitable genre** or type of story. (Will it be contemporary? Futuristic? A thriller? Mystery? Fantasy? A mix of genres?)

Focus for development: Expanding ideas

Here are one student's notes from his laptop, planning ideas for a story based on the ending given. His chosen genre is a thriller. Each file has a range of documents, with notes on key details.

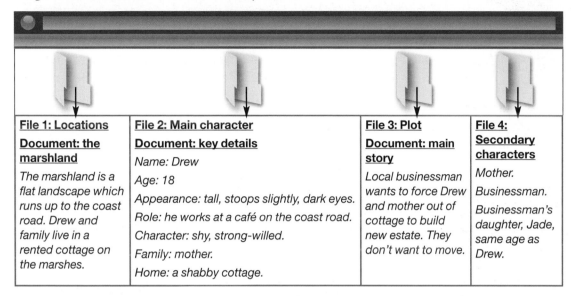

File 1: Locations	File 2: Main character	File 3: Plot	File 4: Secondary characters
Document: the marshland	**Document: key details**	**Document: main story**	Mother.
The marshland is a flat landscape which runs up to the coast road. Drew and family live in a rented cottage on the marshes.	*Name: Drew* *Age: 18* *Appearance: tall, stoops slightly, dark eyes.* *Role: he works at a café on the coast road.* *Character: shy, strong-willed.* *Family: mother.* *Home: a shabby cottage.*	*Local businessman wants to force Drew and mother out of cottage to build new estate. They don't want to move.*	Businessman. Businessman's daughter, Jade, same age as Drew.

ACTIVITY

Choose one of the following and write further detailed notes.

- **File 1: Locations. Document: the marshland** Make notes about its appearance, the natural features, atmosphere, colours, etc.
- **File 4: Secondary characters. Document: the daughter** Produce a file like the one for Drew, adding even more details.

ASSESSMENT FOCUS

You will explore this story further on the next two pages, but try to complete this initial structure based on the sample story above *or* jot down your ideas for a related story:

Introduction: Drew and mother in cottage before he goes off to work

Development: arrival of Jade, businessman's daughter, with news that her dad is sending builders to start work on the land

Further development: Drew sets off to…

Climax/key moment: …

Conclusion: …

Remember

- **Get to know your story inside out before you begin.**
- **Have a clear basic plot structure written down.**
- **Plan as much content as you can before you begin the Controlled Assessment task.**

Structuring a story for effect and impact

Learning objective

- To make your story engaging through structure and variety.

Checklist for success

- You need to make sure ideas and plot-lines are clear enough to follow, but unusual enough to keep readers engaged.
- You need to use a variety of sentences and paragraphs to make your reader want to keep reading.

Below are two openings to the 'Drew' story from pages 224–5.

Grade B response

Drew and his mother sat at their pine kitchen table finishing breakfast. It was 7 o'clock and still not quite light. Drew needed to be at the café by 8, to open up for the passing salesmen and truck drivers who drove along the coast road to the motorway junction.

Then his mother spoke. 'You finished, love?' She stood up, ready to take his cereal bowl.

'Yeah, ta,' he replied, and then got up to finish getting ready for work.

The cottage they lived in was tiny, but it was home, and Drew couldn't imagine living anywhere else, even though at 18 many of his friends were off to uni soon.

This is good because

- we are shown Drew and his mother in their cottage with some visual details
- their relationship (a good one) is hinted at
- we find out information about Drew: his job, his age
- the paragraphs are clear and the dialogue is quite convincing.

However, the sentences are rather dull, for example two begin with 'Drew'; 'Then' isn't really needed; and there are not many visual details.

ACTIVITY

Discuss with a partner how this Grade A response
- conveys the same information
- engages the reader
- adds new information.

The grey light of the marshland morning seeped into the kitchen and across the pine table where Drew and his mother sat finishing breakfast. The café needed to be opened at 8 for the passing salesmen and truck drivers who drove along the coast road to the motorway junction, so Drew pushed his bowl across the table and stood up.

'Think Jade will be round today, love?' asked his mum, picking up the bowl and walking to the kitchen.

'No idea. What I do know is that we'll see her father again soon. He's a right bully.'

Quietly, Drew pulled open the curtain and stared across the flat, coarse, yellowing grass of the marsh. The cottage was tiny but it was home. He couldn't imagine looking out on any other scene, the landscape as familiar as his mother's tired and lined face.

Jade and his friends would be off to uni soon, but this was home.

Focus for development: Writing paragraphs to make an impact

When you plan your story, the information you reveal and how you reveal it are key. The example on the previous page does this well:

- **Paragraph 1**: reveals setting, creates atmosphere, introduces characters, reveals key information but as part of the action (Drew preparing for work)
- **Paragraph 2**: dialogue establishes relationship between characters *and* brings in new information and hints at problem to come (the father as a bully)
- **Paragraph 3**: further description of setting establishes the importance of the cottage to Drew and probably his mother – this ties into the main plot of story
- **Paragraph 4**: a one-line paragraph for impact, stressing the importance of the place.

ACTIVITY

- Plan three more paragraphs that will show the **development phase** of the story (see page 225). They could deal with Jade's father coming to the café to bribe Drew to persuade him and his mother to leave the cottage.
- Think about how the paragraphs can contrast, too (quiet café to violent confrontation? perhaps Jade's dad grabs Drew, or vice versa?).

ASSESSMENT FOCUS

Now write the three paragraphs.

- Use any **dialogue for important information** about the story or characters but keep it short – no need to have lots of introductory 'hellos'.
- Include **visual details** so that it is not just action, for example 'a pile of unwashed dishes, thick with grease, sat in front of Drew as Jade's father entered'.
- **Move the story on** – make sure we know more about the character or plot by the time the three paragraphs are complete.
- **Begin each paragraph in a different way**, for example not just with pronouns or names.
- **Avoid unnecessary linking words** such as 'then' and 'so', unless they are really needed to keep it clear. If the action itself links paragraphs effectively, that is all you need.

Remember

- Concentrate on keeping the plot moving on as you develop your story.
- Use contrasting pace and mood in your sentences and paragraphs to keep the reader interested.

Adding variety and interest

Learning objective

- *To interest the reader with a compelling style.*

What does adding variety and interest mean?

Good writing is more than just interesting imagery and flowery description; powerful verbs and a variety of sentences also keep the reader hooked.

Checklist for success

- You need to use a wide range of sentences for impact.
- You need to select verbs very carefully according to the effect you want to create.

Varying sentences

A range of sentences can convey suspense and keep you reading.

Grade A response

Short sentence stresses man's threat.

Long sentence helps paint clear still image, like a long-held breath

Short sentences match Drew's anxiety

> Drew lay flat by the canal bank. **A huge man with a torch was circling the cottage, shining the light through the blank window panes, as if peering into the soul of the place. He looked a brute.** Suddenly, the man turned. **Swung his torch towards Drew. For a moment, all was still, like a camera shot of them both frozen in time – the man with his torch, Drew a few yards away, pressed to the ground.** Then, the sound of footsteps disappearing. **Had he gone? Yes. Thank god.**

Longer sentence reveals details of man and contrasts his movement with Drew's stillness

Short sentence matches sudden brief movement

ACTIVITY

Write the next paragraph. In it, the man returns with someone else – Jade. Show Drew's continued fear, and the questions he asks himself, by using a mix of short and long sentences.

Focus for development: Using verbs for effect

Powerful verbs can be better than adjectives for adding pace and excitement.
Look at this extract from a **Grade A★** response.

> Drew **raced** down the canal path, his bike's wheel rims **glistening** in the dark. He **swerved around** the clumps of grass and stone that **jutted** from the path, and **skidded** to a stomach-wrenching halt by the road.
>
> No one was there.

Examiner's tip ★

Plan for contrasting situations or twists of plot in your story. This might be, for example, a quiet conversation between two characters followed by a chase or pursuit.

Equally, **more subtle use of verbs** (and adverbs) can make characters come alive, as here.

> Jade **hovered** on the doorstep, waiting for someone to come to the door. Her eyes **flicked nervously** from the pot of dead flowers to the large bell, and she **fiddled anxiously** with the buttons of her woollen coat.

ACTIVITY

Improve this **Grade B response,** which does not convey character or action effectively, by changing the highlighted verbs.

> Drew opened the door. He looked at Jade angrily.
> 'What do you want?'
> Jade turned without a word and hurriedly went back down the dry, cinder path.
> Drew looked at her as she left.
> Soon she was out of sight, and it was at that moment he knew he'd been a fool. His heart beating wildly, he went after her, shutting the door behind him, desperate to get to her before she reached the road.

ASSESSMENT FOCUS

Now invent a character, or use one from a story you are currently working on.

- Choose a location they could be in (a shop? at home? at school?).
- Decide what they are doing. (Why are they in this location? What do they want? What is about to happen?)
- Decide on some basic details about how they feel at this point (determined? frightened? nervous? shy? aggressive?).

Make notes of your ideas then write two paragraphs from this part of your story.

Remember

- Focus on carefully-selected verbs and adverbs to keep the reader's interest.
- Use a wide variety of sentences to convey atmosphere and action (for example, suspense, speed, calm reflection).

Re-creations: changing the viewpoint of a text

What does changing the viewpoint of a text mean?

One way of re-creating a text is to take a different viewpoint. For example, a poem told from the point of view of an old man might be re-created as a short story told by his granddaughter.

Checklist for success

- You need to choose the best form to help you develop your idea. It might be difficult, for example, to turn a reflective poem about love into an action-packed mystery!
- You need to sustain the viewpoint and voice you choose so that you engage and persuade the reader that your character is 'real'.

Changing form and perspective

Here is a brief summary of the poem 'Cold Knap Lake' by Gillian Clark, followed by the first two verses.

The poet (as a child) and her parents see a crowd of people pull a girl from a lake, apparently drowned. The poet's mother gives the kiss-of-life to the child, and she recovers. The poet's father takes the girl home where she is beaten by her parents, presumably for getting into trouble.

> We once watched a crowd
> pull a drowned child from the lake.
> Blue-lipped and dressed in water's long green silk
> she lay for dead.
>
> Then kneeling on the earth,
> a heroine, her red head bowed,
> her wartime cotton frock soaked,
> my mother gave a stranger's child her breath.
> The crowd stood silent,
> drawn by the dread of it.

The poem is told from an adult's perspective, looking back on an incident from their childhood.

ACTIVITY

- Note down anyone else who could have told the story from a different point of view.
- Which, in your opinion, would have been the most interesting choice? Why?
- What particular changes would you need to make to turn the poem into a story? (A poem is often a snapshot in time, or may be written in an unusual order using particular language.)

Focus for development:
Developing different viewpoints

When you write from one person's perspective, their experience of the events will be different from another person's. The **voice** they use will be different too.

A student writes…

How do I make the voice of each character different?

Answer…

Focus on character, with subtle hints: the sympathetic mother who saves the girl's life thinking about her own child; the girl's parent's cruelty, calling her a 'little cow'. Try to write as the person would speak, but avoid stereotypes.

ACTIVITY

Who is writing each of these paragraphs? How do you know? What is distinctive about the voice they use in each case?

> All I remember is being on that long branch stretched out over the lake. It was a dare, and Jimmy told me I was a 'scaredy-cat', so I started to creep along it when…

> I knew I had to do something. The poor girl could have been my own daughter, but the crowd were doing nothing, so…

> There was this knock at the door. We don't get many visitors on the estate – too scared mostly. But it was some man with our Rosie soaked to the skin. The little cow, in trouble again! I pulled her into the house…

ASSESSMENT FOCUS

- Choose one of the perspectives above and write a story from that character's point of view.
- First read the whole poem from the AQA *Moon on the Tides* anthology, noting down any key details that may help you with your story, for example the wartime setting or details of the lake (mentioned in the final verses).
- Decide what else you need to add that is not in the poem.
- Finally, work out the structure for your re-creation. (See pages 224–227 to remind yourself about story structure.

Remember

- Be clear about your character's role in the story – what they see or don't see, and how they feel about it.
- Get your character's voice right.
- Make sure you have used the conventions of story form, but remember you will still need strong language, imagery and atmosphere.

Grade Booster

Extended Assessment Task

Generate ideas, plan and write a response of about 700 words to this task.

> **Write a creative piece that leads up to these final two sentences:**
> *The room was completely empty. Not a trace remained of anyone having ever been there.*

Start by generating ideas using a format you find useful, such as a spider diagram like the one on page 216.

Evaluation – What have you learned?

With a partner, use the grade checklist below to evaluate your work on the Extended Assessment Task.

- I can write a sustained, vivid piece of original or re-creative writing which engages and delights the reader.
- I can make full and varied use of a wide and ambitious range of language devices, structures and effects, including the full repertoire of sentence and paragraphs.

- I can write a sustained, vivid piece of original or re-creative writing which engages the reader and often delights through ambitious use of language devices, structures and effects.
- I can use a wide variety of sentences and paragraphs, always for effect.

- I can write a well-developed piece of original or re-creative writing, with conscious use of a range of language devices and structures to create effects and impact.
- I can use sentences and paragraphs fluently and creatively.

- I can write a clear and well-structured piece of original or re-creative writing, which uses some language devices and structures for purpose and effect.
- I can use clear and sometimes varied paragraphs and sentences.

- I can write a piece of original or re-creative writing which mainly matches the task I have been set and is generally accurate and clear, but sometimes undeveloped.
- I can use only a limited variety of vocabulary and sentence and paragraph structures.

You may need to go back and look at the relevant pages of this section again.

Me. Myself. I.

Introduction

This section of Chapter 5 shows you how to

- explore the area of creative writing linked to 'Me. Myself. I.' – writing about personal experiences
- understand what a Controlled Assessment task in this area is asking you to do
- develop writing from experiences you have had, or memories of places and people.

Why is learning about this area important?

- This is one of the three areas of the creative writing unit from which you will choose two tasks to respond to.
- The skills you develop here will feed into your other reading, writing and speaking and listening tasks and responses.

A **Grade C** candidate will

- convey personal feelings and impressions clearly and in a structured way
- use consistently the main conventions of creative texts suited to writing about personal experiences
- try consciously to achieve certain effects in his or her writing to interest the reader, for example through vocabulary choices
- use clear paragraphing and sentences, which are sometimes varied.

C

A **Grade A/A★** candidate will

- convey personal feelings and experiences in ways which engage and delight the reader
- exploit the chosen form, or conventions which suit writing about personal experiences, for effect and impact
- use a wide range of language devices for effect
- use varied and sophisticated vocabulary, sentences and paragraphs
- write with ambition and imagination.

A **A★**

Prior learning

Before you begin this section, think about

- your memories of your life five and ten years ago, focusing in particular on places, people or events that stand out
- autobiographies, or accounts by people (famous or not) about events from their lives and their childhood.

> Where were you living? What was your house or flat like at the time?

> Try to find some and read them, if you are not familiar with any. Do you think famous people are mostly proud of their background, or pleased to escape it?

Writing about personal experiences

Learning objective

- To learn how to make personal anecdotes or experiences interesting to the reader.

What does writing about personal experiences mean?

It means writing about events, people and places that have featured strongly in your life.

Checklist for success

- You need to develop what might be quite small moments into something more significant and worth reading.
- You need to use many of the conventions of good story writing but apply them to real situations.

ACTIVITY

- In a small group, take turns to tell out loud a short anecdote from your life. You must not speak for more than four minutes. It could be
  - a funny or serious incident
  - something that changed how you felt about the world or other people
  - a memorable encounter with someone.
- When you tell your anecdote, try to
  - interest your listener with the way you speak: vary your voice, use emphasis, speak clearly
  - paint a picture in their minds: don't expect them to be able to see what's in *your* mind
- When you have finished, think about your anecdote and the others you listened to. What made the better ones interesting? Was it what happened in the story? Or the way it was told?

ACTIVITY

- Read the autobiographical extracts on pages 12 (Richard E Grant) and 74 (Julie Myerson).
- How do they bring these experiences to life and make them interesting to the reader?

ACTIVITY

Using a spider diagram, create a word-map of all the elements of your anecdote and add the details that would make it a 'proper' story. If you wish, embellish them (add some details which you can make up), like this.

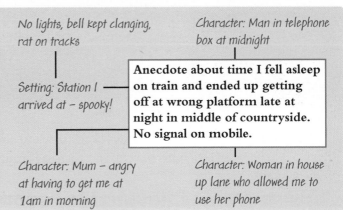

No lights, bell kept clanging, rat on tracks

Setting: Station I arrived at – spooky!

Character: Man in telephone box at midnight

Anecdote about time I fell asleep on train and ended up getting off at wrong platform late at night in middle of countryside. No signal on mobile.

Character: Mum – angry at having to get me at 1am in morning

Character: Woman in house up lane who allowed me to use her phone

Focus for development:
Losing the plot

When you are writing about personal experiences, concentrate on bringing the setting and people to life.

Here is an example of a student writing about a memorable event from his childhood.

ACTIVITY

With a partner, make some quick notes:

- How well can you picture the situation? Has the writer provided enough visual detail?
- What do we find out about the other people involved?
- Does this anecdote have potential for development? Why / Why not?

Improve it by adding a paragraph in which you describe in detail the effect of the rain on the site. Start like this:

> The effect of the rain on the campsite was catastrophic. My parents' tent ...

Grade C response

> The campsite we stayed on was awful: it had no facilities and it rained nearly every day. However, it was near a river and we spent most of the time trying to cross it by building a stone bridge. This took up nearly all the holiday and it was only on the last day that we got it completed. By then the river was really high. The crossing was quite dangerous but one by one, everyone managed it and then it was my turn ...

ASSESSMENT FOCUS

- Now, either take your anecdote from earlier, or choose your own 'memorable event' from your childhood.
- As before, create a spider diagram of the key elements.
- Then, for each element, write two paragraphs describing the people and the places.
- Use vivid description, adding detail to nouns: 'tent weighed down by huge, icy pools of water'.
- Plan how your anecdote will begin.
- Think about how you will finish – maybe with a flashback, or a reflection on the beginning?

Remember

- **Personal anecdotes only make interesting stories if they are developed.**
- **Focus on character and place as much as you would in a completely 'fictional' story.**
- **Be constantly aware of what your story is trying to show the reader.**

Writing about memorable people

Learning objective

- To understand how focusing on specific character features can engage the reader.

You may be asked to write about people you know well or have met who have made a lasting impression on you.

Checklist for success

- You need to convey what is different and special about them through interesting or unexpected details.
- You need to consider everything about them: their appearance, behaviour, how they speak, and how others describe them and react to them.

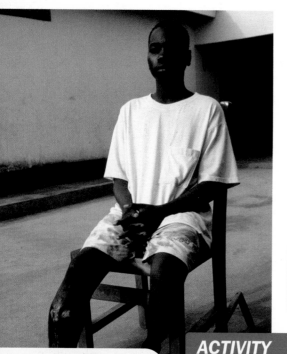

Read this opening to a piece of writing by the BBC reporter, Fergal Keane, about meeting a survivor of the Rwanda massacres.

> *Like nearly every other survivor of the genocide I have met, Placide always looked away when answering questions about what had happened to him. He did not look into my face, but rather into some unreachable distance, in whose limitless spaces he seemed lost. Yes, he could tell me his story and he could remember names, dates, places and incidents. But he would not meet my eyes and so that most fundamental of human contacts evaded me through the long hour I spent with him. Later, I would find out why. But only after I had made a very foolish and hurtful mistake.*
>
> A Boy Called 'Grenade'

Examiner's tip

Try to come up with an original simile or comparison. For example, a look could be like a shaft of sunlight into your heart; a person might roll a cigarette as if it was a work of art, and so on.

ACTIVITY

Discuss with a partner:

- What particular feature of Placide's behaviour does Fergal Keane choose to tell the reader about?
- What words or phrases describe the powerful effect this has on Keane?
- In what other way does he draw the reader into his account? (Think about what he *doesn't* tell us.)

Now, write two paragraphs about someone you know well, concentrating on one feature alone. It could be how they move, dress, speak or a particular expression they have.

Focus for development: Revealing Information

When writing about someone memorable, you can emphasise their importance by structuring the text to delay information for impact.

Look at this extract from a **Grade A** response.

> I have known Uncle Joe all my life – literally. In fact, 'Uncle' Joe isn't really what I should call him. You see, when I was just six months old, **my father put on his coat and walked out, never to come back.**

The important, hard-hitting information comes at the end of the third sentence, almost like a punch-line.

This high grade poem does a similar thing, but here it is *who* the memorable person is that is left till last.

> I remember your hands, so much bigger than mine
> My little fist was tiny when I fell;
> You picked me up, Joe.
> When my father took his coat, and walked right out
> You walked right in,
> **You were there when he was not**
> **Made 'uncle' seem a pointless name.**

We have to think about what the poet is implying – that his 'uncle' was really a father to him.

ACTIVITY

Write an opening paragraph, or first verse of a poem, about someone you know well. Try out this technique of holding back the most important thing about the person until near the end.

ASSESSMENT FOCUS

Write an extended first draft of the same text, developing your opening paragraph or verse if you wish.

Remember

- **Focus on one or two specific details or features of this person to make your description personal and real.**
- **Keep the reader interested in what you have to say by delaying key information.**
- **Draw on what you have learned in other sections about impressive writing techniques, such as using imagery or variety of sentences lengths.**

Refining personal writing

Learning objectives

- To improve the structure of your writing.
- To use symbolism to interest the reader.

What does this involve?

By refining your personal writing, you can avoid generalised statements, and write as concisely and creatively as you would for other more obviously imaginative texts. For example, you could

- show contrast in narration between the older, more reflective you, and the younger you who experienced these events
- use literary techniques such as symbolism, to explore the significance of a thing, time or place.

Here is an example of the former.

We were ushered into the small room, and there he was – my favourite singer, my favourite person – my idol. **He took off his dark shades and I almost fainted!** ← In the moment!

'What's your name, honey?' he asked.

Looking back, I realise I had stars in my eyes. I **had been** blinded by the soppy records, the posters, the stories in the gossip magazines. **How could I have ever liked him?**

- In the moment!
- Reflecting back
- Use of tense shows things have changed
- Rhetorical question shows she has grown up!

⭐ Examiner's tip

Contrast can help you convey feelings clearly. For example, swap between **active, immediate writing** *('She was wearing a green wig!') and a more* **reflective tone** *('I wonder now…', 'Could it be that over the years…'.*

ACTIVITY

Write your own two paragraphs in which you reflect back on a person you once met or on an experience which you now feel differently about, for whatever reason.

Paragraph 1: Start by recalling the moment at the time when you saw this person, or experienced something. It can be effective to describe this scene as if it was from a story with vivid details and descriptions (as above).

Paragraph 2: Develop by reflecting on your changed or different perspective now. Try altering tenses as in the example ('had been blinded', 'had thought that').

End with a rhetorical question you ask yourself now.

Focus for development: Using symbols

Often, when writers reflect about past experiences, certain items, objects or locations take on a symbolic importance.

In this extract, Ted Hughes recalls a pair of scissors (a wedding present) he and his wife cut daffodils with, and eventually dropped somewhere. Many years later, after her death, he writes:

> But somewhere your scissors remember. Wherever they are.
>
> Here somewhere, blades wide open,
>
> April by April
>
> Sinking deeper
>
> Through the sod – an anchor, a cross of rust.
>
> *from 'Daffodils'*

Glossary

Symbol: usually, an object or natural feature that brings to mind powerful feelings or connotations, such as a rose symbolising love.

ASSESSMENT FOCUS

Write about a significant object or item from your past. Decide what it symbolises but don't spell it out in your writing; let the reader work that out. You could describe

- a favourite childhood book
- your first bike
- an item in your garden or flat/house.

Choose your own form – either verse or prose for this task.

Here, a Grade A★ student has chosen to 'extend the metaphor'. What is the symbolic object being described, and how has she developed the central idea?

> Giant iron gates
> Opened on the school and all its noise,
> Great limbs to let me in or shut me out.
> Through the years the giant shrank
> Under the spell of time
> As like a beanstalk I grew towards the light.

ACTIVITY

With a partner, make some quick notes:

- What might the scissors symbolise?
- Why do you think Hughes uses the metaphors of an 'anchor' and a 'cross' to describe them?
- Is there any significance to the scissors 'sinking deeper' in the earth, or the mention of 'rust'?

Remember

- **Consider all the ideas (feelings, connections) associated with the item or object and try to imply these in your description, perhaps through similes and metaphors.**
- **Describe the symbolic item in detail to paint a vivid picture.**

Grade Booster

Extended Assessment Task

Using the ideas and the skills you have learned from this chapter, write a 700-word response to this task.

> *Write about a place that is memorable or has made an impact on your life for whatever reason. You can choose the writing form that best suits what you have to say.*

Make sure you

- write vividly, bringing the place to life through wide and varied vocabulary, sentence and paragraph use
- show your past feelings and your feelings now
- keep the reader engaged by holding back information
- refine your writing through the use of symbols and metaphors.

Evaluation – What have you learned?

With a partner, use the grade checklist below to evaluate your work on the Extended Assessment Task.

- I can write a personal sustained, vivid and original piece based on my own experience, which engages and delights the reader.
- I can make full and varied use of a wide and ambitious range of language devices, structures and effects (such as subtle symbols), including the full repertoire of sentences and paragraphs.

- I can write a personal, sustained, vivid and original piece which engages the reader and often delights through ambitious use of language devices and structures.
- I can use a wide variety of sentences and paragraphs for effect.

- I can write a personal, well-developed creative piece with conscious use of a range of language devices and structures to create effects and impact.
- I can use sentences and paragraphs fluently and creatively.

- I can write a clear and well-structured creative piece based on my experiences, which uses some language devices and structures for purpose and effect.
- I can use clear, sometimes varied paragraphing and sentence use.

- I can write a creative piece which mainly matches the task I have been set and is generally accurate and clear, but sometimes undeveloped.
- I can use only a limited variety of vocabulary and sentence and paragraph structures.

You may need to go back and look at the relevant pages of this section again.

Controlled Assessment Preparation

Introduction

In this section you will

- find out the exact facts about, and requirements of, the Controlled Assessment task: Producing Creative Texts
- read, analyse and respond to three sample answers by different candidates
- plan and write your own answer to a sample question
- evaluate and assess your answer and the progress you have made.

Why is preparation like this important?

- If you know exactly what you need to do, you will feel more confident when you do the real task.
- Looking at sample answers by other students will help you see what you need to do to improve your own work.
- Planning and writing a full sample response after you have completed the whole chapter will give you a clear sense of what you have learned so far.

Key information

Unit 3 Section B is 'Producing Creative texts'.

- The controlled part of the task will last **three or four hours**, and is worth **40 marks**.
- It is worth **20%** of your overall English GCSE mark.

What will the task involve?

- You have to complete **two** written tasks.
- The recommended **number of words** for the two pieces is **1400 in total**.

What does the task consist of?

You will complete two different tasks, which will have been chosen from two out of three possible areas:

- Moving images (writing related to moving images such as film)
- Re-creations and prompts (using a text or prompt to develop writing)
- Me. Myself. I. (writing from personal experience)

The two responses do not need to be of equal length so, for example, you might write 800 words re-creating a poem as a short story, and 600 words writing about someone who has made an impression on you. These tasks will be prepared in advance and then written in 'controlled conditions', possibly in your own classroom or the school hall over a period of up to four hours.

Here are some example questions based on the general task areas set by the exam board.

Moving images	Watch the first 5 to 10 minutes of a film. Using what you have seen as your inspiration, write a creative piece which aims to capture a similar atmosphere.
Prompts and Re-creations	Look at the poems from the English Literary Heritage section of the Anthology. Choose a poem and use it as a starting point for your own story, but write it from a different perspective from the original.
Me, myself, I	Write about a place that is important to you. It can be a natural space, a building, an area – your choice. The place should be the title of your writing.

The Assessment

The assessment objectives for this unit (AO3) state that you must:

- Write clearly, effectively and imaginatively, using and adapting forms and selecting vocabulary appropriate to task and purpose in ways that engage the reader.
- Organise information and ideas into structured and sequenced sentences, paragraphs and whole texts, using a variety of linguistic and structural features to support cohesion and overall coherence.
- Use a range of sentence structures for clarity, purpose and effect, with accurate punctuation and spelling.

Targeting Grade A

Some of the key differences between a Grade C and Grade A response are as follows:

Grade C candidates	See example on pages 243–4
<ul><li>use a range of sentences and a varied vocabulary to maintain the reader's interest</li><li>write in clear paragraphs that link well; punctuate and spell accurately in general but vary structure for effect on the reader less often</li><li>demonstrate clear understanding of form and genre</li><li>develop subject matter appropriately to keep the reader's interest</li><li>use a range of language features, such as imagery, in an attempt to have a conscious effect on the reader.</li></ul>	(C)

Grade A/A★ candidates	See example on pages 247–8
<ul><li>grab and engage the reader's interest and sustain it throughout</li><li>organise ideas and content for conscious impact on the reader</li><li>write vividly and with originality, delighting the reader with a wide and ambitious range of language techniques and effects, such as symbols and metaphors</li><li>use the full repertoire of sentence and paragraph structures, with a clear sense of how these will affect the reader's reaction</li><li>demonstrate accurate spelling and punctuation throughout.</li></ul>	(A) (A★)

Exploring Sample Responses

ACTIVITY

Read the extract below from a response to this 'Moving Images' task.

> *Watch the first 5 to 10 minutes of a film. Using what you have seen as your inspiration, write a creative piece which aims to capture a similar atmosphere.*

As you read it, think about whether it is closer to a C, B or an A/ A★ grade, and why.

Consider these key elements an examiner would look for:

- how well the writer has engaged the reader by creating atmosphere through his/her choice of vocabulary, language devices and other decisions about content
- a clear understanding of what makes a creative story work in terms of structure, developing ideas and detail
- accurate and, where appropriate, creative use of punctuation, sentences and paragraphing.

Example 1: Moving images

Opening takes us straight into the story →

Pippa Hawkins looked at her brother's gravestone. Joshua Hawkins had died five years ago to the day after going missing on the marshes while fishing. His body had never been found but his parents wanted a memorial so this was it.

She found it difficult to understand at the time because she was only ten. Now

A lot of information is 'told' to us here: could it be shown →

that she was fifteen she missed him a lot which was natural and OK. But she had this sneaking feeling that he was still there. Often she would go into her room and an object would be missing.

Once she had gone upstairs in her family's old cottage and the window was wide open. She swore she could see someone at the end of the garden. But her parents said she must be wrong and that she was just a silly girl. 'I'm not!' she told them

Nice visual detail ⌐

and ran off crying.

*Now here she was putting **some withered flowers** by his gravestone. Her family was poor as there was not much work on the river. Her father was a fruit-seller in*

Good development of details about the graveyard including a simile

Covent Garden but it took him nearly two hours on horseback to get to work and two hours to get back so she hardly ever saw him.

The graveyard was deserted and freezing cold because it was so close to the river. There was only one big tree for shelter and that

A bit informal →

*looked **dead frightening** with bark that*

ctd.

243

looked **like a face**. The tree seemed to be staring at her.

    Suddenly a hand grabbed her! She wasn't expecting anyone and she cried out ⟵————— Good change of pace
terrified. She turned right round. There was a tall thin person standing right there.
He had his face covered in a scarf.

    'Don't say anything!' he whispered in a horrible way. ⟵

    'I won't say anything,' she replied. ————— Dialogue could be sharper

    'Do as I say and you won't be harmed,' he said. ⟵

    Then he took off the scarf. To her surprise she saw it was her brother. He looked ⟵
older but it was definitely him. She felt sick inside. Perhaps it was a ghost? But she ——— Good variety of sentences and use of question
touched him and he was real.

    Joshua. Is it really you?' she asked him.

    Joshua held her by the hand.

    Yes,' he said. 'I'm really sorry I frightened you but I was worried you would cry out
and they would catch me.'

    'Who would catch you?' she questioned.

    'It's a long story,' he replied. 'I'll tell you all about it.'

Examiner feedback

This is a generally accurate response to the task, which attempts to recreate some of
the atmosphere of the original film. Unfortunately, some informal usages such as
'OK' are a little out of place. The structure is clear and paragraphs are used to
develop the story. Speech is accurately punctuated but it is not always necessary to
add the speech tag (i.e. 'questioned', 'asked') as this can disrupt the flow. There are
some nice moments of description when the writer tries to create a picture in our
minds but rather more of this would help, and vocabulary could be a little more
varied. There is a good simile ('bark that looked like a face') but language techniques
are a little limited. All in all, this is a clear and well-managed response to the task.

Suggested grade: C

ACTIVITY

Rewrite the response above. Focus on the following:
- Improve the general description – give more detail, use imagery and any other language techniques you think are appropriate.
- Sharpen up the conversation; cut out some of the question 'tags'.
- Remove any informal usages.
- Improve impact on reader by adding at least one shorter sentence.
- Check all spellings.

ACTIVITY

Read the extract below from a response to this 'Re-creations' task.

> *Look at the poems from the English Literary Heritage section of the*
> *Anthology. Choose a poem and use it as a starting point for your own*
> *story, but write it from a different perspective from the original.*

As you read, look at the annotations around the text. Note down any
observations of your own about what the writer does well.

Example 2: Re-creations and prompts
Poem choice: 'My last Duchess'

Opening 'tells' rather than 'shows' →

When I married the Duke I did not know what kind of man he was.
He was kind enough and although much older than me seemed
delighted that I would take on his famous family name.

The trouble began when we **employed** local people to help pick
the fruit from the orchards we owned outside the castle. I was
bored. The Duke would often leave and travel for days and all I
had to **occupy** me was reading or playing the grand piano. So,
one sunny afternoon in late September I **strolled** in the orchard
as the workers gathered the fallen golden apples.

— Good range of vocabulary

Then I saw him. A handsome young man who was kneeling by a
large, wicker basket picking the
apples from the ground.

He looked up, and nodded his
head.

Fits the style and tone of the story →

'Good afternoon, your
ladyship,' he said.

I blushed and turned scarlet,
and was unable to speak. He was
about the same age as me, much
younger than my husband. I
turned and hurried off without
a word.

What was I supposed to do?
My husband, the Duke, was a
fiercely jealous man. I was
worried that if I showed my
feelings openly everyone in the

ctd.

245

village would gossip. Then my husband would find out.

Of course he did anyway. One day later in the week I passed him in the corridor. It was night and lamps were burning **like fiery eyes** on the solid stone walls. I bowed my head and smiled at him. But he stopped and grabbed me by the arm.

'Why do you smile like that?' he shouted nastily.

'Like what?' I replied, innocently.

'Your smile is false!'

Then he threw me against the stone wall, and cracked my head open. As I lay on the floor **I knew** I was dying. He had done it on purpose **and I knew** that he had been spying on me for ages.

He laughed openly as my mind began to go blank.

'Soon all you will be is a painting on the wall who looks down on visitors!'

In fact I am more than that. Yes I am dead but I now haunt the castle, watching my murderous husband's movements. Perhaps I will be able to warn his next wife about him. I don't know. It will depend if I can send messages from the other side **like a poltergeist** to get my revenge on him, and join the young handsome man from the village. We will see what will happen.

Powerful simile →

Dialogue short and effective ←

A little repetitive →

Seems to want to turn the story into a supernatural tale →

Ending to this section is the weak point – too much information and 'telling' ←

Examiner feedback

This is a fluent and well thought-out response which takes the perspective of the murdered Duchess and tells her story. In general, the tone of voice of the Duchess is conveyed effectively and the language fits the style of the piece. The story engages us as readers although the structure could have been better – the opening and ending are both a little weak, telling us rather than showing us what happens – but the way the characters are described is excellent, as is the dialogue. There are some good uses of language – the 'fiery eyes' of the lamps, the varied vocabulary and a range of short and long sentences for effect. Overall, an atmospheric piece of writing whose structure needs more work.

Suggested grade: B

ACTIVITY

Rewrite the last paragraph of the response, removing the reference to a poltergeist. You could describe

- how you will move around the castle
- the places and rooms you will watch over
- the next young woman whom the Duke pursues. Do you try and warn her about him?

Read the response below to this 'Me. Myself. I.' task.

> *Write about a place that is important to you. It can be a natural space, a building, an area – your choice. The place should be the title of your writing.*

As you read, consider the annotations around the text. You could note down any observations of your own about what the writer does well.

Example 3: Me, Myself, I

The Colonnade

The colonnade is a **crescent-shaped building** and looks out to the sea, **like a half-moon in colour and form**. Concrete and grey-white, it was a soul-less place in winter with its café closed. Usually on a winter's day only a few brave walkers with their scruffy dogs **haunted the promenade**.

But for us, on summer evenings, it was the place to be. The place where we met, laughed, joked – a sort of home from home.

Why was it so special to me back then? Well, I didn't have my own room at home, and had to share with my little brother, so I craved a place where I could meet my friends. The colonnade was ideal. On summers' nights we would 'borrow' the deck-chairs once it had got dark, and put them in a circle. The beach was only a few feet away, so often we'd often race down, kick off our trainers and muck around in the foam-topped breakers.

One time, Simon (my best friend) and I dared each other to swim to the nearest buoy although the waves were

ctd.

Evokes the scene with specific vocabulary and a simile

Short paragraph has immediacy and introduces new tone

Verb 'haunted' appropriate for the winter

Rhetorical question good way to start a reflective paragraph

Please Do Not Feed The Birds

Well-chosen physical simile → *pounding like boxers' fists on the shoreline*, and there was stormy weather coming.

We were both strong swimmers, but the current was a **murderous magnet** pulling us away from the buoy, and halfway there we gave up and turned back. Both of us felt the same moment of panic – would we make it? Our friends were too far away to hear us call, and the lifeguards had all gone home. We encouraged each other as the waves churned around us but thank god, we made it to the shore. We lay on our backs staring at the sky panting and laughing, but to tell the truth we had been frightened to the core. **We never did it again.** ← **Effective short sentence emphasises end of drama**

← **Successful use of alliteration and metaphor**

Simon has moved away now. His dad got some job up north so I don't see him, though we keep in contact through Facebook and text each other from time to time.

Funnily enough, I don't go to the Colonnade any more. There are other, younger teenagers there now – I even saw my younger brother with his friends. The council have also opened the café all year round and repainted the concrete. Now it's all sparkling and trendy, and at night-time, **more people walk along the promenade, not just men with their dogs!** ← **Links back structurally to the start**

To me it will never be the same again. It was probably just one summer or two when we all went there, and there were probably moments when we sat around bored and with nothing to say to each other. But I only remember the good times.

Yesterday I walked down to the beach with our dog. But I don't take him near the colonnade. **When we get to the front by the big nursing home I take a left turn and go in the opposite direction.** It's better that way, I think. The sea is still the same, sometimes grey and choppy, sometimes calm and blue. I wonder if my brother will have the same memories as me as he gets older?

Symbolises having taken a different turn in his life, too ⌐

Examiner feedback

This is an excellent response which paints a detailed and vivid picture of an important place for the writer. There is much to admire, from the detailed and varied vocabulary ('crescent-shaped', 'craved', 'breakers') to the language devices such as simile ('like a half-moon'), metaphor ('murderous magnet') and the sentences for effect ('We never did it again').

The change in the way the writer sees the place – as it was when he went there, and how he sees it now, is also conveyed well and we get a real sense of the writer's personal feelings when he talks about his younger brother and his friend moving away. These little details engage the reader. Finally, the structure is excellent. Perhaps at the start he gets a little confused with his use of tenses, mixing up his memories of the colonnade with how it is different today, but the ending is very well written, with its use of symbolism.

Suggested grade: A★

EXTENDED PRACTICE TASK

Prompts and re-creations

The other day I walked past the house for the first time since that summer. On the outside it looked the same, but I knew it was empty, and why they had left.

Use this as the starting point for a story of your own.

If you only do five things...

1 Read a range of creative texts, especially short stories, and note the ways in which the best writers interest and engage you.

2 Where appropriate, plan for original ideas and different perspectives on the task set; this will make the reader sit up and take notice. Also, develop detailed ideas so that any ideas or scenes you describe can be taken further.

3 Draw on what you know about the conventions of story-telling, but be highly flexible in order to make an impact on the reader, for example by holding back information to keep the reader's interest or build suspense.

4 Use an ambitious range of vocabulary, sentences and paragraph types and don't forget to check the accuracy of your spelling and punctuation.

5 Use a variety of language devices such as similes and metaphors, to make your writing come alive.

ACKNOWLEDGEMENTS

The publishers gratefully acknowledge the permission granted to reproduce the copyright material in this book. While every effort has been made to trace and contact copyright holders, where this has not been possible the publishers will be pleased to make the necessary arrangements at the first opportunity.

Chapter 1 p5, 'Picks of the day', from *The Observer*, 26 July, 2009. © Guardian News & Media Ltd 2009; p5 website reprinted with kind permission of The Coventry Building Society; p6, 'Flood victims will suffer trauma of a war zone, says GP' by Russell Jenkins, *The Times*, 25 November, 2009 pg 13. © NI Syndication; p7, 'After the rain, here comes The Sun' *The Sun*, 25 November, 2009. © NI Syndications; p9, courtesy of Sky News; p10, extract from *New York Encounter* Lonely Planet 2007 © 2007 Lonely Planet; p11, Text and images courtesy of NYCVP (New York City Vacations Packages) website; p12, extract from *Withnails: the Film Diaries of Richard E Grant* published by Picador Macmillan; p14, 'Birth of Asian Elephant is trumpeted by Zoo', *The Times*, 29 July, 2009. © NI Syndication; p15, Marriott Hotel courtesy of Marriott Hotels; p16, Transun Arctic Spirit advert reprinted with kind permission; p18, extract from *The Backwash of War* by Ellen la Motte published by Dodopress; p23, 'The day of the vulture' *The Independent*, 5 September, 2009; p24, 'Er, does this thing have a reverse gear?' *Daily Mail*, 27 July 2009. Reprinted with permission of Solo Syndication; p25, WaterAid ad reprinted with kind permission of WaterAid; p27, 'It's wonderful to see you all: re-united with the evacuees' by Chris Green, *The Independent*, 5 September, 2009; p28, problem page from *Woman's Magazine Annual*, 1935. Reprinted with permission of IPC Media; p30, 'Barbed Ire - Allotment fence 'might injure vandals' Euan Stretch, *Daily Mirror*, 5 September 2009; p36, Harley-Davidson advert © Harley-Davidson Europe. (Prices are not current, this is an old advert.); p40, 'Academies are the only way forward' *Oldham Advertiser*, 24 September 2009. Reprinted with permission of MEN Syndication; pp42-43, 'Let's Rejoice in the Rain' by Andrew Grimes, *Manchester Evening News*, pg 8, 31 July 2009. Reprinted with permission of MEN Syndications; p43, 'What a He Row' by Ben Ashford, *The Sun*, 25 November, 2009. © NI Syndication; p45, Dracula leaflet for Northern Ballet Theatre's production of Dracula at the West Yorkshire Playhouse, 2009; pp46-47, screengrab courtesy of Folk Alley homepage; p50, 'Champion of the word: Keith Waterhouse' (written by Anton Antonowicz), *The Mirror*, 5 September, 2009; p50, 'Farewell Keith, King of Fleet Street' (written by Sam Greenhill) *Daily Mail*; p55, 'Grizzly bears starve as fish stocks collapse' by Tracy McVeigh, *The Observer*, 20 September, 2009. © Guardian News & Media Ltd 2009; p56, 'From Russia With Love' from *Sky Magazine*, October 2009; p57, extract from *A Short History of Nearly Everything* by Bill Bryson published by Random House; **Chapter 2** p74, Short extract from 'TV dinners: Chops, mash and Mad Men' by Julie Myerson, *The Observer*, 21 June, 2009. Copyright © Guardian News & Media Ltd 2009; p88, 'Oceans of Clichés' by A.A. Gill published by *The Times* November 16 2008; p89, Short extracts from 'To Groom or not to groom' by Kathy Lette, *Good Housekeeping*, August 2009. This was written by Kathy Lette, author of ten best-selling novels; p100, extracts from 'The right to die or not' by Brendan O'Neill, *The Big Issue*, August 17-23 2009; **Chapter 4** p192-3 extracts from *Of Mice and Men* by John Steinbeck published by Penguin Books 2000 Copyright © John Steinbeck 1937, 1965. Reprinted with permission of Penguin Books and Curtis Brown Limited; p199 'Praise Song for my mother' by Grace Nichols from *The Fat Black Womans Poems* published by Virago part of Curtis Brown; p200 'Thoughts on my father' by James Berry published by Fractured Circles; **Chapter 5** p230 'Cold Knap Lake' by Gillian Clarke courtesy of Gillian Clarke; p236 A Boy called 'Grenade' by Fergal Keane from *Letters Home* published by Penguin 1999; p239 'Daffodils' by Ted Hughes from *Birthday Letters* published by Faber & Faber.

The publishers would like to thank the following for permission to reproduce pictures in these pages:

Advertising Archive: p35; **Alamy:** pp62, 64, 67, 107, 110, 118, 127, 139, 150a, 150b, 162, 167a, 167b, 173, 183, 207, 211, 228, 236, 245; **Alton Towers Resort:** p115; **BBC:** p152b; **Bridgeman Art Library:** pp178 'London', plate 38 from 'Songs of Experience', 1794 (colour printed etching with w/c), Blake, William (1757-1827) / Yale Center for British Art, Paul Mellon Collection, USA / The Bridgeman Art Library, 179 Portrait of William Blake (1757-1827) Leaning Forward, 1820 (pencil on paper), Linnell, John (1792-1882) / Fitzwilliam Museum, University of Cambridge, UK / The Bridgeman Art Library; **Cavendish Press:** p43b; **Corbis:** pp19, 75, 79; **Getty Images:** pp23, 43a, 55, 112, 113, 114, 116, 120, 123, 132, 141, 145, 157; **iStockphoto:** pp10, 12, 13, 37, 38, 44, 69a, 69b, 72a, 72b, 74, 76, 77, 78, 82, 85, 86, 87a, 87b, 90, 92, 93, 95a, 95b, 97a, 97b, 98, 100, 101, 108, 124, 125a, 125b, 134, 136, 140, 148b, 148c, 151a, 151b, 170a, 170b, 192, 195, 199, 200, 209, 214, 230, 238, 239, 243; **Mary Evan's Picture Library:** pp21, 180; **Movie Store Collection:** p160; **North News and Pictures:** p7tr; **News Team International:** p7cl; **PA Photos:** p7br; **Photolibrary:** pp2, 66, 83, 91; **Rex Features:** pp14, 26 (Kelly Hancock/UCF), 50 (Ray Tang), 89, 118 (CSU/Arhcv/Everett), 122 (Steve Hill), 130, 144 (c.20thC.Fox/Everett), 147a, 147b (c.20thC.Fox/Everett), 148 (Alastair Muir), 152 (Brian J. Ritchie), 158 (Giuliano Bevilacqua), 164, 169 (Courtesy Everett Collection), 182 (c.W.Disney/Everett Collection), 184 (ITV), 186 (ITV), 190 (Courtesy Everett Collection), 216a (ITV), 216b (ITV); **Ronald Grant Archive:** p194; **Shutterstock:** pp8, 219, 224, 226, 231, 237, 247.).